MADAME BOVARY'S OVARIES

Madame Bovary's Ovaries

A Darwinian Look at Literature

DAVID P. BARASH

and

NANELLE R. BARASH

DELACORTE PRESS

MADAME BOVARY'S OVARIES
A Darwinian Look at Literature
A Delacorte Press Book / May 2005

Published by Bantam Dell
A Division of Random House, Inc.
New York, New York

Book design by Ellen Cipriano

Delacorte Press is a registered trademark of Random House, Inc.,
and the colophon is a trademark of Random House, Inc.

Library of Congress Cataloging in Publication Data is on file with the publisher.

ISBN: 0-385-33801-5

Printed in the United States of America
Published simultaneously in Canada

www.bantamdell.com

BVG 10 9 8 7 6 5 4 3 2 1

To the memory of
Nat Barash
1915–2005

CONTENTS

Madame Bovary, c'est moi.

—GUSTAVE FLAUBERT

1

THE HUMAN NATURE OF STORIES

A *Quick Hit of Bio-Lit-Crit*

———

Othello isn't just a story about a jealous guy. Huckleberry Finn isn't just a rebellious, headstrong kid. Madame Bovary isn't just a horny married woman. As students, we are told about various ways to understand fiction: that Othello may also teach us about deceit and loyalty (among other things), how Huck will tell us about the American national character, that Madame Bovary will help reveal the meaning of social transgression. In addition, those who get deep and sophisticated enough may be urged to examine what they read from various perspectives: those of Marx, Freud, Jung, or maybe the French literary theorists Derrida or Foucault, not to omit feminist and "queer" studies, socioeconomic analyses, and the historical facts of each author's personal biography. The list is nearly endless: New Criticism, old criticism, new historicism, old historicism, critical theory, and sometimes crackpot theory.

It's all fine, up to a point. No one has a monopoly on how to read what others have written. There is much to be said for examining literature as a reflection of class struggle (Marx), unconscious drives (Freud), power relations (Foucault), social mores, sexual repression, historical forces, or even—as postmodernists often insist—of "texts" that signify nothing more than themselves. But in fact, *Othello is* a story about a jealous guy. Huck Finn *is* a rebellious, headstrong boy. And Madame Bovary *is* a horny married woman.

The reason *Othello* is still being read and performed five hundred years after Shakespeare wrote it is because this play tells us something timeless and universal . . . not so much about a fellow named Othello but about ourselves. It speaks to the Othello within everyone: our shared human nature. *Othello* the play is about a jealous guy, and, as we shall see, jealousy is a particularly potent and widespread human emotion, one to which *men* are especially vulnerable. That's precisely why it's okay to talk about Othello or Madame Bovary or Huckleberry Finn in the present tense: they live on, at least in part, because they have distinctly human characteristics that transcend the artistry by which they were depicted. Their tribulations, responses, loves and hates, fears and delights are in some way recognizable to all readers, to marvel at, agree or disagree with, learn from, or be shocked by.

It may be startling to some—especially those who have not kept up with recent advances in biological science—but the evidence is now undeniable that much of human life is not socially constructed. In short, even though learning and cultural traditions exert a powerful influence, there also exists an underlying human nature, universally valid and characteristic of all *Homo sapiens*. People live in many different places, following many different traditions and cultural trajectories, but beneath this wonderful diversity there is something else that is equally wonderful, and maybe even more so: a common thread of recognizable humanity, woven of human DNA and shared by everyone who reads and writes (as well as those who don't). Othello's jealousy, Huck's rebelliousness, and Emma's urges are just three examples of that common thread.

In his advice to the traveling players, Hamlet suggested that the role of the artist is to hold a mirror up to nature—not, as some theorists would have it, to hold a mirror up to another mirror and thereby reflect only the infinite emptiness of mirrors. The "nature" at issue here isn't wild animals, pretty landscapes, or magnificent wilderness, but *human* nature. And human nature isn't like a unicorn or some other mythical beast. It exists. It does so because human genes exist and have produced a different kind of creature than horse genes or hyacinth genes have. "Read deeply," writes Harold Bloom in *How to Read and Why*, ". . . not to believe, not to accept, not to contradict, but to learn to share in that one nature that writes and reads."

As Bloom intuits, connecting literature and human nature isn't really all that new. Until recently, in fact, our most enduring images of human nature have resided in literature. Where better to find it? Psychology, for instance, didn't even exist until scarcely a hundred years ago, and during most of the twentieth century, it was torn between two equally unhelpful poles: the semimystical mythologizing of Freud and the sterile behaviorism of John Watson and B. F. Skinner. Anyone wanting to get a sense of human nature in, say, the Bronze Age can do no better than to excavate among the words of Homer, or for the Elizabethan Age, Shakespeare.

Universal human nature was perceived thousands of years ago by our greatest storytellers, from the early authors of the Hindu *Mahabharata*, the Babylonian tale of Gilgamesh, and Homer's *Iliad* and *Odyssey* to Virgil's *Aeneid* and the writings of Dante, Cervantes, and Shakespeare. It wasn't until Charles Darwin, however, that the scientific basis for human nature was identified. Actually, some of the most important breakthroughs didn't occur until a century and more *after* Darwin, when the genetic basis of evolution by natural selection was discovered and its implications for human behavior were made clear.

These breakthroughs haven't had much direct effect on the conscious *creation* of literature, but we hope to show that they can be immensely useful in its *interpretation*, since they help the reader to see what was always there, albeit generally unacknowledged by writers and readers alike. Roland Barthes's celebrated essay "The Death of the Author" proclaimed that the intentions of an author do not matter in interpreting his or her text. We agree, to a point. It doesn't matter, for example, whether authors are *intentionally* presenting a biologically accurate view of human beings. In fact, it is even more telling if they have no such aim and yet end up doing just that; nature whispers within their work nonetheless. Just as it did among the ancients, biology continues to flourish inside the best of our modern writers.

The key concept is that human beings, like all other living things, are biological critters, products of evolution by natural selection. As a result, people are strongly inclined to behave in ways that enhance their fitness. Not physical fitness, although being strong, smart, and healthy can certainly help. Rather, fitness is the fundamental evolutionary bottom line: a measure of success in projecting genes into the future. If living things seek food when hungry, sleep when tired, have sex when horny, if they scratch when they itch, do a good job of pumping their blood, and learn to keep their heads down when predators are about, it is because those who do so have been more successful in promoting genes for eating, sleeping, mating, scratching, pumping, hiding, and so forth. Such individuals are, in short, more fit than other individuals whose ancestors were less adroit (or, to be more accurate, whose genes were). This means that whatever else they may be—artful manipulators of language and symbol, composers of symphonies, splitters of atoms no less than of logs—human beings are concatenations of genes that have evolved to do their best at copying themselves and then kicking those copies into the future.

This does not mean that everyone is desperately seeking to have as many children as possible, or even necessarily to survive. But since we have inherited the genes of men and women who *did* reproduce and survive, we unconsciously behave in ways designed to enhance our success in doing so, that is, to benefit what biologists call our fitness. These behaviors are the stubborn, indelible core of human nature. To be sure, human beings have also been blessed, or cursed, with unique self-consciousness and the ability to say no (at least on occasion) to their biological inclinations. Breathing, too, is part of our human, and animal, nature. So is digesting. We cannot say no to them. By contrast, people are not absolutely obliged to have children or even to have sex, not to mention engage in the other, more arcane activities we shall shortly explore. Human beings can and sometimes do say no to many of the fitness-enhancing tendencies that make up human nature. But this doesn't mean that those tendencies aren't there. Indeed, even the occasional decision to say no, and the conscious effort it requires, is testimony to the existence of those deep, internal yearnings in the first place; otherwise, there would be nothing to rebel against. All of this means that people, whether they acknowledge it or not, are fitness-focused creatures. And that isn't all. As we shall explore in chapters ahead, an evolutionary view of human nature goes beyond simply identifying the importance of fitness itself to make specific predictions as to how human beings are likely to behave depending on whether, for example, they are men, women, children, parents, someone's friend, or someone else's enemy.

Although evolutionary biology is so new that it deserves in many ways to be called "revolutionary biology," the idea that great literature reflects certain human universals is actually as old as literary analysis itself, having been foreshadowed in the first organized attempt to make sense of fiction, Aristotle's *Poetics*. "Poetry is something more philosophic and of graver import than history," wrote the great Greek himself, "since its statements are of the nature of universals, whereas those of history are singulars." By "poetry," Aristotle meant creative fiction, not just poetry in the narrow sense but also theater (novels were unknown in his day). His point is that the power of poetry lies in its ability to capture fundamental truths about the human condition, including, most notably, the way people act . . . which, in turn, derives from the nature of what people *are*. And this is where a biological perspective has much to offer.

It won't always be pretty. Indeed, throughout *Madame Bovary's Ovaries*, we'll point to a number of inclinations that are regrettable, sometimes downright despicable, but always, as Nietzsche has written, "human, all too human." Men taking sexual advantage of women; women often doing the same thing, although typically in different ways. Competitiveness, whether violent or more subtle. The selfish underbelly of friendship. Nepotism (favoritism toward relatives) often combined with discrimination against strangers. Abuse and neglect of stepchildren. The catalog is intriguing but not necessarily inspiring. Please note that throughout, we offer descriptions, not prescriptions, in the hope of illuminating what people—and their literature—are like, not necessarily how they ought to be. (In fact, a case can be made that part of the burden of being human is to behave counter to some of our all-too-human inclinations, but that is another story.)

Seeking to understand *Homo sapiens*, not to condone ethically unacceptable behavior, a growing band of scientists has been busily unraveling the nature of human nature. They are known as evolutionary biologists, sociobiologists, behavioral ecologists, Darwinian anthropologists, and, increasingly, evolutionary psychologists, an expanding group in which literary critics are not (yet) included. But at last, the nature of human nature is becoming clear. One of its cardinal principles—reflected in literature—is the gravitational pull exerted by what Richard Dawkins first labeled "selfish genes," a force that influences not only what people do but also the stories they tell about themselves, including what they find interesting, boring, perplexing, and frightening.

Dostoyevsky's Ivan Karamazov worried that "without God, everything is permissible." Without human nature, too, everything is permissible. There could be worlds of the imagination in which people don't eat, sleep, communicate with each other, or reproduce. Or in which there is no sexual identity, no predisposition to care preferentially for one's children or relatives, no predictable patterns of love, anger, competition, or cooperation. The result would be a kind of science fiction or wild fantasy, yet it is noteworthy that such imaginary excursions of extreme inhumanness are rarely undertaken, almost certainly because wholesale departures from the recognizably human are not only very difficult to portray but also genuinely incomprehensible and thus unlikely to be interesting. Even the physically bizarre creatures conjured up in the Harry Potter books, Tolkien's *The Lord of the Rings*, or the various *Star Wars* movies (especially the wonderful bar scene in the first film), for all their imaginative anatomic variety, retain demonstrably human motivations and relationships to each other, just as— centuries after their conception—Hamlet, Don Quixote, and Achilles retain their vitality because they retain their humanity.

It has been said that great writers (Shakespeare, Cervantes, Homer, Tolstoy, Dickens, Austen, James, and Chekhov, among others) peopled the world with characters that seem so real that they appear to have existed even before they were written about. Certainly these characters remain "alive"—almost literally—long after their creators have passed away.

This leads to a key notion in nearly all approaches to fiction, but especially in an evolutionary analysis of literature: believability. "The only difference between fiction and nonfiction," observed Mark Twain, only somewhat ironically, "is that fiction should be completely believable." How, then, is this achieved? Fictional characters are believable when they reveal their human nature, which is to say, when they behave in concert with biological expectation. This is what lies behind Falstaff's expansive humor, Heathcliff's obsessive passion, Jane Eyre's spunkiness, Huck Finn's mixture of naïveté and wisdom, Augie March's antic yearning for self-realization. Harold Bloom once more: "[Shakespeare's] uncanny ability to present consistent and different actual-seeming voices of imaginary beings stems in part from the most abundant sense of reality ever to invade literature."

To be sure, literary characters may sometimes behave counter to reality, and thus in defiance of expectation. After all, they are fictional! But such exceptions are notably rare, and also of particular interest; their impact comes from the drama of seeing patterns contrary to our anticipation of how a biological creature—as opposed to a crystal, say, or a robot—would likely act.

"From the crooked timber of humanity," wrote Kant, "nothing straight was ever fashioned." And from the squishy stuff of humanity, nothing nonbiological was ever fashioned. Even the loftiest products of human imagination are, first of all, emanations of that gooey, breathing, eating, sleeping, defecating, reproducing, evolving, and evolved creature known as *Homo sapiens*. We aren't idealized, ethereal essences but genuine biological beings, shaped by evolution and twisted and gnarled by life itself. This is why the most damning observation that can be made about a character in a novel (or play or movie) is that he or she isn't believable, which is another way of saying that for fiction to make sense, it must accord with a kind of evolutionary reality. Too much artificial straightness won't do.

Interestingly, the exceptions—although not proving this rule—provide paradoxical confirmation. Thus for millennia readers have been fascinated by Achilles, despite his unrealistic immunity to injury; significantly, although he is physically inhuman, when it comes to his psychology Achilles is human indeed. His unbelievable invulnerability is combined with other altogether realistic traits, such as intense competitiveness, a penchant for sulking famously when he feels unappreciated, and a tendency toward anger when deprived of a loved one. Or take the character Pilate in Toni Morrison's *Song of Solomon*, who lacked a navel, thereby magically demonstrating her profound independence. Not only can such suspensions of disbelief be consistent with a biological approach to literature, but they also add to its richness insofar as they help italicize the underlying humanity of the characters in question.

Evolutionary psychology isn't currently part of the standard approach to interpreting literature, but perhaps its time is coming. After all, it is their universality, their human believability, that makes Shakespeare's characters readily comprehensible, despite the fact that they are now five hundred years old. Their language may sometimes be dauntingly archaic, but this only emphasizes the fact that, as the French say, the more things change, the more they remain the same.

There is something instantly recognizable about such basic, such obviously natural traits as Romeo and Juliet's hormonally overheated teenage love, Hamlet's intellectualized indecisiveness, Lady Macbeth's ambition as well as her remorse, Falstaff's drunken cavorting, Viola's resourcefulness, Lear's impotent rage, Othello's jealousy, and Puck's . . . well, his puckishness. And when the last concludes wonderingly in A *Midsummer Night's Dream*, "What fools these mortals be," the reader or theatergoer cannot but agree, because deep down she knows what human beings they—and each of us—all are.

Our point is that yes, Virginia, there is human nature, just as there is hippopotamus nature, halibut nature, even hickory tree nature. And the greatest of storytellers have been those who depict it. Let's grant, with Hamlet, that literature holds that mirror up to nature, including the nature of human beings. And so we are led to the assertion that evolutionary biological insights yield a powerful set of instruments with which to understand literature and, in the process, ourselves.

In *Madame Bovary's Ovaries*, we merge two worlds, literature and science, showing how fiction can be illuminated by the single most important idea in biology (evolution) newly applied to human behavior. We hope that our dissection of Madame Bovary's ovaries, Othello's jealousy, Holden Caulfield's alienation, and the like will reveal a novel way to read and understand. Not the *only* way, mind you—our intent is not to sweep away any current literary theories in favor of science—but a new one, a useful tool to add to each reader's kit. Our basic premise is simple enough, although oddly revolutionary at the same time: that people are biological creatures and that as such they share a universal, evolved human nature. Add to this our second basic principle: that evolutionary psychology, a decidedly nonfiction science, has been discovering why human beings behave as they do, and that it offers a raft of refreshing, rewarding, challenging insights into the world of fiction no less than that of fact. You hold the result in your hands: a new set of spectacles for the reader who is discerning, perplexed, or just plain curious and ready for something new.

At this point, it may be tempting to ask why any particular slant, whether theoretical or scientific, is needed in order to make sense of literature. Why not just read the books and let them speak for themselves? The answer is simple: people always use some sort of interpretive lens, whether they admit it or not. John Maynard Keynes wrote, for example, that when economists propose to do their work "without theory," this merely means that they are in the grip of some other, unacknowledged theory. There is no such thing as a truly naive reader, which is why experts in literature have long searched for new and useful ways to approach their subject.

Several decades ago, geneticist Theodosius Dobzhansky gave this title to a now-famous article he wrote for a technical journal: "Nothing in Biology Makes Sense Except in the Light of Evolution." Dobzhansky's dictum applies to the world of letters just as it does to the world of life, because the former is merely one manifestation of the latter: literature is life written down. Accordingly, literary critics—and, more important, garden-variety readers—should profit by adding the cardinal principle of the life sciences to their armamentarium. According to renowned literary theorist Northrop Frye, "Criticism is badly in need of an organizing principle, a central hypothesis which, like the theory of evolution in biology, will see the phenomena it deals with as parts of a whole." Such an organizing principle already exists, however, needing only to be recognized and developed. Ironically, it is the same one that Frye gestured toward so longingly: evolution. Whereas the various warhorses of traditional literary analysis offer intellectual richness, so does Darwin. Moreover, Darwin has this additional appeal: he was right.

Don't get the wrong impression. We are not proposing scientific veracity as the sole guidepost when it comes to approaching literature. After all, physics is also valid (despite what some postmodernists—many of them, incidentally, literary theorists—often claim), and yet it would be pointless and, indeed, comical to base an approach to literature on quantum mechanics, string theory, or general relativity. Even though, for example, suitable calculations of force, mass, and momentum would doubtless yield insights into Anna Karenina's terminal encounter with a train, we suspect that a strictly Newtonian analysis of Tolstoy's great novel would leave out some important (non-Newtonian) dynamics.

Nonetheless, given the near-universal scientific consensus when it comes to the origins and nature of life in general (including that of *Homo sapiens*), one might think that literary critics would long ago have rushed to embrace biology or at least to explore its potential usefulness. This, to our knowledge, has not happened, although from time to time scholars have at least gestured in that direction, and there is a nascent movement among a tiny minority of humanities professors to take Darwin seriously at last.

This is *not* to claim that biological realism should be the touchstone for literary quality (in fact, we doubt that there should or could be any single measure), although we have already suggested that to some extent, believability may be what logicians refer to as "necessary but not sufficient." There will always be room for the uniquely subjective qualities of literature, with its richly imaginative textures. Fictional accounts of what people *might* be like are in no danger of being supplanted by nonfiction representations of what they really do. Great literature is not rendered great simply by accurately portraying human nature; fiction is not ethnography or photography, nor should it aspire to be.

We find it significant, however, that for all the expressive freedom of literature, there is virtually no written equivalent of abstract expressionism, which is to say, arrays of words seemingly disconnected from any reference to the real world. Or think of the vast difference between literature and what psychiatrists call "word salad," the random, chaotic verbalizations of people suffering from a variant of schizophrenia. The point is that literature deals, however impressionistically and subjectively, with people, and the nature of people (just like the nature of their languages) follows certain consistent patterns, even as that nature is relatively open-ended and malleable. Couldn't there, shouldn't there, be room for readers to take this into account?

Literature, when done well, not only is timeless (think of *The Iliad*, *The Odyssey*, *The Aeneid*, *Hamlet*, *Don Quixote*, *War and Peace*, *Madame Bovary*) but also travels widely and deeply. The Japanese adore Shakespeare. Americans read Tolstoy and Dostoyevsky. *Don Quixote* has been translated into dozens of languages. "Nothing can please many, and please long," wrote Samuel Johnson in the preface to his edition of Shakespeare's plays,

> but just representations of general [human] nature . . . The irregular combinations of fanciful invention may delight awhile . . . but the pleasures of sudden wonder are soon exhausted, and the mind can only repose on the stability of truth.

Dr. Johnson is talking here about our old friend human nature—those universals that Aristotle so admired, that same source of "stability of truth" that serves as a kind of unmoving polestar throughout *Madame Bovary's Ovaries*.

Memorable literature owes its greatness to many things, including the artistry and imagination with which characters and situations are portrayed, not to mention the richness of the language employed, all made possible by the genius of the author. But if human nature isn't somehow in or behind the picture, then literature will have less staying power. For this reason alone, it seems certain that despite all the hand-wringing, the Western canon is solid; its grounding in the biology of human nature is what keeps it from becoming a loose cannon. In this regard, we must take issue with one of critic Harold Bloom's more quotable assertions: Shakespeare didn't "invent the human," evolution did.

Arnold Weinstein's book *A Scream Goes Through the House* is a fine contemporary work of more traditional literary criticism, subtitled *What Literature Teaches Us About Life*. It delivers generously on this promise. *Madame Bovary's Ovaries* might have had the reverse subtitle: *What Life Teaches Us About Literature*.

Get ready, in short, to get in touch with your "one nature," the one that not only reads and writes but also lives and is therefore abundantly reflected in the books and stories all around us. Let's see what happens when we marry the rich world of creative fiction to the equally rich world of biological insights. Our approach will be simple enough: we'll describe some of the key concepts in modern, Darwinian behavioral biology and try to show how they flourish in literature. In the process, we'll spread our nets widely, and if successful, we'll come up with an interesting and diverse catch.

We believe that the current offering is new,[1] and also, not coincidentally, going to be controversial. We hope that it will also be productive and—most of all—fun.

---

[1] Well, not entirely new. As already mentioned, some scholars—such as Brian Boyd, Joseph Carroll, Ellen Dissanayake, Nancy Easterlin, Jonathan Gottschall, and Michelle Sugiyama—have begun exploring the potential of "Darwinian literary criticism," but thus far their work has been directed toward a technical audience, and they certainly represent a minority, even among scholars.

2

OTHELLO AND
OTHER ANGRY FELLOWS

Male Sexual Jealousy

———————

Othello is a terrific tale of jealousy, murder, revenge, high passion, and low cunning. The tragedy has fascinated audiences for centuries, to the point that Othello himself has become emblematic of lethal and credulous jealousy, his wife, Desdemona, the embodiment of innocent victimhood, and his "friend" Iago the archfiend and purveyor of deadly disinformation. The play is great because it is wonderfully written, but its timeless, universal appeal may well be due at least as much to the fact that it taps into a deep underlying current of human frailty: sexual jealousy. Indeed, the depth of *Othello*, the play, derives from the extent to which it plumbs the depths of Othello, the deeply human, vibrantly organic creature.

Let's look, therefore, at Othello as a member of the species *Homo sapiens*. As a believable human being. And, most important, as a sexually jealous male.

The story, in brief: Othello is military commander of the armed forces of Venice. He has just married the young and lovely Desdemona. He has also just passed over one assistant, Iago, and named another, Cassio, as his chief deputy. Iago, boiling with hatred and rage, schemes to convince Othello that Desdemona has been unfaithful to him with Cassio. Othello eventually comes under Iago's spell and, driven nearly mad with jealousy, kills Desdemona, then himself. Exit stage right.

Othello wasn't simply jealous, a black African, and a war hero; he was also a *man*. This brings up some important biology. Men are different from women, not simply because of social traditions, the cut of their clothes, or, for that matter, the structure of their private parts. Even the notorious Elizabethan codpiece didn't cover the real meaning of "manhood" (birds, for instance, are unquestionably either male or female, and yet even the most "masculine" feathered fellows, such as hawks or eagles, lack external genitalia).[1] Rather, Othello's maleness stems from something that he and all men share with other male animals: sperm. Males are simply those creatures that produce an amazingly large number of very small sex cells. Whether bird or mammal, Venetian or Moor, this and this alone is how biologists distinguish the two sexes. Females are egg makers; males, sperm squirters. The truly important thing about Othello wasn't the color of his skin, his age, or his war record. Rather, Othello was all about sperm; Desdemona, eggs. So when the evil Iago egged on Othello, he was doing more than one might think. And herein lies a tale.

The most important consequence of the biological difference between the sexes is that one sperm maker can fertilize many egg makers. A female, by contrast, can generally be fertilized by the prompt exertions of merely one male. Therefore, the payoff for an already impregnated female to have additional male lovers is not nearly as great as it is for males to inseminate additional females. A woman's reproductive potential is necessarily limited: she can usually only have one—rarely, two—children every nine months. During that period, more sleeping around won't yield more offspring. On the other hand, consider the man's situation (whether or not his wife is pregnant): if he has sex with another woman, he has given himself the possibility of yet more descendants. If he

---

[1] Nearly all birds have a cloaca, which is a common opening for reproductive and excretory products. There are, however, some interesting exceptions: ducks, geese, and ostriches, for example, have penises. But this really doesn't matter for our purposes.

repeats the process yet again, with someone else, he might conceivably have conceived yet again. And again. And again.

This isn't to recommend such behavior, but to understand it. Moreover, we'll shortly see that women aren't as sexually reticent as just made out, but the general pattern is nonetheless clear: men are more likely to seek multiple sexual partners than are women. Similarly, they are more likely to be stimulated by the prospect of a casual sexual conquest, and also—tragically for both Othello and Desdemona—prone to sexual rivalry with other men as well as sexual jealousy of "their" women.

Another way of looking at all this from nature's point of view: eggs are large, expensive, and relatively rare since they only come one at a time and require a lot of energy if they are to be turned into children. Sperm, on the other hand, are small and cheap, and there is an almost inexhaustible supply. As a result, eggs and egg makers are limiting resources for the success of sperm and sperm makers, which is to say that the number of children a male can produce depends less on him than on how many women he can impregnate (and also on whether or not other males succeed in impregnating the woman or women he associates with).

These simple differences have enormous consequences for the behavior of males and females, men and women, Othello and Desdemona. First, males of most species make the most of their evolutionary prospects by having sex with as many females as possible. Each female is a potential target of opportunity and worth competing over because she is an egg maker, uterus bearer, and potential pregnancy maintainer. Although only one male is likely to hit a woman's reproductive bull's-eye at any one time, many are likely to try. The result, all too often, is trouble, especially among those avid, competing spermatic archers.

Under these circumstances, successful males tend to be those who have excluded others. Moreover, *really* successful males are those who have succeeded in monopolizing the sexual favors of more than one female. (This is equivalent to firing successfully at more than one target, a strategy that makes sense if the arrows are cheap and the rules of the game permit it.)

So what's a male to do? If his species is highly social—as in a variety of mammals, including *Homo sapiens*—he will likely aim at as many females as possible. In short, he'll try to obtain a harem, and when that's not possible, he will likely be prone to sleeping around . . . all the while worrying about the fact that his counterparts are trying to do the same thing. Othello's credulity, although excessive and eventually lethal, is exactly what one might expect from a man who, like most men, has an inkling of the lascivious inclinations of his competitors, in no small part because he doubtless feels them in himself.

After all, human beings are perfectly good mammals, and the evidence—from biology, anthropology, and history—is overwhelming that for most of their evolutionary history, men have aspired to be harem keepers and have engaged in sexually oriented male-male competition. It shows in our bodies, our brains, and our behavior—especially in the differences between men and women. Biologists call this sexual dimorphism (*di* = "two," *morph* = "shape"), which refers to the simple but consequential fact that among many living things, males and females are different, not only in their gametes but also in their anatomy as well as their inclinations.

The general pattern is simple and consistent: among harem-keeping species, males are larger, more aggressive, and more sexually assertive than females. Male gorillas, for instance, are considerably larger and more aggressive than females. Generation after generation, the largest, most aggressive silverback males outcompeted their rivals, and as a result they bequeathed their genes—for largeness and aggressiveness, among other things—to future generations.

To be sure, not all animals, or even all primates, have evolved this mating strategy. Creatures such as beavers, coyotes, or gibbons, for example, are mostly monogamous, and they show very few differences between males and females: very little sexual dimorphism. Chimpanzees, on the other hand, are quite close to human beings—measured by their DNA—but their flamboyantly erotic lifestyle has little resemblance to the more staid love life of *Homo sapiens*. Every species is distinct, some more monogamous and some less so, but certain general patterns nonetheless remain, including the fact that sexual dimorphism of the sort found among gorillas (and many other creatures as well, such as deer and seals) bespeaks males competing for the sexual attention of females.

What, then, about our own species? Human beings are pretty much in between the gibbon and the gorilla: more dimorphic than the former but less so than the latter. Although Judeo-Christian morality, not to mention the restraints of civil law, restricts westerners to monogamy, the biological fact remains that inside the most faithful husband there is a fervent philanderer—and, at least in part, a hopeful harem master—just waiting to emerge. And, by the same token, there is a sexually jealous competitor whose anxiety and anger is all too readily evoked. Just ask Othello.

Most of us are (or claim to be) monogamous, just like the ill-starred Moor. It is an open question, hotly contested among biologists and historians, why Western cultural tradition has overridden our natural polygynous inclinations. One possibility is that since under monogamy each man is more likely to get a wife, whereas polygyny necessitates that for every harem keeper there are frustrated, angry, and potentially troublesome bachelors, monogamy serves to diminish sexual discontent and thus promote social harmony. (Women, by contrast, will generally be mated whether the prevailing system is monogamy or polygyny.) In any event, anthropologists know that harem keeping is closer to our natural state than the current regime of culturally imposed monogamy. Thus, prior to the cultural homogenization of the last few centuries, upward of 85 percent of human societies were preferentially polygynous. For yet more evidence of our polygynous patriarchy, look at boy-girl differences at the age of sexual maturation. Girls grow up several years earlier than boys, a pattern that is consistent with polygyny in other animals: when the social life of a species is characterized by intense male-male competition, it's a bad idea to enter the fray when you are too young, too small, too weak, and/or too stupid to prosper, or maybe even to survive. Hence, in harem-keeping species, males don't start breeding—and, more to the point, struggling with other males for the opportunity to breed—until they are older and thus larger, stronger, and cagier. Moreover, the greater the degree of polygyny (that is, the larger the average harem size and hence the greater the intensity of male-male competition), the greater the disparity between the ages at which males and females become sexually mature.

Put this all together and there is simply no question about it: a Martian zoologist visiting the Earth would take one look at *Homo sapiens* and our sexual dimorphism in body size, inclinations toward violence and having multiple sexual partners, and male-female differences in age of maturation and would confidently conclude that at heart—and body and brain—human beings are preferentially polygynous. And one thing is true about a harem-keeping species: the payoff for success is large and the consequences of failure severe. Since there are roughly equal numbers of men and women, the reality is that the more polygynous the society, the greater the number of men left out in the nonreproductive cold, doomed to be frustrated, resentful bachelors. Most men can be grateful that monogamy is legally mandated: harem keeping is no picnic. The result? A high level of sexual competitiveness, even in a species such as ours, in which serious harem keeping is largely a distant biological memory.

Finally, add to this the fact that any male—whether highly dominant harem keeper or run-of-the-mill monogamist—can be cuckolded, and to top it off, the additional fact that (as explored more lasciviously in Chapter 5) females have their own hankering for occasional infidelity. The result is an evolutionary witches' brew in which men are especially subject to a heavy dose of sexual jealousy. Even if, like Othello as well as the rest of us, he inhabits a society in which polygyny is outlawed, and moreover even if he is not a frequent philanderer, the typical human male has been outfitted by a lengthy evolutionary past with a profound distaste for the womanizing of his fellow men as well as a sensitivity to being cuckolded by his fellow women.

To be sure, females are typically less than delighted if their male courts and inseminates other women. That's why Frankie killed Johnny, why harems tend to be difficult places, and why even in ostensibly monogamous households, woman-woman competition can be pretty intense (think of the movie *Fatal Attraction*). Still, men have more to lose than women when their partners are unfaithful. Once again, biology holds the key. The male's investment in mating isn't much to speak of; there is no comparison between a man's "lovin' spoonful" and a woman's pregnancy and lactation. More important, even if a philandering man ends up providing assistance to his extramarital lover and her offspring, a deceived woman is not going to be deceived as to *her* maternity, although if she also fools around she may have her doubts about the father.

A woman whose husband is unfaithful can still bear her own children, no matter who the father. A husband whose wife is unfaithful could end up in the same situation as a sparrow victimized by a cuckoo: manipulated into rearing someone else's offspring (hence the origin of the antique-sounding but very up-to-the-minute word "cuckold").

And so we return to Othello, a dominant bull elk or silverback male if ever there was one, but who—like the rest of us—has been culturally restricted to just one Desdemona at a time. It should be clear that it doesn't really matter whether such a male is ostensibly monogamous or polygynous: either way, it pays for males to be sexually jealous and thus highly protective of their reproductive prerogatives. During the rut, bull elk are notoriously aggressive and intolerant of each other, while cow elk are comparatively placid; even among monogamous songbirds, males regularly patrol their territories, alert for intruders.

Men have evolved to be similar to bull elk, or maybe even nastier, since women are fertile all year round. Not surprisingly, therefore, the

Othellos (and Cassios and Iagos and Roderigos—the latter a minor character who lusts for Desdemona and is manipulated by Iago into attacking Cassio, twice) among us pant after each other's women while simultaneously ready to be roused to jealous rage by any suggestion that someone else might do unto their woman (or women) as they long to do unto others'. To paraphrase Winston Churchill, men are often jealous beasts, with much to be jealous about.[2]

To make matters worse, Shakespeare's Othello-elk has a "buddy" whispering in his ear, introducing the poisonous pretense that a different young buck—Othello's lieutenant, Cassio—has been "enjoying" his Desdemona. Iago taunts, insinuates, and sets up innocent circumstances that appear to the credulous Othello to prove Desdemona's infidelity.

Of course, Iago is himself male, and thus he is both attuned to Othello's anxiously susceptible jealousy and also afflicted by his own, acknowledging at one point a suspicion that his wife, Emilia, might have been unfaithful . . . with Othello. "I hate the Moor," Iago soliloquizes, "and it is thought abroad that 'twixt my sheets, he's done my office." All in all, a nasty business, enmeshed in yet more intimations of male sexual jealousy via some of the peripheral characters.

It is also worth noting that Othello is considerably older than Desdemona, a pattern that lends itself to an additional slate of evolutionary insights. Yet another biological asymmetry between the sexes is that whereas women go through menopause, men remain potentially reproductive into old age. In addition, older, successful men—such as the rich, charismatic Moor—are further likely to be attractive to women because they offer the prospect of what we might call r-cubed: reproductively relevant resources. At the same time, such men are vulnerable to women seeking to profit from their superior wealth and social prestige, who then cuckold them

---

[2] Churchill once described his political rival Clement Atlee as "a modest man, with much to be modest about."

with younger, more physically attractive specimens. In short, there is a female proclivity to get wealth, power, and protection from one male and sperm from another.

As we'll see later, when we confront Madame Bovary and her sisterly soul mates, this is a very ancient pattern, well ensconced in the animal world no less than in our own, and it leads to yet another variant on the theme of male-male sexual competition: older, more powerful men versus others who are younger and less socially successful—but often more physically attractive—over access to sexually appealing, nubile women. No one should be surprised, therefore, when the middle-aged Othello is prone to anxiety about possibly being sexually supplanted by his young lieutenant.

Othello has plenty of company. Think of King Arthur contending, unsuccessfully, with Sir Lancelot over Guinevere. Or the tale of Tristan and Isolde: King Mark is a bit like Othello—somewhat elderly, albeit influential—and sure enough, his bride-to-be, Isolde, falls for Mark's emissary, Tristan, who is youthful and dashing and whose appeal is also, truth to tell, abetted by Isolde's consumption of a magic love potion. (Isn't it possible, moreover, that the love potion part of this myth is an attempt to explain an attraction that biology interprets more directly and plausibly?) According to Homer's account, Menelaus is older and a king but loses Helen to the younger Paris. Euripides' tragic tale *Hippolytus* recounts the erotic infatuation of Phaedra, wife of the older Theseus, with her eponymous stepson. This story had sufficient resonance, moreover, for Racine to update it in his greatest play, *Phaedra*. It is a dynamic that isn't restricted to tragedy, however, having become the subject of many a barbed comedy of manners, from Boccaccio's *Decameron* to Chaucer's *Canterbury Tales* and the plays of Molière, Oscar Wilde, Tom Stoppard, and Edward Albee.

Put all this together, and Othello's jealousy is not an isolated peculiarity; it reflects an enduring, universal theme. To be sure, the plot—like much of Shakespeare—is overwrought, and yet the audience cannot simply dismiss *Othello* the play as absurd or downright preposterous, because men in particular cannot simply dismiss the plight of Othello the person: sexual jealousy is too much a part of everyone's biological and social experience. George Bernard Shaw managed nonetheless to despise *Othello*, complaining of its "police court morality and commonplace thought." But Shaw's greatest weakness as a playwright lies precisely in his tone deafness to male-female dynamics, which includes, crucially, male-male sexual competition à la *Othello*. As to "commonplace thought," that's precisely the point: nothing is more devastatingly commonplace than male sexual jealousy, especially when it takes a violent turn.

Not surprisingly, sexual jealousy isn't unique to *Othello*. It emerges in much of literature, as in life, and when it does—especially if it is violent—it is likely to be a guy thing. People, like elk, are only human.

For example, male-male competition animates "The Knight's Tale," the first and longest of Chaucer's *Canterbury Tales*. It is the story of two cousins and—until sexual rivalry intervenes—best friends, Arcite and Palamon, who have been imprisoned and who both fall in love with the same woman, whom they ogle from their prison window. One is eventually released and the other escapes, whereupon, in a lovely melding of chivalric propriety with Darwinian sexual competitiveness, they agree to a lethal fight to the finish, with the winner to get the girl. Thus doth best friendship give way to murderous violence, once the best friends have—hath?—become sexual competitors. "The Knight's Tale" being a medieval romance, there is, of course, more: before Arcite and Palamon proceed to hack each other to bits, they are met by King Theseus, who had originally imprisoned them, and whose sister, Emilye, is their shared inamorata. Theseus demands that the two contestants put up their swords and meet one year hence, each attended by one hundred armored knights, to battle it out for the hand of the fair damsel. Which they do.

Shakespeare was evidently taken with the story, so much so that he borrowed it for his last play, *Two Noble Kinsmen*, co-authored with John Fletcher. Others have also been taken with the theme of male-male competition—not surprising, since it takes up so much of human endeavor.

F. Scott Fitzgerald, for example, is generally seen as the great chronicler of the decadent Jazz Age, but he was at least as much a bard of male sexual jealousy, which drives *The Great Gatsby* just as much as Jay Gatsby drives himself and his famed automobile. When, in the novel's ironic denouement, the cuckolded George Wilson kills Gatsby, it is in a fit of sexually jealous rage, thinking—wrongly—that his wife, Myrtle Wilson, had been unfaithful with Gatsby, when in fact Tom Buchanan was the culprit, that same philandering Tom who was married to Daisy, Gatsby's secret flame. Most critics and readers focus on the mystery of Jay Gatsby's past and his quintessentially American striving for money and success, all the while missing the role of male-male competition not only in motivating Gatsby's personal trajectory but also in powering its tragic denouement.

Nor are sexual jealousy and male-male competition necessarily limited to duos, such as Othello and Cassio, Arcite and Palamon, or Tom Wilson and Jay Gatsby. For a case of multiple male sexual jealousy, consider *The Sun Also Rises*, by Ernest Hemingway, a great writer whose star has recently been in partial eclipse within the American literary establishment, partly because of his uninhibited sexism. It is likely, however, that the critical pendulum will once again swing in Papa's direction, due in no small measure to the acuity with which this most masculine of all writers perceived the underlying persistence of sexual tension among men. Thus, in traditional interpretations, *The Sun Also Rises* depicts the "lost generation" between World Wars I and II. But it also does a masterly job of depicting male-male competition, in this case for the beautiful, pleasure-seeking Lady Brett Ashley. Or rather, call it male-male-male-male competition, since the rivals are Mike Campbell (her fiancé, a wealthy Scot), Jake Barnes (an impotent, wounded war veteran), Robert Cohn (an aspiring writer and amateur boxer), and Pedro Romero (a handsome, up-and-coming young bullfighter).

Lady Brett can't keep away from men, who buzz around her like besotted flies. She really loves Jake, who really loves her, too, but can't do much about it. Cohn keeps pestering her, but his insecurity is a big-time turnoff. By contrast, the confident, sexy bullfighter Pedro Romero is definitely a turn-on, and indeed, Brett and Pedro have an affair, but it doesn't last and she ends up going back to Mike Campbell, with his alcoholic, wealthy, upper-class ways. Meanwhile, Cohn—who is an accomplished boxer—picks fights with Jake, Mike, and the erotically charged bullfighter before remorsefully leaving town just as the story seems to be heading for an impressive climax of passion and jealousy. In Hemingway's hands, the "lost generation" is so lost that even sexual rivalry can't energize it. Othello might well wish for a bit of the lost generation's ironic indifference. But in fact, the pugilistic Robert Cohn—who beats up Romero, Mike Campbell, and even the nonthreatening Jake Barnes—more accurately reflects the male sexual style.

Recall that sperm are cheap and easy to replace. So it has been biologically advantageous for males to spread their seed widely, or at least to give it a try. As with Robert Cohn, this may involve punching people in the nose if they think it will help, or, in the case of Pedro Romero, engaging in high-risk, flashy activities (e.g., bullfighting) as a way of getting noticed—and, if possible, bedded—by the ladies. Or being rich and upper-class, like Mike Campbell. But not to get shot in the balls, like Jake Barnes! By the same token, a cuckolded husband is widely considered pitiable; he is a loser, not only socially but also biologically. Indeed, he is a double loser, since on top of the injury of being potentially nonreproductive is heaped this heavy material insult: he may well end up expending time, effort, and expense in the rearing of someone else's child. No wonder there are Othellos, Gatsbys, jilted lovers, and jealous husbands of all kinds echoing in our literature: they resound no less in our biology. The real wonder is that there aren't more.

Actually, there are. Threatened adultery pops up as a theme in many other depictions, not least those of Shakespeare. It abounds, for example, not only in *Othello* but also in *Much Ado About Nothing*, in which young Claudio makes much ado about what seems to him something indeed: his perception (entirely incorrect, it turns out) that his bride-to-be, a heroine aptly named Hero, has been "unchaste." Interrupting their wedding, Claudio denounces Hero as promiscuous: "she knows the heat of a luxurious bed," or so he claims, and it requires much of the rest of the play to clarify that she is altogether innocent in every sense of the word.

Claudio is young, inexperienced, and easily confounded.[3] The same applies to another male Shakespearean creation whose credulity falls for yet another false report of female infidelity: Posthumus, husband in *Cymbeline*—which, incidentally, lays claim to flaunting the most preposterous of all Shakespearean plots, the only believable component of which is Posthumus's anguish when he is led to believe (falsely, once again) that his wife, the faithful Imogen, has had sex with the devious Iachimo (shades of Iago). Iachimo bets Posthumus that he can seduce Imogen. He fails—Imogen is as pure as Hero, or Desdemona—but succeeds in smuggling himself into Imogen's bedchamber, after which, by describing its contents (including Imogen, whom he evidently ogled most indecently), he persuades Posthumus that he won the bet:

> Under her breast—
> Worthy the pressing—lies a mole, right proud
> Of that most delicate lodging.
> By my life, I kissed it, and it gave me present hunger
> To feed again, though full.
> You do remember
> This stain upon her?

---

[3] Actually, there is a far more interesting couple in *Much Ado About Nothing*: Benedick and Beatrice, who are older, wiser, and wittier. Their byplay speaks less to male sexual jealousy than to matters of female choice in particular, à la Jane Austen, which we take up in the next chapter.

At this, Posthumus is thrown into a paroxysm of grief and rage, proclaiming his wife as suffering from "another stain, as big as hell can hold." Posthumus goes on to torture himself by imagining Iachimo as superstud: "Perchance he spoke not, but, like a full-acorned boar [i.e., one whose "nuts" are intact], . . . cried 'O!' and mounted."

And so, like Claudio denouncing Hero, Posthumus rejects Imogen, even scheming to have her killed. Fear not: everything is straightened out in the end. But Shakespeare knew, as well as Darwin, that it will happen again, that men are not only sexually jealous and often violently so, but astoundingly willing to believe the worst, especially if it involves a threat to what they fancy as their sexual monopoly over a woman.

Such violent sexual credulity is hardly limited to the young and callow, neither in nature nor in Shakespeare. Our exemplar, Othello, was a middle-aged specimen, "declined into the vale of years." And in *The Winter's Tale*, we see another man in the throes of a sexually charged middle-aged crisis. The play begins with King Leontes unaccountably—and again, falsely—accusing his faithful wife of committing adultery with his childhood friend, then visiting Leontes's court. It ends with forgiveness and reconciliation. Ditto for *Much Ado About Nothing* as well as *Cymbeline*. These plays have all been criticized for their bizarre plots (seeming statues that come to life, a headless corpse mistaken by the faithful Imogen—of all people—for her husband), which are literally incredible. Yet even the most carping critic or jaded theater patron is likely to agree that these plays, amid all their absurdity, remain stunningly believable in one respect, and probably only this one: each paints a realistic picture of male sexual jealousy.

Of course, male-male competition has been going on for hundreds of millions—perhaps billions—of years, and Shakespeare wasn't the first to write about it.

Legend has it, for instance, that the Trojan War was set in motion when Paris (son of the Trojan king) ran off with Helen (wife of Menelaus, a major Greek king). At its end, the victorious Greeks kill the male Trojans and divvy up the women—a bloody, inhumane, but all-too-human resolution that occurred often in the Old Testament as well and is powerful testimony to the persistence of the competitive impulse. Over and over, whether in the Bible or *The Iliad*, men fight other men, with women as the prize; indeed, the earliest descriptions of war involve male-male competition far more than faceless armies maneuvering against each other. In such cases, two goals are at stake: direct access to fertile females and achieving social status.

Make no mistake: underlying both is the promise of male competitive success, and especially sexual—and thus reproductive—fulfillment. At one point, when the Greek army is especially demoralized, the wise and aged Nestor cheers them up by reminding them that Zeus has promised victory, which means that no Greek will have to "hurry to return homeward until after he has lain down alongside a wife of some Trojan." But even in such simplistically sexual situations, men are typically also maneuvering for status and prestige, mostly because where status and prestige are found, women are not far behind.

An animal parallel comes to mind: when choosing among possible mates, female red-winged blackbirds elect to nest with males whose territories are especially desirable, which means, for this species, that they contain predator-proof nest sites. Not surprisingly, this motivates male redwings to compete for access to those desirable territories. And who gets such access? Those who are socially dominant. Nor is this pattern unique to blackbirds. In essentially every species that forms a hierarchy of social dominance, the individuals at the top get the lion's share of the ladies. Even among chimpanzees, which don't partake of a simple, linear dominance hierarchy or an easily depicted sex life, high-status males tend to have more offspring than do subordinates.

The famous wrath of Achilles—an undoubtedly dominant male—is kindled by the fact that Agamemnon, brother to Menelaus and chief military honcho among the Greeks, had taken the gorgeous Briseis from Achilles. Not insignificantly, Briseis had been "given" to Achilles as a reward for some of his earlier heroic exploits, all of which involved killing other men. It is made clear, however, that Achilles isn't so much enamored of Briseis as he is of his own reputation. His anger derives from the threat to his social status and prestige, which is inextricably linked to his sex appeal.

Combat isn't simply mano a mano by force of arms alone; it also involves one-on-one verbal jousting, with extensive taunts, threats, and boasts, all of which are attempts to diminish the other and enhance oneself. Moreover, such vigorous competition is only marginally less intense within the armies on each side.

As anthropologist Robin Fox describes it, "The Greek warriors, beached on the sands of Troy, very much resemble giant elephant seals angling for upward mobility in the social and reproductive hierarchy. Those who top the hierarchy are men like Achilles, Ajax, Odysseus, Agamemnon, and Diomedes—they are huge, sleek, bellicose animals."[4] Just as alpha elephant seals get the most females, so do the most dominant warriors. Such dominance is typically established by contests staged among members of the same army. Robin Fox once again:

> The games are designed to award the talents typical of elite warriors: speed, guile, martial art, level-headedness, muscular bulk, and power. As on the battlefield, there are arguments, spear-thrusting and hurtling, punching and grappling, flying feet, clattering chariots, rock hurling, and arrow-shooting. . . . A very similar dynamic plays out in all other intra-army confrontations. They include all varieties of manly posturing, posing, rumbling, bellowing, flexing, chest puffing, and teeth baring.

---

[4] "Sexual Conflict in the Epics," *Human Nature* 6 (1995): 135–44.

All this is not to claim that men are *just like* elephant seals; rather, they are *like* elephant seals. Whether men, or women, like it or not.

At one point in the games of *The Iliad*, Diomedes and Ajax have at each other in a ritualized spear and sword fight that becomes so potentially deadly that the observers have to separate the two. Then there is a boxing match involving someone named Epeios, who proclaims that he will thoroughly destroy his opponent: "Utterly will I break apart his flesh and crush his bones. Let his mourners, who are his kin, wait in a throng so they can carry him away after my hands have broken him."

And these guys are supposed to be on the same side!

Nor is such posturing limited to literary depictions of the heroes of yore. Moreover, it isn't even necessary that women be the immediate prize. Like stallions rearing and snorting in a stable even with no mares nearby, men will often posture and puff themselves up even in an all-male environment. In such cases, women are nonetheless the behind-the-scenes motivators. Here, for example, is Mark Twain's account of a fight witnessed by Huckleberry Finn, when he had stowed away on a barge making its way down the Mississippi. A dispute broke out between two "rough-looking men," and one of them

> jumped up in the air and cracked his heels together again and shouted out: "Whoo-oop! I'm the original iron-jawed, brass-mounted copper-bellied corpse-maker from the wilds of Arkansaw! Look at me! I'm the man they call Sudden Death and General Desolation! . . . I take nineteen alligators and a bar'l of whisky for breakfast when I'm in robust health, and a bushel of rattlesnakes and a dead body when I'm ailing. . . . Stand back and give me room according to my strength! Blood's my natural drink and the wails of the dying is music to my ear. . . ."
>
> Then the man that had started the row . . . jumped up and he began to shout like this: "Whoo-oop! Bow your neck . . . for the massacre of isolated communities is the pastime of my idle

moments, the destruction of nationalities the serious business of my life! The boundless vastness of the great American desert is my enclosed property, and I bury the dead on my own premises! . . . Whoo-oop! . . . the Pet Child of Calamity's a'coming!"[5]

In Twain's hands, male-male competition is larger than life, filled with bluff and bluster, and comically absurd, whereas in Homer's, it is tragic. This may be due in part to the simple fact that in *Huckleberry Finn*, the competition occurs in the absence of women; it is men's entertainment, but also deadly serious and undergirded—as is all male-male competition—by the portentous prospect of who comes out on top. Hence the whooping and hollering, the speaking in exclamation points, and if need be beating each other over the head. Once men have established their dominance hierarchy, the likelihood is that a parallel hierarchy of reproductive access and thus evolutionary success will follow.

It isn't necessary, incidentally, for the participants to understand the connection between male aggressive bravado and reproductive success. It isn't even necessary that immediate sexual triumph follow from competitive social success. The key connection is that in the past, men who succeeded in besting other men were likely, as a result, to succeed in conveying their genes into future generations, either because they won more women directly or because they won prestige and social success, which in turn resulted in their being chosen by more women as well as deferred to by subordinate men.

Reading Twain, one cannot help laughing, but with a rueful recognition of the plausibility that underlies such absurdly excessive posturing. But the posturing isn't merely an arbitrary artifact of frontier America. Reading Homer, it is similarly easy to assume that one is eavesdropping on culture-specific behaviors that have

---

[5] We thank Steven Pinker and his book *The Blank Slate* (New York: Viking, 2002), for making us aware of this quotation.

nothing to do with animals, but dig deeper in either case—beneath the veneer of nineteenth-century America or classical Greece—and you strike underlying roots in biology, a bedrock that all human beings share with elephant seals, elk, gorillas, and much of the animal world.

To an extent only rarely appreciated by social scientists, and essentially not at all by self-proclaimed experts in literature—including classicists, whose contact with the raw ferocity of the blood-soaked Homeric epics should have taught them better—the human and animal estate are now, and have ever been, fundamentally identical.

Sometimes the violent outcome of male-male sexual competition is wildly exaggerated, although the underlying motivation rarely is. Let's turn briefly to *The Odyssey*, whose grand finale features a classic—in more ways than one—case of male-male competition over women, in this case the famously faithful Penelope and the mob of 108 (count 'em!) ill-mannered suitors, whose primary ill-manneredness consists of the fact that they have been lusting after another, higher-ranking man's woman. In the climactic scene, that horny horde of heavy-handed bachelors is challenged to string Odysseus's great bow, a test of physical strength and ancient manliness. Of course, only Odysseus can do it, whereupon, with the help of his son Telemachus, he proceeds to slaughter all the upstarts and reassert his claim to the throne, and to Penelope.

In the animal world, there is no end to the competitive hijinks in which males will engage, struggling to supplant each other in order to get their Penelopes. At the same time, it must be acknowledged that male-male competition, whether animal or human, needn't always generate violence. Sometimes it merely festers, leaving its participants marinating in a hormonal broth of equal parts anxiety, frustration, and barely repressed jealousy.

Take Marcel Proust's *In Search of Lost Time*, a masterpiece of great art distilled from memories and recalled perceptions. It is difficult to imagine two worlds of literature that are more disparate than the blood-soaked, brain-bespattered, lusty epics of Homer— dating from several thousand years ago—and the delicate, mannered, cultivated, and almost painfully fussy recollections of a rather effete and retiring scion of the French upper middle class at the onset of the twentieth century, who spent much of his adulthood carefully crafting his words in a darkened, cork-lined room. And yet they be of one blood, Homer and Proust.

Much of the richness of Proust's oeuvre consists of its evocation of—you guessed it—male sexual jealousy. Thus, *In Search of Lost Time* (more popularly mistranslated as *Remembrance of Things Past*) recounts the obsessive competitive anguish of three major characters regarding the sexual infidelities of their lovers. Saint-Loup, Swann, and Marcel cannot shake off the worries and woes associated with their lady friends. Marcel, for instance, spends much of his early adulthood tracking down the multihued love life of Albertine, the love of his young life, not at all daunted by the fact that by this time she had been killed in a horseback riding accident.

As Arnold Weinstein describes it in *A Scream Goes Through the House* (New York: Random House, 2003),

> the narrator continues to imagine, with ever more frenzy, scenes of betrayal committed by Albertine, acts of sexual independence that can (now) never be corroborated or disproved because the actress is no longer available for interrogation (not that much was ascertained even when she was). The dead Albertine romps through her imagined sexual repertory, thanks to the prodigiously creative jealousy of her grieving lover.

Nor is Marcel's jealousy diminished by his discovery that Albertine was a lesbian. One might expect that insofar as sexual jealousy is reproductively driven, homosexual infidelity to one's heterosexual partner would be of little account, but this fails to reckon with the powerful emotional undertow of motivations driven by evolution. When biology confronts the need to implant a potent response—as is certainly the case for sexual jealousy—it is likely to do so by linking that response to behaviors that are powered by emotion, rather than by reason, and that are quickly and reliably aroused. The fine-tuning of whether infidelity is same-sex (and hence, less likely to have reproductive consequences) is less important than the simple, blunt, and powerful panhuman abhorrence of a partner's infidelity, period. Especially when the "infidel" is female.

By the same token, one might expect that heterosexual infidelity could also be easily ignored, so long as the unfaithful partner used a condom. Of course, it isn't that simple. After all, birth control is very new on the evolutionary horizon; there isn't time for *Homo sapiens* to have evolved a suitably nuanced response to it. And sex with someone else, even avowedly nonreproductive sex, cannot help conveying a threat of restructured affection as well as the prospect of further infidelity in the future.

Sexual competition dies hard, if it ever does. In Proust's huge multivolume novel, as in this brief selection from one of its components, *The Captive*, the dogged persistence of sexual jealousy is the reason jilted lovers insist on "ransacking the past, in search of a clue," a search that may well turn up nothing, but continues nonetheless:

> Always retrospective, it is like the historian who has to write the history of a period from which he has no documents; always belated, it dashed like an enraged bull to the spot where it will not find the dazzling, arrogant creature who is tormenting it and whom the crowd admires for his splendour and cunning. Jealousy thrashes around in the void.

To be sure, even men can get along. And literature isn't shy about depicting it. Significantly, however, in such cases, the two (rarely more) collaborating Y chromosome carriers usually have a clear dominance relationship: Don Quixote and Sancho Panza, Robinson Crusoe and "his man" Friday, the Lone Ranger and Tonto.

Social equals in similar situations are expected to fight, or at least to strut and posture and act like jerks on occasion. They might well display their professed "manliness" like Charles Bukowski, whose writing reflected a persona that was self-consciously hard-drinking, wildly womanizing, heavily gambling, two-fisted, usually unemployed, abused, and abusive. Bukowski's first collection of short stories was given the memorable—and biologically appropriate—title *Erections, Ejaculations, Exhibitions, and General Tales of Ordinary Madness.* Most of its erecting, ejaculating, exhibiting, and otherwise maddening behavior takes place in a male-dominated context, in which, not surprisingly, various aspects of male-male domination figure prominently. For another, even more recent array of male-male violence (typically over one or more women, but sometimes with sex in the background . . . although never very far), pick up Cormac McCarthy's *Blood Meridian* or any of his Border Trilogy: *All the Pretty Horses, The Crossing,* and *Cities of the Plain.*

And of course, there is nothing like competition over a woman to drive a wedge between men who might otherwise be the best of friends. Probably the iconic modern example in this case is *McTeague,* a classic example of literary naturalism written by Frank Norris and published in 1899. The eponymous hero is physically imposing but not especially bright, charming yet also prone to drunkenness and violence. McTeague works as an unlicensed dentist, sometimes extracting teeth with his bare hands. His best friend is Marcus, who is engaged to Trina. But McTeague also falls for Trina, and vice versa, whereupon Marcus obligingly steps aside and the two marry.

All is not well, however. Barely repressed sexual jealousy and competitiveness between the two men bubble just beneath the surface. Their buddyhood inevitably and irrevocably dissolves. While attending a picnic at which wrestling matches are held, McTeague and Marcus are the two winners. When they face each other,

Marcus bites off part of his "friend's" ear, and McTeague responds by breaking Marcus's arm. Shortly after, McTeague is barred from practicing dentistry: someone had informed the San Francisco authorities that McTeague was practicing without a license. It was Marcus.

McTeague becomes increasingly alcoholic and violent, physically abuses Trina, and eventually kills her. He flees to Death Valley, California, where he is eventually confronted by a man with a gun: none other than Marcus, who had volunteered for the manhunt to capture Trina's killer. The two men—friends no more—struggle, during which Marcus is mortally injured, but before dying he succeeds in handcuffing himself to McTeague. Exposed to the broiling desert sun, without water, and lethally linked to his sworn enemy, McTeague, too, will die.

McTeague is in part a critique of American acquisitiveness and materialism; in 1924, director Erich von Stroheim adapted it into a renowned silent film titled *Greed*. But Frank Norris's novel may be even more powerful as a depiction of the destructive effects of male-male sexual competition. Thus, when the reader first meets McTeague, he is basically gentle and harmless, a "draft horse, immensely strong, stupid, docile, obedient." After being sexually awakened by Trina, however, his brutishness is aroused, tragically revealing itself in his treatment both of her and of his erstwhile friend, Marcus. When Marcus bites McTeague's ear during their wrestling match, this evokes "the hideous yelling of a hurt beast, the squealing of a wounded elephant. . . . It was something no longer human; it was rather an echo from the jungle." Here, author Norris missed a crucial point: echoes from the jungle are often profoundly human, especially when they involve males struggling with each other over females.

Nor are females necessarily passive, as we have already noted. They are more than capable of stimulating male-male competition; in fact, a frequent pattern involves the femme fatale encouraging her lover to kill another man, not uncommonly her current husband. It has become almost a genre unto itself: sexy, somewhat sociopathic drifter dude meets equally sexy, alienated wife of boring or downright beastly husband, whereupon drifter/lover kills husband, with encouragement—either covert or overt—of wife. For example, James Cain's *The Postman Always Rings Twice*, an explicit tale of adultery and murder, and a sensation when it appeared in 1933, employs a kind of tough-guy, Mickey Spillane objectivity to describe the murderous outcome when Frank Chambers, a young drifter, seduces Nora Papadakis, wife of service station owner Nick Papadakis. In this lurid tale, Frank and Nora decide to murder Nick (obese, middle-aged, and no longer appealing to his young wife) and collect the insurance money. Consider how rare, by contrast, is the mirror image: sexy woman meets unhappily married man and then proceeds to murder his wife. It's not that women don't compete, but rather that they generally do so with more subtlety and less violence. What do you think of, for example, when you consider the well-known fact that girls or women commonly engage in "telephone aggression"? Perhaps this: that they are likely to employ catty, undermining gossip. Now think about men or boys making hurtful use of a telephone: likely by hitting one another over the head with it.

At the same time, female-female competition is no less real than its male-male variety; as will be seen in the following chapter, it has its own peculiar flavor and style, less violent than the ill-fated Othello or McTeague, but nonetheless more vigorous than that of mere cheerleaders egging on their male counterparts. Accordingly, we turn next to females, and ask: what does the nature of femaleness, and thus womanhood, teach us about those women we meet within the stories we tell ourselves about ourselves?

3

THE KEY TO JANE AUSTEN'S HEART

What Women Want, and Why

———————

Freud famously asked "What do women want?" but didn't even try to answer. Biologists have a pretty good idea, however. So do the world's great novelists.

Take Jane Austen. Her scope was remarkably limited—in geography, in events, in diversity of people: just a few middle- and upper-class families in one or another rural village in England during the late eighteenth and early nineteenth centuries, when the author herself lived. Add to this the fact that Jane Austen is, of all famous novelists, perhaps the *least* interested in nature, animals, and biology; she barely even bothers with basic physical descriptions of her characters. (Were they tall or short, thin or fat, brunette or blond?) And yet Austen captured universal truths, making her one of the English-speaking world's most beloved writers. So here we have the redoubtable Ms. Austen, writing about a very restricted range of human experiences, yet touching on one of the most fundamental and universal of all situations.

That situation is simply this: finding the right mate. All of Jane Austen's novels are love stories; all of them are concerned with getting the major characters suitably married; and in all of them, things work out eventually. Sounds boring—especially, perhaps, to men—but it isn't! Austen understands that the stakes are high, the outcomes weighty. And regardless of gender, the reader can't help sharing in her sense of bemused urgency, since the personalities are handled in such a masterly way, their characters lively and compelling, and, of course, because they are dealing with something that has obsessed our own species (and most other living things) for millions of years. Darwin called it sexual selection, and as we have seen, when it involves competition between individuals of the same sex, and particularly when those individuals are male, things can get aggressive, even violent.

At the same time, there is another side of sexual selection, namely, mate choice. Males and females "hooking up" isn't just a matter of pushy, angry, potentially violent Othellos competing with each other and occasionally even murdering their consorts; it's also a question of Desdemonas carefully and often peacefully choosing their Othellos. We have already described how, in the most dramatic cases, males push and shove and otherwise seek to overmaster each other for the biological bottom line: the reproductive payoff that comes from getting a mate. (Or, if they are especially lucky or well positioned, several mates.)

Jane Austen's domain is less confrontational but, in its way, no less dramatic, and certainly no less important. It is the female-oriented realm of sexual selection: choosing a mate and getting chosen. Just as males have largely cornered the market on violent same-sex competition, females occupy the spotlight when it comes to the choosy component of sexual selection. Why this difference? Essentially, it's because females have something that males want. Since males are comparatively eager and more or less sexually undiscriminating ("easy come, easy go" is a biologically accurate account of male sexuality, on several levels), females are often in the driver's seat: mate choice is largely their province. Of course, mate choice can be a female prerogative only among those species in which mate choice occurs at all. The typical female elephant seal, gorilla, or elk—creatures that for various reasons have thrown in their lot with a large-harem strategy—have woefully little opportunity to exercise sexual preferences. As we saw in the last chapter, species in which males keep big harems are those in which males are, well, particularly big, and generally rather nasty to boot. Cow elephant seals, female elk, and lady gorillas therefore have little choice but to mate with the master.

But then there are those other species, such as human beings, that still possess various stigmata of harem keeping but are also somewhat predisposed to pair bonding. In such cases, although male-male competition is an unavoidable fact of life, females also get to have their say, all the more so because they are the keepers of what biologists call "parental investment." This refers to eggs and everything that follows: a placenta, pregnancy, lactation, a high probability of maternal devotedness, and so forth. By contrast to this rich bounty of female attractions, male mammals have little to offer but their sperm, and so, in a strictly anatomical sense, they are beggars looking for a handout. In fact, a singles ad placed by males might read, "Nearly naked packages of DNA looking for a suitable home." Biologically, females are the wealthy ones; all males, even those with the fattest wallets, are paupers. So in our own species as well as many others, females get to exercise choice, deciding who among the eager suitors is to get their hand . . . and their breasts, vagina, and most crucially uterus, with all that entails.

As a result, women are in a position to drive a hard bargain, saying essentially, "You can have my goodies, but only if you provide assets of your own in return." What assets? Money, social prestige, good genes, a guarantee of parental assistance, what we referred to in the last chapter as r-cubed: reproductively relevant resources.

As part of courtship, men the world over commonly ply their dates with flowers and seek to impress them with fancy cars, expensive clothes, and elegant restaurants, often expecting sex in return. Rare is the man who doesn't see sex as a desired (if often unfulfilled) goal at the end of a date. Women, in turn, send countermessages. By acquiescing sexually, they are signaling that the man has what it takes to win their affection; by refusing, they may be saying either that he does not or that they are simply not sure, or they may be emphasizing that their own investment is so valuable that it cannot be obtained quickly. Women are exercising their choice, toting up the available r-cubed, waiting for the right fellow to come along.

And this is where Jane Austen shines. She is the poet laureate of female choice. Selection of the right marital partner is central to her writing, more so than for any other major novelist. Nearly always, Austen's women are in the driver's seat (and never more so than when they adroitly lead a man to think that *he* is). Darwin suggested that female choice is the motive force behind sexual selection; he pointed especially to the elaborate tail feathers of male Argus pheasants and peacocks, suggesting that such seeming absurdities evolved because generations of females have preferred to mate with the more elaborately bedecked males. (As we'll see, there are two major reasons why this peculiar preference might have evolved. For one, fancy males may be healthier as well as genetically better endowed than their plainer compatriots. For another, by preferring males who are appealingly ornamented, a female makes it likely that she will produce sons whose ornamentation will be similarly appealing to their own future mates. The result? She will have more grandchildren; her choosiness causes more of her genes—including those for choosiness—to be passed on.)

In any event, bright colors, pendulous wattles, shiny plumage, an elaborate song repertoire, or large canines or horns or antlers have come to characterize the males of many species. Whenever fancier males are preferred by females, natural selection will automatically ramp up the fanciness of males, simply because the plainer models are more likely to go unmated, and thus their plainness dies with them.

Modern biologists understand that this applies not only to physical characteristics but also to such traits as intelligence, generosity, and "control of resources" (which is to say, wealth and social standing). There is an old, sarcastic saying that the rich get richer and the poor get children. In the biological world, things are a bit more complex and even less fair: the rich get children, and the poor get next to nothing. Thus, "wealthy" blackbird boys—that is, those who own desirable, predator-free territories—get more blackbird girls and, in turn, more offspring. The "richest" male woodchucks, whose burrows are deep and safe and who occupy good feeding areas, attract the healthiest, womanliest woodchucks, with whom, once again, they have more offspring. Evolution rewards immediate success (including but not limited to wealth and social prestige) with reproductive success, and one way it does so is by instilling a female preference for successful males. Or at least a preference for males who are more successful than they are.

"If I were a carpenter, and you were a lady," asks the male voice in a popular folk song, "would you marry me anyway, would you have my baby?" To this, the female responds reassuringly (especially for carpenters) in the affirmative. But the truth is that most women, throughout most of history, would have answered with a resounding "No way!"

Jane Austen showed how it actually works among human beings. She wrote six novels, each justly famous today. In every one, the reader quickly meets the ideal mate for her heroine, but along with him are introduced many other characters, some of them plausible partners but each flawed in some crucial way.

And so we watch and wait, in a mixture of fascination, delight, and even on occasion a shiver of fear, as her protagonists work their way through their inevitable patches of sexual quicksand or hack through innumerable threatening thickets of social entanglements. Just as in our shared evolutionary past (and present), sexual choice for Austen's characters takes place in a social environment, chockfull of possibilities, and the tension mounts as we wonder who will end up with whom and whether the heroine will recognize that her own best interest lies in connecting with one fellow rather than another, often despite the urgings of society and family. Austen provides us with just enough obstacles and alternative outcomes to leave things uncertain, often until the last few pages.

What do Jane's young ladies look for in a mate? The same traits that female animals generally look for in their swains. Call them the three goods: good genes, good behavior, and good stuff. In other words, looks, personality, and money, although not necessarily in that order. Once again, given that males bring very little, anatomically and physiologically, to the reproductive marketplace, it is only natural—literally—that females choose among males based on what they *do* have to offer: the quality of their genes, their ability and inclination to be a good partner, and the quantity of their r-cubed—the size not of their penis but of their wallets.

It deserves to be repeated: wealth isn't merely a human construct. Among living things generally, parents who have valuable stuff—food-rich or predator-free territories, good nest sites, a den that lends itself to successful birth or hibernation, and so forth—can count on having a larger number of more successful offspring. And in turn, they can count on being preferred by members of the opposite sex for precisely this reason. This approach also suggests why human wealth—especially in its more arbitrary forms, such as gold or fancy trinkets—is considered desirable at all: because in the past at least, those who possessed it were able to exchange it for evolutionary success, even if such a transaction is less reliable in today's world.

Of the three goods, r-cubed loomed especially large in Austen's day and—despite the supposedly liberated twenty-first-century world—in ours. Thus, human beings, no less than blackbirds or woodchucks, find wealth appealing, not only as a goal for themselves but also as a sexual attractant when present in a potential partner. As already mentioned, resource-rich males of nearly every species become remarkably attractive at a level that often goes beyond (or beneath) conscious awareness. And in this regard, *Homo sapiens* may well take the cake.

"It is a truth, universally acknowledged," writes Jane Austen in the famous opening sentence of *Pride and Prejudice*, "that a single man, in possession of a good fortune, must be in want of a wife." She goes on:

However little known the feelings or views of such a man may be on his first entering a neighborhood, this truth is so well fixed in the minds of surrounding families that he is considered the rightful property of some one or other of their daughters.

In *Pride and Prejudice*, Mrs. Bennet—mother of five daughters—is laughably obsessed with "eligible" men, that is, single gentlemen possessing such fortunes. Indeed, part of Austen's genius has been to identify, dissect, and at the same time give life to this "truth," which other writers have more often accepted as simply embedded in the social landscape, so taken for granted as to go unremarked upon.

Pride and Prejudice opens as a country estate has been rented to Mr. Bingley, a wealthy London gentleman, which greatly encourages Mrs. Bennet to hope that her chief goal in life—finding suitably wealthy husbands for her marriageable daughters—will attain fruition. Mr. Bennet has the temerity to suggest that perhaps Bingley hasn't rented Netherfield Park with the express intent of marrying one of the Bennet daughters. (But we all know better.) As it happens, Bingley hits it off splendidly with Jane, the oldest Bennet daughter; moreover, he has a close friend, as rich as he is unmarried, named Darcy. Darcy, however, is very proud, and he initially insults Elizabeth Bennet, the second oldest sister; Darcy's pride evokes corresponding prejudice in Elizabeth, the sprightly, attractive, clever, and altogether admirable heroine. He also evokes something else. (More on this in a moment.)

Other characters appear: Mr. Collins, a ridiculously pompous clergyman who is also a conceited bore, but who will shortly come into possession of the Bennet property because Mr. Bennet has no male offspring; Wickham, a dashing officer who is an immediate hit with the ladies but who, we are led to understand, is something of a bounder, not above misrepresenting his assets as well as his intentions; Charlotte Lucas, a friend of Elizabeth's who is getting a bit long in the tooth (all of twenty-seven years); Elizabeth's three younger, rather ditzy sisters, Mary, Kitty, and Lydia, who are led more by their hormones than their heads; and an array of others. Eventually, Lydia runs off with Wickham, the regrettable Collins marries Charlotte Lucas, and—after many on-again, off-again embarrassments, annoyances, near misses, and misunderstandings— Bingley becomes engaged to Jane Bennet. Darcy's pride is sufficiently humbled and Elizabeth's prejudice adequately mollified so that Darcy and Elizabeth, too, announce their forthcoming nuptials.

A useful term for much of this is *hypergamy*, literally "marrying up." Men try it, too, but given the biology of male-female differences, it makes sense that hypergamy is a female specialty. This is to say that women can—and often do—insist on mating only with the best male if possible, one who represents some sort of improvement over their present condition. After all, since one male can fertilize many females, there is a certain logic to females insisting—insofar as they have choice in the matter—that their mate be an especially good specimen. Compared to many other species, human beings are often able to exercise such choice, which, when the opportunity arises, comes down to women choosing men who are particularly well-off. Dominant, wealthy, well-positioned males therefore not uncommonly mate with subordinate, poorer, less-advantaged females, and not the other way around. In fact, marriages in which women are wealthier or otherwise "above" their husbands generally have a poor long-term prognosis, whereas for women, "marrying up" is a widespread goal, perhaps even the norm.

In fact, this pattern is so well established—in the animal world generally and the human one in particular—that dominant, healthy seals and elk, as well as wealthy, upper-class people, are more likely to favor their sons, while the socially disadvantaged tend to invest more in daughters.

In F. Scott Fitzgerald's *Tender Is the Night*, we are given a masterly depiction of reverse hypergamy (we might call it "hypogamy," although, significantly, such a term doesn't even exist). Here, the beautiful, exceedingly wealthy Nicole Warren is married to up-and-coming psychiatrist Dick Diver. He is bright enough and attractive, but given that she—not he—is the wealthy one, the relationship would likely be biologically unstable, except for one fact: Nicole is mentally ill (the victim, we later discover, of childhood sexual abuse) and Dick is/was her shrink. As time goes on, however, Nicole gets stronger—and even richer when her father dies—while Dr. Dick gets weaker. His comparative poverty is increasingly evident, he has an affair with a much younger woman, and he begins to drink excessively. Dick Diver's downward spiral is matched by Nicole's upward progress, culminating—not surprisingly—in her leaving him for the dashing soldier Tommy Barban. Dick Diver dives indeed, into obscurity.

Another, related take on *Tender Is the Night* relies on the possibility, in twentieth-century America, for women to accumulate resources through inheritance, which in turn facilitates reverse hypergamy (women associating romantically with men who are "below" them). Nicole Warren is the one with the money; Dick's the one with the looks, personality, smarts, and, relatively speaking, good mental health (i.e., likely good genes). But the Warren-Diver duo is still not the norm, a situation of reverse hypergamy that is emphasized when Nicole's condition improves, whereupon her relationship with Dick becomes increasingly untenable.

Untenable relationships are sometimes maintained nonetheless, as memorably portrayed, for example, in Edward Albee's *Who's Afraid of Virginia Woolf?* Here we witness the painfully dissatisfied marriage of Martha, daughter of the local university president, to George, a middle-ranking, middle-aged disappointment (at least to Martha) who, as she likes to point out, is *in* the college's history department, as opposed to *being* the history department. George has failed to live up to both Martha's and her father's expectations; her marriage, like that of Nicole Warren to Dick Diver, is another case of reverse hypergamy, with a predictably rocky outcome. Martha explains her feelings toward her husband as follows:

> "He was the groom . . . he was going to be groomed. He'd take over some day . . . first, he'd take over the History Department,

and then when Daddy retired, he'd take over the college . . . you know? That's the way it was supposed to be. . . . And Daddy seemed to think it was a pretty good idea, too. For a while . . . Until he watched for a couple of years and started thinking maybe it wasn't such a good idea after all . . . that maybe Georgie-boy didn't have the *stuff* . . . that he didn't have it in him! . . . So, here I am, stuck with this flop . . . who's married to the President's daughter, who's expected to *be* somebody, not just some nobody, some bookworm, somebody who's so damn . . . contemplative, he can't make anything out of himself, somebody without the *guts* to make anybody proud of him."

George and Martha seem unlikely to divorce, although in Albee's lacerating depiction of the pain generated by such role reversals, the audience cannot help wishing that they would.

For a more traditional account of hypergamy "as it ought to be"—or at least as evolutionary biology would predict—take one of the most famous depictions of a female adventuress: Becky Sharp in Thackeray's *Vanity Fair*. Published several decades after the works of Jane Austen, *Vanity Fair* presents a much less sympathetic portrayal of Becky's hypergamic efforts. Whereas Jane Austen's heroines are smart, plucky, deserving, and socially sensitive, Becky Sharp is scheming, unethical, and selfish, but nonetheless exceedingly attractive to men. She sets her cap for Rawdon Crawley, son of a very rich family, and marries him secretly, but in the process she ends up alienating his wealthy father and even wealthier aunt, who—horror of horrors—disinherits her nephew.

At this point, a biologically attentive reader is likely to anticipate trouble. Sure enough, growing impatient with her husband's "reduced circumstances," Becky becomes the mistress of rich old Lord Steyne, eventually taking up with the prosperous Jos Sedley, brother of her closest childhood friend. Jos unwisely takes out a large insurance policy with Becky as beneficiary, and then—surprise—dies under unexplained circumstances, leaving Becky Sharp a wealthy woman at last.

Hypergamy triumphs.

But not everyone cheers. It is likely not a mere coincidence that Thackeray, a man, takes a much darker, more critical view of hypergamy than does Austen, a woman. Readers can't help siding with Jane's heroines, so sympathetically portrayed in their efforts to get the right man, whereas Becky Sharp may well represent male distrust of scheming hypergamous females. Especially considering that she ends up with all the stuff without having provided the female side of the bargain: offspring, . . . or even sexual fidelity.

Often, "marrying up" is at least as much a goal for a young woman's family as for the sweet innocent thing herself. Gabriel García Márquez's *Love in the Time of Cholera* is a love story beginning with the death of an elderly doctor, whereupon his equally elderly wife, Fermina Díaz, is the surprised recipient of protestations of eternal love from a comparably aged gentleman, Florentino Ariza. As the story unfolds, we learn that nearly fifty-two years earlier, Fermina and Florentino had been young lovers, but, in a fit of Austenesque bio-logic, she rejected him as unworthy. Shortly after, Fermina's father pressured her to marry the doctor—an especially "good catch" because he was already a prestigious physician—and the two lived together, although with more stability than happiness, for upward of five decades. Fermina's earlier hypergamy sets the stage for the ensuing novel, which follows the renewal of affection between Fermina and Florentino once the doctor (the object of Fermina's father's hypergamic lust by proxy) has died.

We also learn, interestingly, that during the ensuing five decades between Fermina's rejection of Florentino and their late-life reunion, Florentino had numerous affairs, despite vowing a kind of distant fidelity to Fermina, and that he had also become a successful businessman in an effort—ultimately rewarded—to make himself attractive to her. Throughout this marvelously evocative and bittersweet novel, love is equated with illness (including but not limited to the cholera of its title), but it is also presented as a disease that can be ameliorated, if not cured, with enough "medicine" in the form of money and social prestige.

Let's be clear, however. Whereas successful hypergamy can indeed be a winning ticket for a woman (and, of course, for men such as Fermina's physician-husband, who constitute the jackpot), it can be a disaster for guys at the bottom. Had Florentino remained as fiscally unprepossessing as he had been fifty-two years previously, the widowed Fermina never would have considered taking him as her geriatric lover. Someone who is unable to seduce a woman by his physical or intellectual charms alone (this includes most men) and who also lacks money is unlikely to make it with the ladies, regardless of his age. In *Down and Out in Paris and London*, George Orwell wrote perceptively about the situation of the English hobo, or "tramp":

> Any presentable woman can, in the last resort, attach herself to some man. The result, for a tramp, is that he is condemned to perpetual celibacy. For of course it goes without saying that if a tramp finds no women at his own level, those above—even a very little above—are as far out of his reach as the moon. The reasons are not worth discussing [note: we beg to differ on this point!], but there is no doubt that women never, or hardly ever, condescend to men who are much poorer than themselves. A tramp, therefore, is a celibate from the moment when he takes to the road. He is absolutely without hope of getting a wife, a mistress, or any kind of woman except—very rarely, when he can raise a few shillings—a prostitute.

In *Vanity Fair*, the matrimonial desirability of the various male characters varied predictably as their wealth ebbed and flowed, but at least people were pretty much what they seemed. (Except for Becky Sharp, whose male victims are consistently blinded by her coquetry and beauty.) In other cases, people actively misrepresent their resources; when they do, for some reason they are much more likely to err on the side of appearing richer! In the world of most living things, neediness isn't especially attractive; wealthiness is.

Edith Wharton's *The Custom of the Country*, one of her most notable books, introduces one of literature's strongest if most unpleasant characters, Undine Spragg, whose pursuit of money rivals Becky Sharp's. We can do no better than to repeat the following by critic Harold Bloom (*How to Read and Why*, New York, Scribners, 2001), who—all the more appropriately for our purposes—summarizes Ms. Spragg's hypergamic frenzy without knowing that he is doing so:

> The story of Undine Spragg, as created by Edith Wharton, has epic dimensions and thuggish protagonists, a contrast that keeps it lively. Undine is an unstoppable sexual force, almost occult in her destructive drive. . . . [She] boils up out of Kansas into New York City, where she marries the wealthy socialite and would-be artist Ralph Marvell. Later, she gives herself to Peter van Degen for a two-month affair. After rejecting poor Marvell, inducing his suicide, Undine devours a French aristocrat, Raymond de Chelles, and then returns to her first, secret Kansan marriage with Elmer Moffat, now a New York billionaire. That is the gist of Wharton's fable; Elaine Showalter sees Undine as the answer to Freud: "While Freud asks, 'What do women want?,' Wharton replies, 'What have you got?' "

Edith Wharton was a snob, an anti-Semite, and an apostle of wealth and social class who, in *The Custom of the Country*, appropriated Thackeray's Becky Sharp and brought her up to date. Hypergamy, however, needs no updating. It is older than the human species. And its depiction leaves a well-trodden trail.

One of the earliest English novels, *Moll Flanders*, by Daniel Defoe, provides a marvelously picaresque account of attempted hypergamy, with an added double cross. This book, published in 1722, actually bears the following remarkable—and descriptive—title: *The Fortunes and Misfortunes of the famous Moll Flanders, who was born in Newgate, and during a life of continued variety, was twelve years a Whore, five times a Wife (thereof once to her own brother), twelve years a Thief, eight years a transported Felon in Virginia, at last grew rich, lived honest, and died a penitent.* The story of Moll, the world's best-known "picaroon," is one of unrelieved efforts at hypergamy. At one notable point, she leaves a banker with whom she had been flirting to marry Jemmy E., a wealthy Lancashire gentleman. Moll had led Jemmy to believe that she, too, had "means," although she didn't. And sure enough, she soon discovers that Jemmy was similarly leading her on! The two rogues, well matched, turn out to be a congenial couple after all.

Fast-forward nearly three hundred years to a much lesser novel, but one that continues the hearty hypergamous tradition: *Maneater*, by Gigi Levangie Grazer. It tells the story of Clarissa Alpert, a twenty-first-century California girl whose sole purpose in life is to bag a rich husband. She sets her sights on Aaron Mason, checks him out on Google, decides he'll do just fine, and marries him, but soon ends up leaving this frantic phone message: "Mommy, it's Clarissa. There's been an emergency. Aaron is poor."

If the matter of good resources is so obvious as to require little elaboration, the question of good behavior is so complex that it is impossible to do it justice. For one thing, resources are pretty much obvious: it takes money to buy—or even to rent—a gracious country estate, to maintain an elegant team of horses, to afford to do nothing with one's days beyond attending balls, going on hunting parties, or visiting one's equally well-to-do neighbors. Sometimes, though, behavior (whether good or bad) is equally obvious: Collins, the soon-to-be-wealthy minister in Austen's *Pride and Prejudice*, is also a here-and-now pompous jerk, too pompous and too much a jerk to hide it. But on occasion behavior can be faked. For example, Wickham, the military officer, is a liar and a blackguard. And so it behooves Elizabeth Bennet—as with other female mammals whose precious parental investment is at stake—to be a careful comparison shopper: squeezing the Charmin, checking for signs of good or bad behavior beneath the surface.

One especially important trait to assess in a would-be mate is what we identify as parenting potential, notably a man's inclination and ability to take care of kids, either his own, perhaps by a previous relationship, or someone else's. After all, human beings are extreme among mammals in the degree to which their babies are born helpless, as well as in the amount of subsequent parental care they require. Any woman prospecting for a reproductive partner can therefore be forgiven—nay, expected—to evaluate whether he seems suitable in this regard. Speaking biologically, it is a matter of predicting a partner's likely level of parental investment—which requires not only that a presumed investor has the wherewithal to invest, but also the inclination to do so. (Note, by the way, that such assessments are likely to be hardwired into the human psyche, not at all attenuated by a possible commitment to intentional childlessness.)

Significantly, it isn't lost on Elizabeth Bennet that for all his superior airs, Darcy extends protection to Elizabeth's sister, Lydia, when she is vulnerable. Elizabeth also learns to discriminate the realities of character when it may be hidden behind peculiar or idiosyncratic behavior; for example, she learns that Wickham may be agreeable enough, but that he is lacking in conscientiousness. Similarly, she must detach herself from her father (who is lamentably careless, despite his pleasant, cultivated ways) and affiliate with Darcy, who, albeit stiff-necked, is also more responsible. Much of the mating game à la Austen—and also à la Darwin—is carried out by assessing personality structure by way of telling incidents, which help separate likely dads from cads.

To understand what appeals to many women, listen to Czech novelist Milan Kundera as he describes a male conquest that was powered by a young man's expressed interest in a young woman and his solicitude for her:

On that fateful day, a young man in jeans sat down at the counter. Tamina was all alone in the café at the time. The young man ordered a Coke, and sipped the liquid slowly. He looked at Tamina. Tamina looked out into space.

Suddenly he said, "Tamina."

If that was meant to impress her, it failed. There was no trick to finding out her name. All the customers in the neighborhood knew it.

"I know you are sad," he went on.

That didn't have the desired effect either. She knew that there were all kinds of ways to make a conquest, and that one of the surest roads to a woman's genitals was through her sadness. All the same she looked at him with greater interest than before.

They began talking. What attracted and held Tamina's attention was his questions. Not what he asked, but the fact that he asked anything at all.

Incidentally, in Kundera's novel it didn't hurt that the young man was also driving an expensive red sports car. Resources, anyone?

Why is it seductive to be a good questioner? Or even a questioner at all? Almost certainly, the mere act of inquiry says something about one's solicitude for the person being interrogated. Consider the joke about the self-obsessed movie star who in the course of a date during which he has spoken continually about himself finally announces: "Let's talk about you now. What did you think of my latest movie?"

It is seductive to be a good listener no less than a questioner, and once again we suspect this is because listening is another sign of reproductively relevant good behavior: taking the time to really listen to someone indicates attentiveness and hence a greater probability of committing oneself to the person being attended to, of being more likely to stick around and help out when things get tough, and so forth. A cartoon in the *New Yorker*, titled "Male Prostitute," featured a well-dressed man on a street corner, speaking with a woman: "Oh yeah, baby, I'll listen to you. I'll listen to you all night long!"

Then there is the question of good genes. When it comes to the courtship antics of animals, genes are typically on display in the size, color, and style of one's body, as well as via the ability to sing an elaborate courtship song, bellow loudly, patrol a hotly contested territory, and so forth. Austen barely notes her characters' physical appearance except for observing whether they are "pleasing" or "plain." At the same time, she is hardly unaware of the consequences. Elizabeth Bennet's friend Charlotte Lucas is described—somewhat offhandedly—as homely. When the lamentable Mr. Collins proposes to Elizabeth (who rejects him, much to her mother's consternation and her father's approbation), Collins proceeds immediately to make the same offer to the less attractive Charlotte, who promptly accepts. Here once more is Jane Austen as a discerning, intuitive biologist who understands what modern researchers have only recently discovered: that animals are capable of remarkably accurate self-assessment. Dominant, desirable specimens are likely to drive a harder reproductive bargain, insisting on comparably desirable mates. Those such as Charlotte Lucas are less discriminating. Beggars can't be choosers. Or at least, they are often obliged to be less choosy.

If Jane Austen's heroines seem overtly unimpressed by their suitors' physical appearance (in the early nineteenth century, it would have been more than a bit unseemly to comment on a guy's nice buns; a "square, manly jaw" was about as far as one could go), they more than compensate by their awareness of the minutest details of each other's behavior and speech. In fact, one of the special delights of *Pride and Prejudice*, as well as Austen's other novels, is the witty repartee, the clever observations, the insightful comments of the major characters, which is to say, the verbal and thus mental adroitness of the heroine and her anointed husband-to-be.

In a now-famous study of sexual attitudes in thirty-seven different societies, evolutionary psychologist David Buss found that men and women differed consistently in their preferences for a partner, with men emphasizing youth and physical attractiveness and women being especially focused on wealth and reliability. Relatively little attention has been paid, however, to what Buss's research found about the shared preference of both men and women: for kindness and intelligence. For kindness, substitute "good behavior," and for intelligence, "good genes." Moreover, in a highly social species such as ours, mental functioning can readily be assessed by competence at conversation. Here again, Jane Austen provides a textbook case of sexual selection in action, as her protagonists reveal their intellects—while stimulating the readers'—via their verbal adroitness.

We've already mentioned the peacock's tail, so intriguing to Darwin (as well as to the peahen). Darwin was looking for an explanation for why animals—especially males—would grow such ridiculously ornate structures when they don't seem to add to success in the travails of daily life; if anything, in fact, they are liabilities, since fancy feathers and the like take time and energy to construct and, in the case of telltale tails, make it more difficult to hide from predators as well as possibly precipitating an awkward or even life-threatening tangle in the bushes.

The key is that while peahens are indeed looking at the peacock's tail, their motivation is more practical than Darwin's: they are on the prowl for signs that whoever they choose as a sperm donor is up to the job. This means that the male in question is strong, healthy, and more or less free of parasites and disease. What better way to ascertain this than to lose your heart only to males who are able to construct a veritable Taj Mahal of a tail? Although it's clear that the best way to a peahen's eggs is by a whale of a peacock's tail, that appendage is really a signifier of something else: male quality. A peacock who is struggling to fight off diseases or internal parasites would have a hard time also devoting the thousands of calories needed to grow such a fancy structure. So a well-ornamented peacock is either comparatively pathogen-free or genetically well endowed (in somewhat old-fashioned human discourse, he must have a "strong constitution").

Moreover, feather-based fussiness on the part of the peahen conveys an extra benefit: a peacock who passes muster would also be likely to bestow comparable anatomical architecture on his (and thus her) offspring. As a result, when the next generation of peacocks and peahens go a-courting, any male offspring of a choosy peahen will probably have a tail that is a chip off the old cock's block, and thus he, too, will attract his share of starry-eyed peahens. This argument—known as the "sexy son hypothesis"—has received strong support from theoretical biologists, who have tested it via computer simulations, as well as fieldworkers, who have observed it among many different species.

In his book *The Mating Mind*, evolutionary psychologist Geoffrey Miller has proposed that the mind of *Homo sapiens*, elaborated as it is far beyond the straightforward necessities of survival and reproduction, represents the human equivalent of a peacock's tail, with mental agility serving as an indicator of competence, whereby the capacity to charm members of the opposite sex—as by constructing elaborate, syntactically accurate, suitably polysyllabic, and intellectually stimulating sentences, perhaps such as this one!—is an evolutionary consequence of a process not dissimilar to what Jane Austen's heroines and heroes engage in so brilliantly. (And which we imitate at our peril.)

Evolutionary geneticists refer to "runaway sexual selection," in which preference for a trait can take on a biological life of its own, whereupon something in the opposite sex will be preferred simply because it is preferred. Thus, like peahens choosing a peacock with a fancy tail because their ancestors did so, and thereby producing sons with fancy tails that were preferred in their turn, Austen's people—and people in general—probably choose others with a fancy vocabulary not only because this indicates intelligence, mental health, and education but also because it suggests that the fancy talkers' offspring will themselves be fancy talkers and thus verbally seductive in their own right when show-off time comes around for the next generation.

In any event, it is nearly impossible not to be charmed by the intellectual alacrity of Austen's courting couples, just as the couples themselves are presumed to have been. If people were peacocks, we expect that Jane would be dilating with enthusiasm upon the glories of visually contrasting spots, especially when combined with the shimmering effulgence of natural iridescence.

For another example of sexual selection and Austen in action, consider her novel *Mansfield Park*. Here is the tale of Fanny Price, a poor relative fostered to the wealthy Bertram family, where she joins her cousins Edmund, Tom, Maria, and Julia, and—of course—their various suitors. These include Mr. Rushworth, as rich as he is stupid, and Henry Crawford, charming but self-centered and unprincipled, as well as Henry's sister, the shallow and frivolous Mary Crawford. Maria Bertram loves Henry but is engaged to Rushworth. Henry falls for Fanny (the novel's heroine), who secretly loves Edmund, who thinks he loves Mary. Fanny turns down Henry, thereby showing her spunk but also angering the elder Mr. Bertram, who can't understand why she should refuse such an "advantageous match." Maria, who eventually gives up on Henry, marries Rushworth, then runs off scandalously with Henry, while sister Julia elopes with another eligible bachelor and man of fashion, Mr. Bates. Got it?

But things work out reasonably well. The Bates dude turns out to be a tolerably good catch after all, since he has fewer debts and more income than Julia's father had supposed, while Maria eventually leaves her disreputable union with Henry. Moreover, Edmund comes to realize that Mary Crawford isn't for him: she didn't appreciate the seriousness of the transgression committed when her brother ran off with the already married Maria, thereby suggesting that Mary herself might well be less than reliable as a potential wife. Most important, it finally dawns on Edmund that he actually loves Fanny, who early on had recognized that stalwart, wealthy, intelligent, and thoughtful Edmund was just the man for her. We all breathe a sigh of relief.

It surely is noteworthy that the first *Mansfield Park* character to marry, Maria Bertram, chooses Rushworth, the richest guy in the county. Maria lacks Fanny's keen judgment and ability to see beyond Rushworth's "good resources." After all, she isn't the heroine. Fanny, on the other hand, has the strength of character and perspicacity of judgment to resist pressures that she accept the caddish Henry Crawford and to recognize Edmund's superior overall value.

Most readers find it easy enough to arrive at a similar recognition. Why shouldn't Austen's characters be equivalently perspicacious? Indeed, they often are. And so, just as in real life it is not unknown for two or more women to choose the same man, in literature, too, we find women facing off over men. Add to this the fact that people are unusual among mammals in that fathers/husbands often provide a fair amount of parental investment (protecting the family from predators, getting food, helping rear children, and so forth). The upshot is that good men may indeed be hard to find, and worth competing over.

The study of female-female competition among animals has long taken a backseat to concern with its male-male counterpart, in large part because the latter is more eye-catching and decibel-raising, as well as ear- and skull-splitting. But increasingly, biologists are discovering a rough edge to the former. For example, when female monkeys "babysit" each other's offspring, their apparent solicitude is often mixed with a substantial dose of child abuse. And among many species, including wolves, dominant females inhibit the ovulation of subordinates. To be sure, there are even cases of female-female violence, as with this discovery: when a male house sparrow dallies with an otherwise unattached females send olfactory cues that the male's "lawful" mate will occasionally kill any offspring that result. More often, however, female-female competition is less obvious but perhaps no less effective. Among starlings, for example, if a mated male begins showing sexual interest in any of the local bachelorettes, his "wife" typically ramps up her own sexual receptivity, thereby monopolizing his amorous attention (or at least trying to).

Female-female competition features prominently in Greek mythology, particularly among the goddesses Athena, Aphrodite, and Hera. The last, in addition, seems to spend much of her time getting even with the various nubile earthly women who have been the recipients of her husband Zeus's extracurricular visitations. Nor is the Roman version lacking in comparable competitiveness. Virgil's *Aeneid* is underpinned by a constant struggle between Venus (Aeneas's mother and protector) and Juno (his sworn foe) as the two goddesses vie to undermine, outsmart, and outmaneuver each other, using human beings as proxies.

Goddesses, however, don't kill each other, although we hesitate to present this as evidence that female-female competition is less violent than the male-male variety (after all, one of the perquisites of divinity is immortality, and even the male gods don't typically murder one another). To be sure, there are lethal manifestations of female-female competition in the world of letters, although they are less frequent and less prominent than their male-male counterparts. Regan and Goneril, murderous daughters of Shakespeare's *King Lear*, both lust after the equally vicious Edmund, as a result of which they alternately poison and stab each other. Mostly, however, the literary imagination pictures rival women as schemers and bad-mouthers who limit their backstabbing to the metaphoric. Consider, for example, the hilarious vitriol heaped upon each other by Hermia and Helena, both of whom have developed a love-potion-induced infatuation with the same young man, in Shakespeare's *A Midsummer Night's Dream.* Or the comic dressing-down served up by Polly Peachum and Lucy Brown in Brecht's *Threepenny Opera* (which was based, in turn, on an eighteenth-century play, *The Beggar's Opera*). Polly and Lucy, rivals for the affection of Mack the Knife, compare waistlines and bustlines and argue over whose ankles are the slenderest.

Jane Austen, not surprisingly, is fully up to showing us how female-female competition works, in the process weaving it carefully into her beautifully realized depictions of female choice. Toward the end of her novel *Emma*, such competition emerges with the suddenness of a literary lightning bolt. Up to this point, our eponymous heroine had been unavailingly meddling in the love lives of everyone around her. Then Emma's protégée, Harriet Smith, reveals that she has lost her heart to George Knightley, a longtime friend of Emma's family, surpassingly rich, woefully above Harriet's social station, but—as every reader discerns early on—just right for Emma herself. No sooner does Harriet announce her "unseemly attachment" than Emma realizes that she herself loves Knightley and that she couldn't possibly imagine him married to anyone else!

Incidentally, studies of mate selection in fish have shown that a male guppy initially rejected by females will suddenly become highly attractive to guppy gals after the experimenter rigs things so that it appears that other females have been attracted to him. It seems to be the sexy-son hypothesis in action, with females clamoring to mate with a male once he is identified as popular. Perhaps it is the piscine equivalent of the George Knightley effect.

Back in the world of human beings and Jane Austen, female-female competition is depicted in *Mansfield Park* as well as in *Emma*. Maria threw in her lot with Rushworth because of his money, then realizes her error when Henry Crawford shows up; in fact, the early phase of the novel is taken up with the courtly catfight between sisters Maria and Julia over Henry, who has both money and brains (although he is a bit underfunded in the scruples department). There is also another—and more significant—case of female-female competition in the works between Fanny Price and Henry's sister, Mary, over Edmund. Initially, Fanny seems too insignificant (too poor, too dependent, too young) to compete with Mary, but eventually she triumphs. When Henry Crawford decamps—he wasn't really interested in either sister—Maria goes ahead and marries Rushworth, so when Henry returns, he turns his charm upon Fanny. Henry is a thoroughgoing rake, but his masculine wiles are not adequate for him to win over our Fanny, who remains sufficiently discerning to hold out for Edmund.

Back at Mansfield Park, once Henry has been rejected by Fanny, he runs into Maria in London; this is when he gets her to run off with him. Maria's tale is thus a mini *Madame Bovary*, but our attentions are elsewhere. Henry's sister, Mary, refuses to be "shocked, *shocked*" at her brother's behavior—behavior that involved Edmund's sister, no less—and so she reveals herself as insufficiently attuned to the merits of female fidelity, not only in the reader's mind but in Edmund's as well.

Why are Mary's attitudes about fidelity so important to Edmund? Or any man, for that matter? And wouldn't any woman be equally concerned about Henry's fidelity? Well, yes and no. Here's the biological angle: women get pregnant, not men, and as a result, men can be cuckolded—induced to rear someone else's offspring—whereas women are at least guaranteed to be genetically related to their own children. So in all human societies, a woman's marital fidelity is considered (by men) as far more important than a man's to a woman. The double standard, which is essentially pancultural, is not due so much to patriarchal churlishness as to the biology of internal fertilization, which is equally universal. If, as is the case, female infidelity is often punishable by death and its male counterpart by a slap on the wrist, this is likely underpinned by the fact that philandering by the two sexes is asymmetric in its genetic consequences. Thus, it is noteworthy that although philandering by a married man is typically not seen as a big deal in most cultures, it is a transgression not only moral but potentially mortal if the woman in question is married, in which case it is seen as a crime against the husband . . . largely because, on an evolutionary plane, it is a crime against his confidence of paternity.

Consistent with these concerns, Edmund listens to his own internal whisperings of biological doubt, which suggest that Mary Crawford might well turn out to be the female equivalent of tomcatting Henry. It is then that he notices Fanny—not just as a pleasant companion but as a prospective mate—and the two are married.

Like all of Austen's best characters, Edmund and Fanny excel at reading the social dynamics around them and are ultimately rewarded for their acute assessments. Biologically sophisticated readers will translate this into a genetic reward not unlike that of a discerning peahen or a gullible guppy. This, in turn, means that Fanny's characteristics—including not only her wise assessment of Edmund but also her success in female-female competition—will likely be projected into the future, abetted by Edmund's resources and good behavior.

Pride and Prejudice and *Mansfield Park* are widely acknowledged among literary critics as prototype Regency romances, in which a proud, rich, sometimes overbearing, and wealthy aristocrat (typically male) eventually marries the comparatively poor, good, intelligent, spunky young girl. *Jane Eyre*, which came several decades later, is closer to the Gothic genre: the plucky heroine, terribly alone, arrives in a gloomy and threatening place and encounters a hero who is equally gloomy and threatening; he is initially distrusted but eventually wins the girl's love, and she his. If the mechanics have changed (admittedly not a lot), the basic biology hasn't. In *Jane Eyre*, the austere Mr. Rochester has a terrible secret: he is married, and to a frightening madwoman, Bertha Mason, who lives in the attic and periodically attacks him with demonic fury. And yet Rochester shows unmistakably good behavior in that he commits resources to caring for his crazy, scary wife.

It is worth noting that Rochester's prior marriage does not itself make him any less suitable as a partner for Jane Eyre; by contrast, however, prior sexual experience on the part of a woman—the impregnated sex—is typically much more troublesome (see Chapter 4). Rochester is obviously not a virgin, but we can all safely infer, as he doubtless does, that Jane is. The novel comes to a close with Bertha safely dead and Rochester—albeit blinded and crippled by the fire she started—finally free. Moreover, in attempting to rescue Bertha, despite all her liabilities, Rochester demonstrated no small amount of devotion as well as courage. *Jane Eyre* ends with this famous statement: "Reader, I married him."

Reader, now you know why.

From Jane Austen to Jane Eyre is a transition from female choice in an environment of delicacy and propriety to one that is considerably darker and more fraught. *Wuthering Heights*, by Emily Brontë (sister of Charlotte, who wrote *Jane Eyre*), continues this trend and if anything accelerates it. We are transported, on one hand, to Thrushcross Grange, a civilized, pleasant, sheltered place in the valley inhabited by the Lintons, who are appropriately civilized, pleasant, and sheltered, and who could have made an appearance in any of Austen's novels. On the other, we encounter Wuthering Heights: bleak, ferocious, subject to violent winds, and occupied by the Earnshaws, who are as crude, violent, passionate, and quintessentially male as the Lintons are sophisticated, soft, gentle, and iconically female. From the perspective of a "choosing" female, one can hardly imagine two more contrasting options. Catherine Earnshaw is hypergamically scheduled to marry the higher-class Edgar Linton. But Heathcliff, the rough-and-ready orphan who had been taken in by the Earnshaws, possesses a passionate, animal nature that cannot forgo Catherine any more than she, in the end, can give him up.

It might seem at first glance that Catherine Earnshaw's enduring embrace of Heathcliff over Linton runs headlong into our argument about what women want, but not so fast! After all, part of the fascination and excitement of literature comes specifically from the tension it reflects between our desires and those preferences instilled by social tradition. Our wants don't always correspond with what is best for us or what society permits. Herein lies tragedy.

It is not uncommon for women to yearn for a guy who is at least a little bad, offering the thrill of an unpredictable, forbidden animal attraction and uncontrollability. Consider this, from a typical Harlequin romance published in 1995:

Faith looked as innocent as an angel in her plain white blouse and midcalf blue chambray skirt. Her hair was drawn back in a loose ponytail at the nape of her neck, tied with a yellow bandanna that left little wisps and tendrils free to frame her face like a halo. He looked like the ragged end of an all-nighter, towering over her, dark and disreputable, with his uncombed hair and screaming eagle tattoo and beard-stubbled jaw. Together, they looked like something out of a fifties movie: the Earth Angel and the Bad-Ass Biker.[1]

Women buy—and read—more novels than men do. Although not all of them are "romance" novels, a remarkable proportion deal with the trials and tribulations of finding the right man. These difficulties often involve a conflict described with admirable succinctness by Richard Dawkins as involving a choice between dads and cads. Dads are those males who promise good resources and good behavior; cads lack staying power but are likely to dazzle with attractive appearance and other stimulating indications of good genes. You might think that women should have evolved to see through the latter and choose the former, and to a large extent they have. But there is a catch: good genes have staying power, too! Remember, those good genes can indicate underlying bodily health, and—through the interposition of sexual selection's runaway process and the production of sexy sons—offer the prospect of ongoing reproductive success in future generations. In other words, if you can get Bill Gates, Hugh Grant, and Jane Eyre's Mr. Rochester all rolled into one, you're in luck. But what do you do if you must choose one and reject the others?

So just as men are said to suffer from a "madonna/whore complex" (more on this in the next chapter), there is a predictable tension within women, deriving from the attractiveness of both dads and cads. Catherine Earnshaw felt it and stuck with Linton, a dad,

---

[1] Candace Schuler, *Lovers and Strangers* (New York: Harlequin Temptation, 1995).

while yearning for her cad, Heathcliff. Jane Austen's heroines consistently feel it, too, but with equal consistency they opt for dads.

Although most women might dispute Erica Jong's infamous endorsement of the "zipless fuck" (a sexual consummation, presumably with a cad, so quick, so spontaneous, and so "in the moment" that unzipping isn't even called for), contemporary writing seems, if anything, more likely to celebrate—or at least to describe—the appeal of cads. According to Jong's heroine, the vivacious Isadora Wing, a zipless fuck is a "platonic ideal," a perfect encounter in which "zippers fell away like rose petals, underwear blew off in one breath like dandelion fluff." It seems unlikely that modern women are more likely to couple with cads—ziplessly or not—than their predecessors were. Maybe they are simply more likely to acknowledge the temptation.

In any event, from Jane Austen to the present day, women—and especially women writers—have been moved to note the dad/cad tension, albeit without the nifty verbal shorthand. Perhaps the optimum (biologically, if not ethically) is to marry a dad but mate, surreptitiously, with a cad. But at the same time, there looms the danger of being seduced and abandoned by a cad; after all, that's why they're called cads!

Consider, for example, *Bridget Jones's Diary*, the 1990s bestseller by journalist Helen Fielding that began as a column in the London *Independent* newspaper and then expanded into a hilarious novel (and a pretty good movie, too). Bridget Jones isn't only wonderfully clever and funny; she also strikes a familiar chord in her obsessive worries about—surprise!—finding a mate. Bridget vows that she will keep away from "misogynists, megalomaniacs, adulterers, workaholics, chauvinists, or perverts," but, interestingly, not paupers. That goes without saying. It is hard to imagine Elizabeth Bennet emulating Bridget Jones and drinking, smoking, or even eating too much. But the pursuit of self-improvement and of a male with r-cubed? That's another story.

Generations of XX chromosome carriers (and even a few XYs)

can also sympathize with Bridget's aversion to the intolerable "smug marrieds" professing concern for her and her fellow "single-tons." Bridget/Fielding points out, "We wouldn't rush up to *them* and roar, 'How's your marriage going? Still having sex?' " Neither would Jane Austen. Jane would also no doubt sympathize with Bridget's parents, who want her to marry glamorous lawyer Mark Darcy. (Does that last name ring a bell?) But Bridget compounds her comical ineptitude by being rude to Darcy, the inverse of what transpires in *Pride and Prejudice*. It may be stretching things to picture Mrs. Bennet in the position of Bridget's mom—sorry, Mum—starting a new career as the host of the TV program called *Suddenly Single* and then disappearing with a Portuguese gigolo. But nearly two centuries post-Austen, some things haven't changed. Good genes, good behavior, good resources: Mark Darcy has them all, and finally Bridget gets it . . . and him, and thus them. The benefits of a cad and of a dad, all wrapped up in one sexy guy.

It is noteworthy that the premier scribe of "what women want" was herself a woman. It is also beyond dispute that women typically read books about relationships, while men choose stories of adventure. By contrast to accounts of female choice, modern novels—and movies and magazine articles—that cater to male sensibilities tend to be more directly violent and explicitly sex-laden, often adventures of the search-and-destroy genre, filled with casual erotic conquests. Picture James Bond, pulling out his gun and his penis with about equal frequency. It is also noteworthy that 007 and his ilk feature in numerous sequels, since there is little in the male sexual imagination that limits a desirable love life to just one partner; by contrast, the world of romance novels—which caters almost exclusively to women—necessarily must create new characters with every book, since the typical climax of these tales involves a satisfying and presumably monogamous union between heroine and hero.

Sadly, things don't always end up that way. Natural selection operates by the gradual accumulation of whatever works—it does not guarantee perfection. After all, more than 90 percent of all species that ever lived are now extinct. Not surprisingly, even though evolution has equipped both men and women to be adroit intuitive biologists, neither sex has a perfect track record when it comes to assessing the desires of the other. Women, for instance— especially in modern-day America—consistently overrate the importance of slenderness as a sexual turn-on for men, most of whom prefer their partners to look healthy rather than anorexic.

And men have historically ended up wide of the mark at one extreme or the other when it comes to sizing up the sexuality of women, either seeing them as sexually rapacious and unutterably lascivious and thus responsible for the world's evils (thereby almost certainly projecting their own lust onto the ladies) or seeing women as altogether chaste, albeit chased.

Thus at one time, Talmudic scholars entertained such an overblown estimate of women's sexuality (and society's responsibility to repress it) that widows were forbidden to keep male dogs as pets! At the other extreme, an influential nineteenth-century Victorian tract by one Dr. William Acton announced that "the majority of women (happily for society) are not very much troubled with sexual feelings of any kind. What men are habitually, women are only exceptionally."

The truth, of course, is that women are neither sexually rapacious nor downright asexual. Central to that truth is the role of female as sexual chooser.

But male befuddlement as to what women really want hasn't stopped them from guessing, worrying, and often fantasizing, frequently about their own anatomy. The reality is that nearly always what women want is not what men think—or fear—that they do. *Lady Chatterley's Lover* is a perfect case. D. H. Lawrence thought he knew what turned women on, but he was wrong. The story, in brief:

Lady Chatterley is married to Lord Clifford Chatterley, rendered impotent by a war wound. She finally finds sexual satisfaction with Mellors, the virile gamekeeper. Maybe the fantasy of Lady Chatterley going gaga over her lover's erect penis—which she does with almost boring repetition—was a turn-on for Lawrence, and for many men who mostly read the "dirty parts," but it doesn't do nearly so much for women:

> The sun through the low window sent in a beam that lit up his thighs and slim belly and the erect phallos rising darkish and hot-looking from the little cloud of vivid gold-red hair. She was startled and afraid.
>
> "How strange!" she said slowly. "How strange he stands there! So big! and so dark and cock-sure! Is he like that?"
>
> The man looked down the front of his slender white body, and laughed. Between the slim breasts the hair was dark, almost black. But at the root of the belly, where the phallos rose thick and arching, it was gold-red, vivid in a little cloud.
>
> "So proud!" she murmured, uneasy. "And so lordly! Now I know why men are so overbearing! But he's lovely, *really*. Like another being! A bit terrifying! But lovely really! And he comes to *me*!—" She caught her lower lip between her teeth, in fear and excitement. . . . And he was helpless, as the penis in slow soft undulations filled and surged and rose up, and grew hard, standing there hard and overweening, in its curious towering fashion. The woman too trembled a little as she watched.

We have no problem with D. H. Lawrence as a creative and imaginative writer (although we are more than a little troubled by his protofascism), and we applaud his willingness to challenge prudish conventions as to what constitutes "obscenity." But Jane Austen, for all her nineteenth-century restraint and delicacy, was a much better evolutionary psychologist, and a far sexier writer. And even Bridget Jones—not to mention Charles Darwin—knew more about what makes women, as well as peahens, tick.

4

HOW TO MAKE RHETT GIVE A DAMN

What Men Want, and Why

———

Let's start with the "madonna/whore complex." (The madonna of the Bible, not the *Billboard* charts.) According to tradition—and biology—men fool around readily enough with whores but prefer to marry virgins. These days, the expectation of premarital female chastity is more than a bit quaint, and perhaps less realistic than ever. And in an age of AIDS, sex with prostitutes can be downright dangerous. But the caricature stands: what men want for a night's entertainment is one thing, what they want in a spouse is another. In other words, men like bad girls but marry good ones. Which brings us to *Tess of the d'Urbervilles*.

Written by Thomas Hardy in 1891, this modern classic tells the travails of Tess, a young, poor, inexperienced lass who, in a moment of weakness, allowed herself to be "possessed" by a dapper young cad named Alec d'Urberville. As a result, Tess became pregnant; her baby died, but Alec kept pestering her for more "possession." Tess escapes to a dairy farm, where she works as a milkmaid while falling in love with a fellow named Angel Clare, who reciprocates her feelings. Angel is especially attracted to Tess's "innocence," an innocence that is, ironically, quite genuine, and which made her susceptible to Alec's earlier advances in the first place. Angel proposes marriage. Initially, Tess turns him down, feeling in her heart of hearts that she is too impure to marry this earthly angel, but later she accepts. The night before their wedding, Tess writes a letter to Angel, confessing her one-night stand with Alec d'Urberville, feeling glumly confident that with this knowledge, Angel will change his mind. But the next morning, Angel is as loving as ever.

Tess delightedly assumes that, soiled as she is, Angel has nonetheless decided to accept her as his bride. It turns out, however, that Angel never found the letter. He tells her about a night of debauchery in his own past, whereupon she tells him of hers. Tess forgives Angel; Angel, however, cannot bring himself to forgive Tess, saying, essentially, that he couldn't possibly live as husband to someone so besmirched. Angel goes off to Brazil. Tess returns to hard work as an itinerant farm laborer, barely avoiding starvation. At this time, the pesteringly possessive Alec d'Urberville shows up once again, claiming to have reformed his ways and behaving generously toward Tess's indigent parents. Tess writes to Angel, begging him to take her back and save her from her previous possessor and present pursuer. But it takes several months for her letter to reach Brazil, during which time Tess concludes, in misery, that Angel has abandoned her for good. Then, sure enough, Angel returns to England, ready to accept Tess at last . . . only to find that, despairing of his forgiveness and desperate to escape a life of poverty, she has moved in with Alec. Tess completes the tragedy by stabbing Alec and then confessing her deed to Angel, with whom she finally reconciles, enjoying a few days of bliss before she is arrested and taken away to be hanged.

Tess of the d'Urbervilles is a grim, compelling story of class differences, economic desperation, and the helplessness of good people caught in bad circumstances. For many, it is primarily a tragedy of errors, notably Tess's assumption that Angel had read her letter and forgiven her prior sexual encounter, whereas in fact he had not. (And when he found out, he could not.) Tragedy ensued. Seen through modern eyes, Angel admittedly did not live up to his name, although for late Victorians, his stiff-necked adherence to the double standard made perfect sense. For Hardy and his audience—many of whom were appalled by the explicit consideration of sex even though no sexual acts as such were described—the tragedy that bound Tess, Angel, and Alec was powered by economic circumstances and social conventions. Like lumbering prehistoric creatures mired in the La Brea tar pits, this unhappy trio was stuck, constrained from moving freely by forces beyond their ken and greatly exceeding their pitiful strength.

At the same time, we can ask why. Why couldn't Angel accept Tess after knowing that she was no longer a virgin? After all, Tess was more than willing to overlook Angel's parallel behavior. It isn't enough simply to point to the double standard, whereby "boys will be boys"—which includes "sowing their wild oats" on occasion—while "good girls don't do that." Of course, some girls do (or else boys wouldn't have the chance to be boys), at least in part because not all are "good." Maybe these looser young ladies are just weak-willed compared to their "better" sisters? Or is it more a question of strategy? If their aim is to mate with the best male available, then do some females intuitively realize that they have less to offer and therefore their best bet is to be more available than the standoffish good girls with their more desirable traits?

What is clear, however, is that in society after society, throughout most of human history, it is far more acceptable for a man to have premarital sexual experience than it is for a woman. The same applies to extramarital affairs. An evolutionary explanation presents itself, one that fastidious Victorians might have found appalling but to which their DNA was already resonating. Recall Othello's rage and its biological underpinnings: if Othello had really had an affair with Emilia, Iago's wife, that could have been a genetic disaster for Iago, who might have ended up rearing Othello's child instead of his own. For Desdemona, it might have been a *social* problem, but not, strictly speaking, a genetic one. Any little Desdemonas would still be hers. Not so, of course, for Othello, if Desdemona really had been making "the beast with two backs" with Cassio, as Iago alleged. We've already seen how this helps make sense of male sexual jealousy generally.

To be sure, most women are not casual about a husband's infidelity. In literature, as in life, women treat the philandering of their mates as a very serious matter indeed, a response that is surely steeped in biology; that is, they're concerned that their mates might divert important resources to the offspring of other females, or even possibly leave them for their new girlfriend. Yet as sexually possessive and jealous as women are, men are even more so. And as much as the divergence between male and female responses to infidelity is undergirded by cultural tradition, both those responses— and even the cultural expectations themselves—are built upon a biological foundation.

In large part, it's a reproductive translation of the old real estate dictum that three things are especially important in determining the value of a house: location, location, and location. When it comes to confidence of genetic relatedness, location once again is key. This time, it's the location of fertilization: internal or external.

Among all mammals, fertilization is internal, taking place deep within the female's body. And among all mammals, babies are cared for—almost exclusively—by their mothers. In every mammal species (including *Homo sapiens*), females do considerably more mothering than men do fathering. Although most people take this parental double standard for granted, it is actually profoundly unfair. After all, a female mammal has carried her offspring for a prolonged period, nurturing it from her own bloodstream, only to undergo the strenuous and sometimes risky process of birth itself. At this point, wouldn't it be fair, and even fitness-enhancing, for her reproductive partner to pitch in and take up some of the slack? In short, why don't men lactate?

It's not that they lack breasts, or even nipples. The sad truth is that not even the most doting father can nurse his offspring, basically because for the past hundred million or so years of mammalian history, not even the most confident father could know for certain that he really was the father. And nursing requires a tremendous expenditure of time and energy; it simply would not be fitness-enhancing for them when "their" child might really have been fathered by someone else. Of course, using this logic we would expect that in species employing external fertilization, with, say, eggs and sperm simply discharged into the surrounding water, males and females should be about equally likely to do the child care. And this is precisely what we find in fish and amphibians.

Back to the tribulations of Tess, now revealed to reflect, in large part, the anguish of Angel and of men generally. Deprived as they are of the serene confidence of genetic parenthood, which is the (literal) birthright of every woman, men in societies as diverse as the Amazonian Yanomamo, the Alaskan Inuit, and the late Victorian English have struggled to increase their confidence. Certain stick in-sects remain *in copula* literally for weeks, keeping other stick insects from inseminating "their" female. Among some species of bees, males actually explode after mating; they die in the process, but only after converting themselves into a postmortem chastity belt by jam-ming part of their genitalia inside that of their lady love. Certain sharks, on the other hand, precede copulation by giving the female a high-pressure saltwater douche via their double-barreled penis, which evidently serves to wash out any sperm that may have been deposited by a prior suitor. Not to be outdone, many mammals (in-cluding most primates) produce semen that coagulates into a rubbery "copulatory plug," which serves as yet another organic chastity belt. Finally, among ringdoves—a species in which males are expected to provide a fair amount of child care after the young have hatched—males actually reject females who reveal, by their overeager receptiv-ity to courtship, that they have already received the amorous attentions of another male. And Angel Clare? He rejected Tess when he learned that she had already had sex with Alec d'Urberville, even though she didn't love Alec and the child hadn't survived.

The biological bottom line is that men, far more than women, have to deal with a heavy dose of sexual anxiety—not so much performance anxiety as the deeper, biologically generated uncertainty of parental confidence. Concern about a potentially wilted penis is nothing compared with concern about one's genetic posterity. Call it "Angel's anxiety," and alleviating it is an important component of what men want. We should pity, therefore, the poor Y chromosome bearers among us. They have fragile biological egos, and for biologically appropriate reasons. What they want, as a result, is reassurance, a neediness that inclines men to crave indications that any prospective mate is likely to be sexually faithful—and, conversely, to be turned off by indications that she isn't, or wasn't, and therefore might not be in the future.

Maybe men want virgins because it gratifies their ego to think that they will not be compared as lovers with anyone else. More likely, Angel's anxiety about Tess was generated by a concern—heightened, to be sure, by nineteenth-century mores—that Tess's earlier dalliance indicated that she might subsequently prove to be a "loose woman," in which case Angel could lose his genetic posterity. It is always possible as well that men have long been attracted to virgin brides because virginity itself generally correlates with youth, and younger women have a longer reproductive future in store. There is little doubt that virgins tend to be, on average, younger than their sexually experienced sisters, but there is even less doubt as to their previous sexual history.

Even Rhett Butler—the epitome of suave, sexually competent manliness and rebellious indifference to traditional values—shows his fragility in *Gone With the Wind*. He desires Scarlett O'Hara and eventually marries her (albeit as husband number three). But even this alluring, dissolute, cynical, unscrupulous war profiteer and blockade runner cannot quite get over his jealousy of Scarlett's nonstop infatuation with Ashley Wilkes. By the story's end, what's really gone with the wind in Margaret Mitchell's celebrated novel (and even more celebrated motion picture) is Rhett's ability to tolerate Scarlett O'Hara's yearning for another man, even though Scarlett and Ashley never do more than kiss. By the novel's end, just as Scarlett is coming to see Ashley for the diminished and weakened figure that he is—and always was—Rhett finally gives up; in his sexual insecurity, Rhett is finally revealed to be as inadequate and insecure as Ashley, although no more so than any male mammal, burdened with the uncertainties of internal fertilization, can be expected to be.

For the evolutionary biologist, men and women are condemned to a delicate mating dance in which the woman must not be too readily available. Sex can be an important way for a woman to demonstrate her love for a man (as well as responding to her own inclinations), but if she is too "free," too sexually avaricious, or even—ironically—too sexually skillful, she runs the risk of turning him off, at least as a potential long-term mate.

In *Humboldt's Gift*, by Saul Bellow, the protagonist, an on-again, off-again successful writer named Charlie Citrine, is alternately fascinated and repelled by his lover, Renata, who is several decades younger than he. Citrine's little monologue reveals a widespread male concern about a prospective mate who may be just a little bit too good in the sack: "As a carnal artist she was disheartening as well as thrilling, because, thinking of her as wife-material, I had to ask myself where she had learned all this." Bellow's hero/narrator is not simply reflecting a stubborn sexist refusal to tolerate as sauce for the goose what he assumes is acceptable in the gander, a puerile inadequacy of the male psyche, or simply a perverse ambivalence. Nor is it merely a refraction of cultural norms. (Because if so, we must ask why it is the cultural norm of virtually every human society; the one thing all human societies have in common is the biology of humanness.)

Recall that in the madonna/whore complex, men are attracted to brief relationships with the latter—mostly because they are available—but prefer to marry someone who is reliable, that is, relatively chaste, who will not squander the husband's resources on another man's offspring. (Recall the ringdoves, among whom the males reject potential mates who may have already been courted, and perhaps inseminated, by another male.)

But what, you might ask, about the saga of the "hooker with the heart of gold," such as in the movie *Pretty Woman*, in which a millionaire falls for a prostitute? First of all, once the viewer accepts Julia Roberts as a prostitute, it is entirely believable that almost any man would lose his heart to her! (Men, as we shall see, are not entirely indifferent to signs of youth and attractiveness in their prospective partners.) In addition, men seem to have a recurrent fantasy of *rescuing* prostitutes through romantic love. This may have something to do with the prostitute—if sufficiently classy—representing the most sexually desirable woman, normally out of reach for the average man. Her previous record of sexual promiscuity is simultaneously a turnoff and turn-on. And significantly, such fantasies always include the expectation that upon being "rescued," the woman's sexual careerism will definitely be turned off, as the "rescuer" manages somehow to appropriate the woman exclusively for himself.

In any event, most viewers would doubtless agree that any story in which a wealthy, high-status man finds marital bliss with a prostitute would be highly unlikely—about as unlikely as a prudish but decent would-be gentleman farmer from the English dairy country finding marital bliss with a young woman who had been courted and inseminated by a rascally smart-Alec.

If sexual fidelity is high on most men's list of female desirables, youth is not far behind. Men want women who are not only young but typically at least several years younger than themselves. As with the saying "I chased her until she caught me," this may simply reflect a wily triumph of *female* choice. This may seem paradoxical since many women bemoan this male tendency. But recall that one of the keys to Jane Austen's heart (Chapter 3) is good resources, which tend to accumulate with age, providing older men with an advantage when it comes to attracting younger women. From the male perspective, at the same time, youthfulness is desirable in a romantic partner because a younger woman offers a longer and thus richer reproductive future. After all, women have a fixed childbearing window that closes abruptly in middle age. Men don't. Should anyone be surprised, therefore, that around the world, husbands are consistently older than their wives? When was the last time you heard someone refer to a May-December marriage in which May was the man and December the woman?

The consequences of this disparity can be as predictable as they are infuriating: middle-aged and even elderly men find themselves attracted to young women, not uncommonly abandoning their middle-aged wives for a newer model. Think, for instance, of *The First Wives Club*, Olivia Goldsmith's 1992 novel in which three middle-aged women (later portrayed on film by Goldie Hawn, Bette Midler, and Diane Keaton), all first wives inhabiting the headier spheres of New York society, were dumped by their husbands in favor of younger, blonder, and more decorative "trophy wives." Not surprisingly, this happened after the men had achieved sufficient wealth and power to be attractive to younger, more fertile women. Incidentally, the three "first wives" eventually find suitable revenge against their heedless husbands, if not against their troublesome biology.

Probably the most dramatic depiction of male preference for youth is Vladimir Nabokov's *Lolita*. Its main character, Humbert Humbert, doesn't leave his aging wife for a younger woman; rather, he marries an older woman in order to be with her preteen daughter and then takes advantage of the fact that his wife dies in an automobile accident to run off with the girl. As hard to believe as it may be, the novel is most compelling simply for its lush language and extraordinary evocation of 1950s America. Yet as a pedophile sexual predator, Humbert is also nothing less than despicable. And while it may seem from their focus on sex that evolutionary biologists are amoral cultural relativists, they, too, recognize something not merely immoral but biologically off base in the hero/villain's obsession with a "nymphet." Nabokov never clearly states whether Lolita has begun menstruating and thus is fertile, and legally this does not matter—Humbert is without doubt guilty of statutory rape. But biologically it does matter.

The unconscious age-related double standard that most people carry within them is italicized in those very rare cases when a young man is portrayed as lusting for an old woman: *Harold and Maude*, for instance. This 1971 film imagined a romance, fully sexual, between a teenager and an octogenarian woman, leaving the audience alternately shocked and amused. Stories in which older men romance younger women capture a chunk of biological reality and hence are not uncommon; *Harold and Maude* captured an audience because it brazenly defied that reality. The truth is that relationships between young men and old women are exceedingly rare precisely because such liaisons do not make reproductive, evolutionary sense, whereas the converse, although occasionally ridiculous, is nonetheless consistent with human nature because it is consistent with nature itself.

Of course, the great majority of men are neither Humbert nor Harold, although more can relate to the former than the latter. Male preference for youthful sexual partners is what anthropologists call a "cross-cultural universal." There is, for instance, no human society in which an eighty-year-old woman is seen as more sexually alluring than a twenty-year-old. The bottom line isn't youth as such, any more than it is virginity per se. Both virginity and youth bespeak the prospect of reproductive success for the man in question: the former as a promise of fidelity, the latter of fertility. Both sexes are turned on by sexual partners who offer them the prospect of the greatest possible reproductive success, even though they typically don't know that this is happening. A man slavering over a *Playboy* Playmate of the Month, ogling an attractive young thing in a strip joint, or admiring the healthy hair and smooth skin of a coworker isn't thinking: "She would probably bear healthy babies." Indeed, the prospect of actual baby making might well be a psychological turn*off* these days, but this doesn't mean that biology isn't driving the system, giving impetus to what men find sexy. In other words, these men need not have reproduction in mind; it is in their genes. Sex is the route, reproduction the destination. Most living things—including human beings—have been programmed to enjoy the trip, giving little or no thought to where it might lead.

Often, they'd rather end up somewhere else. Consider the opening line of *Genesis*, a 2003 novel by Jim Crace: "Every woman he dares to sleep with bears his child." Felix Dern has sex with six different women—voilà, six children! But rather than revel in this evolutionary success, our hero learns that "to be so fertile is a curse." Felix didn't want all these offspring; what he did want, however, was sex with each of the women in question.

How many hungry people of either sex look at a meal and say to themselves: "This looks like an appropriate array of carbohydrates, proteins, and fats, which would optimally satisfy my intracellular metabolic needs"? Instead, a horny man looks at an attractive sexual partner just like a hungry one looks at a well-prepared meal and says to himself: "Yum!"

Not surprisingly, there are certain aspects of the female body that men generally find especially yummy, not least among them breasts. We could fill an entire chapter—perhaps an entire book—with literary references to the attractive female figure, running from "shapely" and "curvaceous" to the Victorian era's "amply provided with womanly charms" to more explicit modern accounts. Any way you write it, men like breasts. It is a near obsession that writers have long acknowledged, although only rarely have they glimpsed the underlying biology as eagerly as they have alluded to the décolletage of their female characters.

What is this all about? Why are breasts so endlessly fascinating—to men, at least? It all has to do with two closely related substances: milk and fat. Add to these a simple fact that we looked at earlier: only women get pregnant. This explains not only why women have a uterus as well as organs of lactation but why men have neither. It also seems to explain why women have a higher proportion of body fat. Extra metabolic reserves, in the form of adipose tissue, almost certainly contributed to the success of our ancestral mothers in carrying healthy babies to term, then providing milk for them afterward. Indeed, it appears that a certain minimum of fat is necessary for women to start menstruating. Serious female athletes even cease having regular periods; when they stop their intense training and, as a result, increase their fat reserves, normal cycling resumes. It is interesting that no similar correlation between body weight, fat levels, and sperm production has ever been demonstrated for males, although the last waxes and wanes according to other things, notably body temperature and frequency of ejaculation. Couples trying unsuccessfully to become pregnant often must be counseled, paradoxically, to *reduce* their frequency of sexual intercourse so as to increase the man's sperm count, but men are not advised to become chubbier so as to become more reproductively competent. The *f*-cubed connection (female, fat, and fertility) makes evolutionary sense because pregnancy and the developing fetus require lots of calories. Moreover, extra body fat represents insurance in the event of lean times. By contrast, the strictly biological demands for a man's reproduction are concluded with an ejaculation.

The likelihood, therefore, is that fat distribution in women has been directly favored by natural selection. At the same time, men's preference for the curvy hourglass figure of sexually mature women almost certainly reflects an unconscious choice of those body types most likely to produce healthy children (for much the same reason that people prefer eating bread over bark, or steak over stones—obviously, the former taste better, but we developed these taste preferences *because* certain things are more nutritious than others). Broad hips, after all, facilitate labor and delivery, and breasts are not just sexual adornment: they provide nourishment for the infant. Not surprisingly, these considerations show up in literature.

Chaucer, in *The Canterbury Tales*, had no doubt what made a woman sexually attractive: "buttokes brode and brestes rounde and huge." And Stephen Dedalus, James Joyce's young fictional hero in *Portrait of the Artist as a Young Man*, came up with this analysis while musing with his friends on the nature of female beauty:

Every physical quality admired by men in women is in direct connection with the manifold functions of women for the propagation of the species. . . . [Y]ou admired the great flanks of Venus because you felt that she would bear you burly offspring and admired her great breasts because you felt that she would give good milk to her children and yours.

To be sure, notions of physical attractiveness reflect social convention and not just biology alone; accordingly, they are far from universal. The full-bodied earth mother goddess or Botticelli beauty has largely been replaced in the United States, for example, by the nearly anorexic fashion model. Among other societies, tattooed faces are de rigueur, or elongated necks, teeth that have been filed to points, and so on. In some places, women typically shave their legs and underarms; in others, they don't.

In a world of scarce food, an ample figure probably did indicate something important about likely success as a parent, while today, in the Western world at least, obstetricians can readily deliver babies by cesarean section, and infant formula can substitute for breast-feeding. Moreover, for those enjoying abundant—often excessively abundant—food, a degree of slimness indicates other components of health, such as sufficient exercise, prudent eating habits, and so forth. But beauty has never really been in the eye of the beholder; rather, it's in the brain, which interprets what the eye sees. And that brain was produced by natural selection. What it interprets as "beautiful"—if "beautiful" means "desirable to mate with"—is whatever contributes to evolutionary success. So it can be predicted that within a spectrum of cultural variation, the basic evolved male desire for large-breasted, slim-waisted women is still at work and is likely to continue. And so those skinny—bordering on scrawny—models have made a booming business of silicone implants.

Human beings are unique among mammals in sporting prominent mammaries when not lactating, and also in making erotic use of them. Why? One intriguing possibility is that for more than 99 percent of our evolutionary past, a primordial battle of the sexes has been under way, with the battlegrounds being the female figure and the male unconscious mind. Let's begin with the assumption that Stephen Dedalus was correct, and well-developed female mammaries have been preferred by men as a promise of subsequent milk for their offspring. This would have led, in turn, to large-breastedness—even when not lactating—on the part of women, because insofar as busty women were especially desirable, they would have been mated by the fittest men, and accordingly would have produced more offspring . . . the daughters of whom were likely to be ample-bosomed themselves.

But the situation is almost certainly more complicated than the simple promise of breasts as milk providers. There is, for example, very little correlation between the size of a woman's nonlactating breasts and her eventual milk production—the greatest proportion of a nonlactating breast is occupied by fat, with virtually no glandular tissue. Milk-producing glands develop only later, during pregnancy, although of course the breasts of a nursing woman are typically full indeed.

Here is one possible explanation: let's assume that long ago, men preferred women with relatively large breasts and hips because the latter indicated room for the baby to be born and the former was at least observed to characterize a successfully nursing mother. This would set the stage for women to have evolved fatty deposits on their breasts and hips, essentially to deceive men. "Choose me," they would have been saying, in the Stephen Dedalus interpretation, "and you will get successful children," although in reality, fatty breasts are no more a guarantee of subsequent milk production than fatty hips truly indicate a wide birth canal. If so, then prominent fatty breast tissue is a case of successful but false advertising. Round one goes to women.

But the sparring need not have ended here. Men could have counterattacked, insisting that their spouses have comparatively small waists as a way of ensuring relatively low fat levels and in the process keeping women honest about what they have to offer. If so, then round two would have gone to the men. Not to be outdone, however, women might have been able to parry their mates' counterattack, arranging their anatomy such that their waists tend to remain slim while fat is deposited elsewhere. The sexually appealing, hourglass figure of women may owe much to deception and counterdeception of this sort.

Devendra Singh, a psychologist at the University of Texas, has explored male preference for the female figure, specifically the ratio of waist to hip measurements. Before puberty, the waist/hip ratios of boys and girls are indistinguishable; then they diverge. Boys lose fat from their thighs and buttocks, while girls deposit fat on their upper thighs and hips. By the time they are adults, women have 40 percent more fat than men in their lower trunk. At the prime of their reproductive years, healthy adult women will have a waist/hip ratio of .67 to .80, while for healthy men, that ratio is between .85 and .95. After menopause, women's waist/hip ratios once again approach that of men. Not surprisingly, hormones seem to be responsible. High levels of estrogen (actually, high estrogen-to-testosterone ratios) stimulate fat deposition around the hips and inhibit it in the abdominal region. Therefore, a low waist/hip ratio signals relatively high reproductive ability, while a high waist/hip ratio can be a sign of illness or a previous or current pregnancy, none of which bodes well for the evolutionary success of men who choose such women.

In a number of studies, Singh has found—as we would expect—that men rated images of women as more attractive the lower this ratio: .80 is preferred to .90, and .70 is preferred to .80. Examining images of *Playboy* centerfolds and of beauty contest winners during the past thirty years, Singh discovered that although preference for overall thinness increased, the ideal waist/hip ratio remained unchanged at precisely .70. (As mentioned, this does not deny that a fondness for total skinniness varies quite a bit: plumpness is valued in societies where resources are scarce, while slenderness is sought after in the affluent West, in which wealthy, healthy people watch their weight and work out.) Regrettably, we cannot apply a tape measure to the female figure as described by the world's creative literary artists, but it's a good bet that if such an assessment could be performed, it would reveal that writers from Ovid to Ian Fleming depicted that trusty, lusty .70.

In any event, it seems clear that female physical traits that men find attractive are heavily weighted toward those that indicate health and, almost certainly, reproductive potential. Regularity of features, skin and hair quality, youth, appropriate physical size, and so forth: all these traits correspond to bodily health. Another feature that is receiving substantial attention is symmetry. Most living things tend to be symmetrical, and human beings are no exception. And yet it is no small trick for a growing body to end up physically balanced. In fact, it is well documented that disturbances during embryology and growth—due to inadequate nutrition, genetic anomalies, and so on—produce disturbances in symmetry. When people are asked to evaluate the attractiveness of human faces that have been computer-altered to reflect differing degrees of symmetry, the results suggest a rewrite of Keats's famous line about the interconnection of beauty and truth. Biologically, we might say, "Beauty is symmetry and symmetry, beauty."

Put it all together and we can at last make sense of the great concluding line to the song "There Is Nothing Like a Dame," in *South Pacific*, when a sailor named Stewpot sings, with deep voice and mounting, robust enthusiasm: "There is absolutely nothing like the frame . . . of . . . a . . . dame."

This story is still told in New Zealand. It seems an Episcopal bishop had been visiting an isolated Maori village. As everyone was about to retire for the night after an evening of high-spirited feasting and dancing, the local headman, wanting to show profound hospitality to his honored guest, called out: "A woman for the bishop." Seeing the scowl of disapproval on the prelate's face, he roared even louder, "Two women for the bishop!"

Clearly, the chieftain was an accomplished evolutionary psychologist. He knew that male sexuality includes a fondness for multiple partners. To some extent, the more the merrier. Lord Byron wondered, "How the devil is it that fresh features / Have such a charm for us poor human creatures?" Biologically, the explanation is obvious: insofar as each prospective partner represents a potential pregnancy—and thus an increase in the reproductive success of the successful inseminator—males generally and human males in particular are partial to "multiple sexual partners." (Not necessarily at the same time; sequentially will do just fine.)

It's that old penchant for polygyny rearing its visage once again. Interestingly, men are often inclined to fantasize about how wonderful it would be if society would only grant them the opportunity to live out their harem-having inclinations, conveniently forgetting that in such a case, other men would also be striving similarly. It is a bit like those people who claim to remember their past lives, in which they were always Cleopatra or Napoleon, never a slave or a peasant. But that doesn't stop men from imagining how it might be if only the world were organized just for them.

Amidst the "oxen of the sun" chapter in James Joyce's *Ulysses*, a horny young man named Buck Mulligan expresses, in comically exaggerated language, a similarly widespread male fantasy: providing sexual services for erotically and reproductively frustrated women, no questions asked and no fee charged.

> It grieved him, plaguily, he said, to see the nuptial couch defrauded of its dearest pledges and to reflect upon so many agreeable females . . . who lose their womanly bloom . . . when they might multiply the inlets of happiness, sacrificing the inestimable jewel of their sex when a hundred pretty fellows were at hand to caress; this, he assured them, made his heart weep. To curb this inconvenience . . . he proposed to set up a national fertilising farm . . . with an obelisk hewn and erected after the

fashion of Egypt and to offer his dutiful yeoman services for the fecundation of any female of what grade of life soever who should there direct to him with the desire of fulfilling the functions of her natural. Money was no object, he said, nor would he take a penny for his pains. The poorest kitchenwench no less than the opulent lady of fashion . . . would find in him their man.

Our young Buck goes on, describing how he would nourish himself so as to maintain necessary strength for the servicing of his imagined clients, to the great approval of his assembled friends. No mention of love or even affection for his partners, and certainly no second thoughts about child care or the maintenance of long-term relationships. The overriding consideration is sexual variety: lots of women, the more they, the merrier he.

Speaking a bit more delicately, W. S. Gilbert, in *Trial by Jury*, alluded to the flip side of the male fondness for variety with the knowing line "Love unchanged will cloy." It isn't necessarily true that monogamy equals monotony, but the biology of male sexuality ordains that novelty itself is a turn-on for men—not simply new positions or new accoutrements, but literally new partners. A few centuries before Gilbert and Sullivan, Shakespeare had described Cleopatra as follows: "Age cannot wither her, nor custom stale her infinite variety." But then, Cleopatra was supposed to have been remarkable precisely because by contrast, "other women cloy the appetites they feed."

One of the first novels to explicitly and directly depict this male penchant for multiple sexual partners, Henry Miller's *Tropic of Cancer*, has been called the most honest book ever written. It is a confessional, autobiographical account of Miller's years as an expatriate in Paris. No punches are pulled in its sexual descriptions, which include a (perhaps unhealthy) dose of gritty reality: accounts of watching a whore use a bidet before sex, of lice, feces, dirt, poverty, mooching off one's friends, cuckolding one's colleagues, trying to create literature while celebrating (or succumbing to; choose your own interpretation) a yearning for multiple partners that would make a Maori chieftain proud and his Episcopal visitor wince (perhaps at least in part out of envy).

As a species that forms pair bonds and in which females—as well as social and religious tradition—exert strong pressure on males to be monogamous, the achievement of serial promiscuity à la Henry Miller is difficult, to say the least. As a result—and for sound biological reasons—not many men have managed to lead the life that Henry Miller did.

Tropic of Cancer was initially published in 1934 but not allowed into the United States until 1961. (Humanity, wrote T. S. Eliot, cannot stand too much reality; in this regard, prudish America may be exceptionally human.) Miller gives his readers graphic accounts of his own exploits with Elsa, Tania, Irene, Llona, Germaine, Claude, even his mysterious wife, Mona (have we left anyone out?), and that's just in the first forty pages. Throughout, Miller's enthusiasm for female flesh—especially when freshly encountered—is undiminished.

In his preface to *Tropic of Cancer*, poet Karl Shapiro called Henry Miller the "greatest living writer," adding, "It is possible that he is the first writer outside the Orient who has succeeded in writing as naturally about sex on a large scale as novelists ordinarily write about the dinner table or the battlefield."[1] The three Fs— feeding, fighting, and fornication—are about as biological as anything gets.

Equally libidinal, and more current, is the Czech expatriate novelist Milan Kundera, several times nominated for a Nobel Prize. Kundera's notorious sexism is said to have worked against him, at least within the Nobel committee's secret deliberations, but at the same time, it has powered much of the compelling honesty of his writing. *The Unbearable Lightness of Being* introduces us to Tomas, a

---

[1] Karl Shapiro, "The Greatest Living Writer," preface to Henry Miller, *Tropic of Cancer* (New York: Grove Press, 1961).

brilliant Prague surgeon who lives happily as an irresistible sexual adventurer. His signature move is to demand of his potential conquests: "Take off your clothes," whereupon they generally do just that. As with D. H. Lawrence's depiction of Lady Chatterley swooning over her lover's erect penis, we suspect that the acquiescence of Tomas's numerous inamoratas is more a reflection of Kundera's overheated imagination than a believable portrayal of what most women are likely to do, but it certainly demonstrates what men want.

Here is another dose of Kundera, from his other masterpiece, *The Book of Laughter and Forgetting*:

> Every man has two erotic biographies. Usually people talk only about the first: the list of affairs and of one-night stands. The other biography is sometimes more interesting: the parade of women we wanted to have, the women who got away. It is a mournful history of opportunities wasted.

Biologists have a term for the male tendency to be sexually stimulated by relations with new female partners: it is known as the "Coolidge effect." It seems the president and his wife were separately touring a model farm during the 1920s. Mrs. Coolidge, commenting on the many chickens associated with a single rooster, commented, "He must be kept quite busy." She suggested that this be brought to the president's attention. Accordingly, when the presidential party arrived later that same day, the guide announced, "Mrs. Coolidge wished me to point out that our single rooster copulates many times each day." "Always with the same female?" asked the president. "No, sir." "Well," said Mr. Coolidge, "tell *that* to Mrs. Coolidge."

Is it just men? Yes and no. Yes: women as a rule aren't turned on by multiple partners. No: males of other species generally act the same way. A ram, for example, left to copulate with the same ewe, will do so several times, then stop, apparently satiated. If he is then presented with a different ewe, his sexual enthusiasm returns, until once again his interest wanes. But each time he is given an opportunity to copulate with a new female, his enthusiasm—and capacity—comes roaring back. A new ewe makes a new him.

This phenomenon was known long before the modern science of animal behavior and before evolutionary biologists understood the consequences of making sperm versus eggs. "I have put to stud an old horse who could not be controlled at the scent of mares," wrote the sixteenth-century essayist Montaigne. "Facility presently sated him toward his own mares: but toward strange ones, and the first one that passes by his pasture, he returns to his importunate neighings and his furious heats, as before."

As a species, human beings generally stop short of importunate neighings and furious heats, but not by much. One of the characters in the musical *Finian's Rainbow* proclaims in song, "When I'm not near the girl I love, I love the girl I'm near." He goes on: "When I'm not facing the face that I fancy, I fancy the face I face." Russell Banks's novel *Continental Drift* includes several infidelities on the part of Bob Dubois, its primary male character. At one point, while Bob is admiring the face of Marguerite, his most recent mistress, he realizes that he can't even remember the details of his wife's face:

> Now he can't recall it. His memory is only of having paid attention to something that has disappeared, . . . so that now, when he . . . remembers it, all he sees is the center of her eyes, as if her face has somehow gradually become invisible without his ever having noticed until after it was gone, lost to him, he is sure, forever.

It is a fascinating irony as well that although men stand to gain more—in terms of producing offspring—from copulations with multiple partners, women are physiologically capable of having more sex than men. Yet social systems are commonly structured the other way around. In his bitingly satiric *Letters from the Earth*, Mark Twain had great fun with this paradox. Here is Twain's Devil reporting his discoveries, after visiting our planet:

Now there you have a sample of man's "reasoning powers," as he calls them. He observes certain facts. For instance, that in all his life he never sees the day that he can satisfy one woman; also, that no woman ever sees the day that she can't overwork, and defeat, and put out of commission any ten masculine plants that can be put to bed to her. He puts those strikingly suggestive and luminous facts together, and from them draws this astonishing conclusion: The Creator intended the woman to be restricted to one man.

Now if you or any other really intelligent person were arranging the fairnesses, and justices between man and woman, you would give the man a one-fiftieth interest in one woman, and the woman a harem. Now wouldn't you? Necessarily, I give you my word, this creature with the decrepit candle has arranged it exactly the other way.

From an evolutionary perspective, it is more logical for one man to mate with multiple women than to have one woman mated to several men. And in this case, evolutionary logic has won out, not only in the great majority of social systems described by anthropologists but also in most of the domestic dramas described by writers.

Another key difference between the sexes is that men are much more susceptible to sexual stimulation than are women. If it's weird sex—involving animals, unusual objects, even the occasional corpse—it's likely to be male sex. Men buy nearly all the pornography. Men visit prostitutes.

Picture the following scene: a man and woman have just spent a pleasant first date together and are now in the privacy of her apartment. She turns to him and, saying nothing, slowly begins to unbutton her blouse, then starts to unhook her bra. All the while, the man watches: fascinated, excited, and delighted. Then she uncovers one breast and he . . .

What is he likely to do? Slap her across the face? Beg her to stop and put her clothes back on? Scream for help? Dial 911? If you were to write a plausible ending to this steamy encounter, it would almost certainly involve a passionate sexual response by the man. The sort of female behavior described above is a definite turn-on for most men.

Now run through the scene again, this time reversing the roles: without explanation, the man suddenly unzips his fly and takes out his erect penis. The likelihood is that in such circumstances the woman would react with something less than delight, fascination, and sexual enthusiasm. Rather than being excited, she may well be repulsed, almost certainly by his social inappropriateness, and perhaps by the sexual organ itself. In any event, she is not likely to be aroused by the visual image of his genitals. By contrast, nearly every heterosexual man is excited by comparable exposure to the intimate anatomy of an attractive woman.

Simply put, women are more often interested in romance, with its implication of caring and commitment (and the promise of follow-through), while men are most interested in sex and immediate availability. This particular gender gap helps explain why women are indignant about being treated as sex objects and why men—often despite their best intentions—keep doing so. In Colette's novel *The Vagabond*, a woman criticizes (and sees through) her admirer as follows:

> If he pretends, cunning as an animal, to have forgotten that he wants to possess me, neither does he show any eagerness to find out what I am like, to question me or read my character, and I notice that he pays more attention to the play of light on my hair than to what I am saying.

What's love got to do with it? Everything and nothing. "Who can explain it, who can tell you why?" ask Rodgers and Hammerstein in their song "Some Enchanted Evening." They conclude, "Fools give you reasons; wise men never try." Well, we have tried. And so have generations of writers. For the biologist, love is a mechanism whereby individuals bond in the interest of maximizing their fitness. What hunger is to metabolism, love is to reproduction. For all its evident irrationality, it is more logical than most people realize. Most writers prefer to treat love—as distinct from lust—as magical, mysterious, inexplicable, and impenetrable, even as they describe its unfolding in precisely the same way that most biologists would predict, albeit adding a twist of the inchoate.

Here is Jay Gatsby acknowledging to Nick Carraway that Daisy Buchanan represents all his hopes and dreams, and recalling their first kiss:

> He knew that when he kissed this girl, and forever wed his unutterable visions to her perishable breath, his mind would never romp again like the mind of God. So he waited, listening for a moment longer to the tuning-fork that had been struck upon a star. Then he kissed her. At his lips' touch she blossomed for him like a flower and the incarnation was complete.

We can struggle against our evolutionary heritage, constantly yearning for a new day, a new success: "Gatsby believed in the green light," notes Nick Carraway, the narrator of Fitzgerald's renowned novel, "the orgiastic future that year by year recedes before us. It eluded us then, but that's no matter—tomorrow we will run faster, stretch out our arms farther. . . . And one fine morning—" What? One fine morning will we outrun, outreach, somehow outperform our evolutionary heritage? Don't count on it. When *The Great Gatsby* famously concludes, "So we beat on, boats against the current, borne back ceaselessly into the past," it is a more distant and more clinging past than Fitzgerald, or most of his readers, ever imagined.

5

MADAME BOVARY'S OVARIES

The Biology of Adultery

When Gustave Flaubert's grand and sexy novel *Madame Bovary* first appeared, readers were shocked, *shocked*. Here was a respectable middle-class woman who had a lover—several, in fact. And she was married! One hundred fifty years later, when students of animal behavior discovered that in nature many babies are fathered by someone other than the mother's social partner, they, too, were shocked, *shocked* (or at least surprised). These upsetting findings all point in the same direction: there is more than a little hanky-panky going on in the world, human as well as animal, and it isn't just a "guy thing." Females—even married ones—are active participants.

To be sure, there is much to be said for marital fidelity. But if you agree with John Milton—who in *Paradise Lost* hailed "wedded love" as follows—

> . . . *mysterious Law, true source*
> *Of human offspring . . .*
> *By thee adulterous Lust was driv'n from men*
> *Among the bestial herds to range . . .*

—then we have a large bridge in Brooklyn that you might want to purchase.

"Adulterous lust" has hardly been driven from men. Or women.

Infants have their infancy, and adults . . . ? Adultery. It "ranges," to be sure, among Milton's "bestial herds," but that's not the only place. The world of great literature, just like the great world of life, is filled with philandering. In addition to *Madame Bovary*, the list stretches from *The Iliad* through *Ulysses*, with numerous stops in between and after. Nor is it ignored by the creators and consumers of not-so-great literature, preoccupying, for example, the suburban occupants of John Updike's "marriage novels" as well as nearly every soap opera ever broadcast.

If monogamy itself is something of a myth, many of our most enduring myths are powered by extramarital events, too: think of the ill-fated Mediterranean house of Atreus (featuring, among others, Agamemnon and his concubine, Cassandra, as well as his wife, Clytemnestra, and her extracurricular lover, Aegisthus), the ancient Teutonic travails of Tristan and Isolde, as well as the Anglo-French exploits of Queen Guinevere and Sir Lancelot while King Arthur stood by. Adultery launched not only a thousand ships to Troy but also the earliest piece of organized literature in the Western world (*The Iliad*) and provided much of the motive force behind Malory's *Le Morte d'Arthur*.

Consider that in all of these cases it is sexual transgression on the part of a married *woman* that generates outrage and, nearly always, her punishment. Consider as well that married women, just as married men, are not only *like* mated animals, they *are* mated animals.

Let's look, then, at a few animals first.

Several decades ago, some intrepid wildlife biologists performed vasectomies on male blackbirds, trying to come up with a non-lethal way of controlling their numbers. The operations were a success, but to the researchers' amazement, female blackbirds kept laying fertile eggs! Evidently, someone other than her "husband" was laying Madame Blackbird. It should have been a wake-up call, at least to the biologists (by all accounts, male blackbirds were—and still are—as naive about their mates' extracurricular activities as the unfortunate Charles Bovary, about whom more later).

Then, in the 1990s, DNA fingerprinting became widely available, and with it, incontrovertible evidence that females of nearly every species engage in EPCs, or extrapair copulations.[1] In other words, they screw around. This was unexpected, since, as we have seen, eggs are produced in relatively small numbers and would seem easily fertilized by just one male, presumably the female's "rightful" mate. This is especially true since males make so much sperm. Besides, additional lovers should only bring additional hassles: an outraged husband could behave violently toward the "errant" wife (remember Othello?) or—equally devastating for any species that relies on shared parental care—renege on his child support payments. After all, it is biologically costly to expend resources on behalf of someone else's offspring (more on this in Chapters 6 and 7). For now, the derivation of the word "adultery" is itself revealing: from the Latin *adulterare*, meaning "to alter or change." To adulterate means to "debase by adding inferior materials or elements; making impure by admixture." From a male's perspective, the crucial admixture is someone else's sperm, which is to say, his genes.

Let's also examine the word "cuckold," which, as we've already seen, derives from the European cuckoo, renowned for its behavior as a nest parasite. Cuckoos lay their eggs in the nest of other species, who then become unwitting foster parents. When cuckoo chicks hatch, they add injury to insult by ejecting the host's biological offspring, thus monopolizing their foster parents' resources for themselves. To be cuckolded is to suffer the fate of those unwitting males who fail to see they have been displaced by a lover and end up not only biological failures but social laughingstocks.

In *Love's Labour's Lost*, Shakespeare gives us this cynical song: "The cuckoo then in every tree mocks married men; for thus sings he, 'Cuckoo; cuckoo; cuckoo; O word of fear; unpleasing to a married ear!' " If a man ends up unknowingly rearing another man's

---

[1] This phenomenon is detailed in *The Myth of Monogamy*, by D. P. Barash and J. E. Lipton (New York: Henry Holt, 2002).

children conceived with his spouse, his love's labor is lost indeed. Even during the French Revolution, at a time when enthusiasm for creating a new society was so great that the names for months of the year were tossed out and replaced with new ones, sexual asymmetries of the old regime were retained in one regard: legal sanctions against a *wife's* adultery.

So evolution should have given us faithful female blackbirds, as well as among nearly every species in which females have little to gain and much to lose by "cheating." And yet the facts are undeniable. In species after species, biologists have found that 10, 20, in some cases as many as 70 percent of the offspring reveal "extrapair paternity"—they're not genetic chips off the old paternal block. Rather, some other male has literally chipped in. In the movie *Heartburn*, Nora Ephron's character complains to her father about her philandering husband (journalist Carl Bernstein), whereupon the elder Mr. Ephron responds, not very sympathetically: "You want monogamy? Marry a swan." Well, it turns out that not even swans are monogamous. And not only males stray. She may be married to a sleek and sober swain, with a lovely house on the lake, yet periodically, Madame Swan is likely to sneak off into the cattails with someone else. It's not quite what Marcel Proust meant by *Swann's Way*, but it is the way of the world.

In fact, the only guaranteed monogamous species appears to be a small worm that parasitizes fish intestines. The males and females of this odd creature, *Diplozöon paradoxicum*, meet in adolescence, after which their bodies literally fuse together, till death do they not part. (We like to imagine that they are happily mated, but in any event they are irremediably united and thus faithful.) For almost everyone else, EPCs are the rule, not the exception.

In *Ars amatoria*, the Roman poet Ovid justifies what is perhaps the most notorious, and ruinous, of all cases of adultery: Helen's affair with Paris, which precipitated the Trojan War and caused unimaginable misery. It seems that Helen's husband, Menelaus, was away at the time:

> *Afraid of lonely nights, her spouse away*
> *Safe in her guest's warm bosom, Helen lay.*
> *What folly, Menelaus, forth to wend,*
> *Beneath one rooftree leaving wife and friend? . . .*
> *Blameless is Helen, and her lover too:*
> *They did what you or anyone would do.*

Ovid's lighthearted view of infidelity so irritated the emperor Augustus that the poet was exiled from Rome. We are less sanguine about extracurricular sexuality than Ovid but less judgmental than Augustus (who had some lingering anxiety about his daughter's erotic predilections). In exploring the biology of extrapair copulation and connecting it to humanity and to literature, our intent is not to legitimize adultery by either sex, nor to stigmatize. Rather, it is to open eyes while stimulating that sexiest part of the human anatomy, the one between our ears.

Biologists have a good idea why males are typically interested in sexual variety, but they are more perplexed when it comes to females. The reason, paradoxically, is that there are many possible explanations, as least some of which also help us make sense of Madame Bovary.[2] First, a female may get a leg up on the evolutionary ladder by mating with a "better" partner, obtaining superior genes to go with the material resources and parental assistance provided by her "official" mate. Or, oddly enough, she may find that another male looks good simply because other females feel the same. As noted earlier, according to this "sexy son hypothesis," females

---

[2] Mark Twain once noted that it was easy to stop smoking: he had done it hundreds of times! Similarly, it is easy to explain female sexual infidelity: there are many explanations.

prefer to mate with males whose traits (bright feathers, large antlers, seductive wattles and jowls, broad shoulders, or a resemblance to, say, Pierce Brosnan) are attractive to other females in general and likely to be inherited by their sons.[3] If so, then a swan or antelope—or human being—who swoons and sighs, "I want to have *his* baby," is doing so because her genes are whispering, "He's *so* cute."

Why such whispers? Because of this unconscious correlation: females who mate with Pierce Brosnan are likely to produce sons who are similarly attractive to the next generation of females, and who therefore will enhance the evolutionary success of their mothers, which is probably why those females were so readily seduced to begin with. In short, in the realm of sexual attraction, nothing succeeds like sexual attraction itself. Once set in motion, it can have a self-maintaining dynamic, quite separate from a male's wealth, social position, qualities as a father, and so forth.

Among birds known as bluethroats, the throats of the males are, not surprisingly, bright blue (females are comparatively drab). When researchers enhance a male's blueness by use of iridescent spray paint, these newly anointed beacons of bluethroat beefcake beauty become very attractive to surrounding females; even already mated female bluethroats start fluttering around, seeking EPCs. Similarly, when a male's throat is artificially bleached to be *less* blue, his "wife" starts looking for another lover. As already noted, appearance counts in the animal world, almost certainly because mating with a sexy-looking partner is likely to produce sexy-looking offspring.

At the same time, there is growing evidence that animal sexiness often reflects genuine healthfulness. A bright, shiny blue throat, for example, isn't easy to come by—in the absence of helpful biologists armed with spray paint—and so individuals who succeed in bluing

---

[3] You may have noticed that this leaves unanswered another question: how did such preferences get started in the first place? This is the subject of vigorous research and equally vigorous debate among biologists. It seems probable that a trait is perceived as sexy insofar as it contributes in some way to the evolutionary success of the perceiver, that is, to begin with, it is an "honest signal." Over time, however, such preferences can take on a momentum of their own.

up are likely to have a strong constitution, an efficient metabolism, a body that is comparatively free of parasites, and so on. As a result, even if other females weren't attracted to such secondary sexual characteristics, any correlation between them and likely well-being would probably be enough to make a bluethroat into a genuine heartthrob. Add to this the likelihood that such preferences can con-tribute to a positive feedback mechanism, and it is not surprising that even a happily married female may have her head turned.

Of course, physical traits are no less important to humans, something that has not been lost on the creators of great literature. Here is Tolstoy's Anna Karenina, contemplating her husband and bemoaning his lack of physical charm:

> "Well, he's a good man; upright, kind, and remarkable in his own line," said Anna to herself when she had returned to her room, as though defending him from attack—from the accusation that he was not lovable. "But why is it his ears stick out so oddly? Or has he had his hair cut too short?"

One can imagine Mrs. Bluethroat—whose mate has just been bleached—engaging in a similar interior monologue.

Physical attractiveness (or its absence) is such an obvious factor in infidelity that it can easily be overlooked. In animal societies that are ostensibly monogamous, females must be "married" in or-der to reproduce, since a partner's assistance is often necessary in order to defend a territory, construct a nest, and provision the off-spring. But this doesn't mean that every female must combine her genes with the male that she has settled for: if she has to have a mate but he turns out to be less desirable than some other, why not set up housekeeping with the former but make babies with the lat-ter? In short, get resources and parental assistance from one and the best possible genes from another.

Guinevere's adultery is said to have undone King Arthur's Round Table, and it should occasion no surprise that Sir Lancelot was hardly a stable boy. Not only was he renowned for his military prowess and his overall goodness, but he was also said to be an extraordinary physical specimen. Thus, according to Malory's account, after iron bars were placed at Guinevere's window to protect her chastity, Lance pulls them apart by sheer strength, in the process wounding his hands and shedding blood that nearly gives him away, after which he spends the night with the queen: "Syr Launcelot wente to bedde with the quene and toke no force of hys hurte honde, but toke hys pleasaunce and his lykynge untyll hit was the dawnyying of the day."

Nor are similar considerations missing from more popular media. In the movie *Unfaithful*, Connie Sumner, a beautiful woman living in what seems to be upper-middle-class bliss—and married to Richard Gere, besides—nonetheless has what turns out to be a disastrous affair with a young, charming, sexy hunk. Why? Because he is a young, charming, sexy hunk, whereupon Mrs. Sumner is swept off her feet and into her lover's bed . . . and couch, and stairway, and the bathroom of a nearby restaurant, and so forth.

Once again, it doesn't matter that this unfaithful woman, just like Queen Guinevere, didn't become pregnant by her EPC partner, nor even that she would presumably engage in strenuous methods of birth control, if necessary, to prevent conception. The point is that human beings, like other creatures, have been endowed with an inclination to have sex with partners who are especially attractive. Delving into that inclination, we see that it is an evolutionary bequeathal from a precontraceptive world when such choices were more directly connected to reproductive consequences. Although the technology has changed, our genes have hardly noticed.

This is not to say that Darwinian urges are necessarily unconscious. Anna and Vronsky know perfectly well they want to have sex. But it's the evolutionary logic behind it—the reproductive payoff and ultimate motivating force—that operates not only below the belt but also below the level of conscious awareness.

By the same token, it is worth noting that Emma Bovary and her beaux—the wealthy rake Rodolphe and the attractive law student Léon—seemed no more eager to reproduce than any of the other renowned lascivious couples of literary or cinematic lore. It would not have been surprising, for example, if Anna Karenina and Count Vronsky had employed the latest advances in nineteenth-century Russian birth control, whatever that may have involved. They wanted each other, not a baby. Biologists understand that a major reason why Emma wanted sex with Rodolphe, Léon, and the marquis (the last unconsummated) was because deep inside (in the DNA of her brain) she heard a subliminal Darwinian whisper that tickled her ovaries, even though she may not have acknowledged it and would likely have even acted consciously against such an out-come. Smart women sometimes really do make foolish choices, and a whiff of Darwin enables us to glimpse some of the reasons why.

Madame Bovary evidently found her various lovers sexually ex-citing, just as a hungry person—even if she knows nothing of diges-tive physiology—can be seduced by a tasty meal. Most people eat not in order to stoke their metabolism but rather to slake their hunger. By seeing such urges for what they are, the modern reader can also see how the prospect of enhancing her evolutionary situa-tion undergirds a beleaguered heroine's erotic hunger. Especially, as we shall soon explore, if she is otherwise undernourished.

This inscription, from Thomas Parke D'Invilliers, begins F. Scott Fitzgerald's *The Great Gatsby*:

> *Then wear the gold hat, if that will move her;*
> *If you can bounce high, bounce for her too,*
> *Till she cry "Lover, gold-hatted, high-bouncing lover,*
> *I must have you!"*

But what makes a woman cry "I must have you"? It turns out that being gold-hatted, no less than high-bouncing, counts for quite a lot. Aside from being turned on by physical attractiveness, female animals often look for lovers who are especially wealthy and willing to share that wealth with sexual partners (male animals with a rich territory will often allow their mistresses to forage there in exchange for sexual favors), including when their "official" mate is a lax provider. For example, an osprey female whose husband is a failure at bringing home the salmon is especially liable to copulate with other males while he is gone; in return, these obliging gents help provision her and her offspring.

Other zoological Madame Bovarys appear to use their adulterous unions to establish a possible bridge to a new relationship, a behavior that is assuredly within the human repertoire as well. But one of the most interesting theories of female infidelity is that primates in particular may do the monkey equivalent of Emma's carnal carriage ride as a way of purchasing infanticide and child abuse insurance. This isn't about, as one might think, a maternal response to an abusive simian husband. Rather, it involves males other than the parent: among many primate species it is not uncommon for males to kill the offspring of others and then reinseminate the mothers, a brutally effective case of getting rid of the other guy's genes to make room for yours. Thus, it would make sense for a female to be generous with her sexual favors so as to induce the neighborhood males to "think" that they might have fathered her offspring, which, in turn, makes the males less likely to murder the juveniles. (Presumably, a male chimpanzee who encounters a female with an infant is likely to say to himself: "Isn't that my old flame, with whom I had such a hot time behind the baobab tree? Cute little tyke with her, too. Looks just like me!")

There just isn't a single, simple answer to the question of why females are sexually unfaithful, although accumulating evidence strongly suggests that infidelity by either sex occurs when it increases the likely evolutionary success of the "infidel." This area of investigation is one of the newest, most exciting realms of research in animal behavior and evolutionary biology; the above discussion only skims the surface. But it helps open a door upon one of the oldest, most pervasive themes in literature. Just as evolutionary in-sights help us understand Othello's jealousy, a dollop of biology sheds light on Madame Bovary and her soul mates. If we are cor-rect, then Emma Bovary is a reflection not only of what goes on "out there" in the animal world but also of what exists "in here," within our own hearts . . . and genes, and gonads. And what has accordingly found its way onto the printed page as well.

And so we come to Emma Bovary herself, literary poster woman for female infidelity. How well does Emma's behavior conform to biological expectations? Very well indeed. Emma's father was a farmer, and her marriage to Charles Bovary is a typical example of "marrying up," or hypergamy, whereby women seek to pair with men who are socioeconomically above them (recall the thrust of many a Jane Austen novel, described in Chapter 3). Flaubert tells us that Emma's father was in debt and "losing money every year." With the family in bad financial shape, Charles Bovary therefore seemed a good catch, at least to Monsieur Rouault, his prospective father-in-law:

> Charles was a bit namby-pamby, not his dream of a son-in-law; but he was said to be reliable, thrifty, very well educated, and he prob-ably wouldn't haggle too much over the dowry. Moreover, Rouault was soon going to have to sell twenty-two of his acres. . . . "If he asks me for her," he said to himself, "I won't refuse."

This is precisely what happens in many species. Given the exis-tence of competition among males, the winners are those who are a bit smarter, stronger, richer, and better connected, who offer a better deal to the females (and, in the case of human beings, their families). Or—another way to look at it—women have been able to insist on mating preferentially with only the most desirable men, which means that women should be more likely to marry up than down. If harem keeping were the current norm, the result would be a relatively small number of socially, financially, and/or physically dominant men monopolizing most of the women. By contrast, in a social system of ostensible monogamy, as currently found in the West, the stage is set for female infidelity, as some women seek to better their situation. As we have already suggested, this pattern also suggests an especially poor prognosis for marriages that go the other way, when the woman is more competent, educated, or otherwise desirable than her mate.

This might seem to augur well for the Charles/Emma union, and initially it did. But twenty-first-century readers need to realize that the situation of a physician in nineteenth-century France was not all that impressive. Moreover, Charles Bovary wasn't even a physician; it is quite clear from the novel that he was an *officier de santé*, a "health officer," and thus one step below an actual doctor: less training, less skill, and less renown, more like a licensed practical nurse. And so Charles Bovary, although initially a good catch for lower-class Emma, is not *that* good. Especially not when her expectations expanded. Plus, Charles is depicted as rather boring and dull-witted, lacking the human equivalent of a bright blue throat or fancy tail feathers:

> By working hard he [Charles] managed to stay about the middle of the class; once he even got an honorable mention in natural history. . . . He understood absolutely nothing of any of it. He listened in vain: he could not grasp it. In the performance of his daily task he was like a mill-horse that treads blindfolded in a circle, utterly ignorant of what he is grinding.

Nor was Charles Bovary especially ambitious:

> Emma looked at him and shrugged her shoulders. Why didn't she at least have for a husband one of those silent, dedicated men who spend their nights immersed in books and who by the time they're sixty and rheumatic have acquired a row of decorations to wear on their ill-fitting black coats? She would have liked the name Bovary—her name—to be famous, on display in all the bookshops, constantly mentioned in the newspapers, known all over France. But Charles had no ambition! . . . "It's pathetic!" she whispered to herself, despair in her heart. "What a booby!"

We cannot help noting, with some irony, that "booby" also refers to several species of oceangoing birds; there are blue-footed, red-footed, pink-footed, and brown-footed boobies, among others. And within these species, females are especially prone to copulating with other males when their mate is, well, a genuine booby. It is also noteworthy that Emma Bovary had a sharp eye for the differences among men. Having seen one booby, she would doubtless conclude, you have not seen them all.

Thus at one point (before Emma's first affair), the Bovarys are invited to a ball at the elegant home of a marquis:

> She thought of Les Bertaux [the farm where she grew up]: . . . and she saw herself as she had been there, skimming cream with her finger from the milk jars in the dairy. But amid the splendors of this night her past life, hitherto so vividly present, was vanishing utterly; indeed she was beginning almost to doubt that she had lived it. She was here: and around the brilliant ball was a shadow that veiled all else.

Here in the marquis's home was something closer to her idealized life of perfection, and both the marquis and another aristocrat, a viscount, came much closer to Emma's ideal than did Charles: "However she imagined him [her perfect husband], he wasn't a bit like Charles. He might have been handsome, witty, distinguished, magnetic—the kind of man her convent schoolmates had doubtless married." Emma didn't enter into an affair with either the marquis or the viscount, but if she could have, she probably would have. After all, in comparison Charles was poor not only in resources but also in intellect (which is to say, probably offering genes that are less than stunning):

> Charles's conversation was flat as a sidewalk, a place of passage for the ideas of everyman. . . . He couldn't swim or fence or fire a pistol; one day he couldn't tell her the meaning of a riding term she had come upon in a novel. Wasn't it a man's role, though, to

know everything? Shouldn't he be expert at all kinds of things, able to initiate you into the intensities of passion, the refinements of life, all the mysteries? *This* man could teach you nothing; he knew nothing, he wished for nothing. He took it for granted that she was content; and she resented his settled calm, his serene dullness, the very happiness she herself brought him.

Sure enough, Emma proceeds to have an affair with Rodolphe, wealthy, witty, debonair, and something of an accomplished sexual predator:

> Monsieur Rodolphe Boulanger was thirty-four. He was brutal and shrewd. He was something of a connoisseur: there had been many women in his life. This one [Emma] seemed pretty, so the thought of her and her husband stayed with him.
>
> "I have an idea he's stupid. I'll bet she's tired of him. His fingernails are dirty and he hasn't shaved in three days. He trots off to see his patients and leaves her home to darn his socks. How bored she must be! . . . A compliment or two and she'd adore me, I'm positive. She'd be sweet! But—how would I get rid of her later?" . . . [After thinking about his present mistress:] "Ah, Madame Bovary is much prettier—and what's more, much fresher. Virginie's certainly growing too fat."

When their affair is in danger of being revealed to Charles, Rodolphe reveals himself to be, for all his faults, attractive to Emma because of his swaggering courage:

> "Have you got your pistols?"
> "What for?"
> "Why—to defend yourself," said Emma.
> "You mean against your husband? That poor . . . ?"
> And Rodolphe ended his sentence with a gesture that meant that he could annihilate Charles with a flick of his finger.
> This display of fearlessness dazzled her, even though she sensed in it a crudity and bland vulgarity that shocked her.

But Rodolphe eventually dumps her, at about the same time that Emma's husband experiences a major professional reversal. A treatment that Charles attempted on a patient had a disastrous outcome, causing him humiliation and lowering his stature in the community as well as in his wife's eyes:

> He was sitting quite calmly, utterly oblivious of the fact that the ridicule henceforth inseparable from his name would disgrace her as well. And she had tried to love him! She had wept tears of repentance at having given herself to another!

It isn't just Emma Bovary who is especially likely to be unfaithful when her mate has suffered a decline in status. A recent study of black-capped chickadees, for instance, found that whereas females are generally faithful, they occasionally stray, but only with males who are socially dominant to their husbands. When a male chickadee experiences a reversal in his dominance stature, he had better look to his "wife." Charles Bovary might have been similarly advised.

Meanwhile, things have been going from bad to worse in the Bovary household. Emma predictably begins another affair, this time with young, handsome Léon Dupuis, an aspiring attorney, at the same time that Charles Bovary is going deeply into debt, largely because of Emma's profligacy. Recall that Charles was boring and intellectually dull. By contrast, Léon radiated mental sprightliness, a characteristic that is "romantic," in large part because it suggests the presence of good genes in a prospective mating partner. (Recall also our earlier look at Jane Austen's heroes and heroines and their crucially witty repartee.)

Although Monsieur Bovary was a dutiful husband, he was decidedly unglamorous, smelling of medicines and body fluids instead of fancy perfumes. By contrast, Léon

> was thought to have very gentlemanly manners. He listened respectfully to his elders, and seemed not to get excited about politics—a remarkable trait in a young man. Besides, he was talented. He painted in water colors, could read the key of G,

and when he didn't play cards after dinner he often took up a book. Monsieur Homais esteemed him because he was educated; Madame Homais liked him because he was helpful: he would often spend some time with her children in the garden.

Emma eventually commits suicide as her debts mount and neither Rodolphe nor Léon will pay them. Charles subsequently discovers letters between her and her former lovers, whereupon he, too, dies brokenhearted.

It is said that Flaubert struggled for weeks to craft the perfect phrase for each sentence, and much of *Madame Bovary*'s impact comes from the exquisitely evocative language in which it is written. At the same time, much of the impact of *Madame Bovary* comes from Madame Bovary, the woman whose struggles with monogamy could have been written by a knowledgeable evolutionary biologist (if he or she were also a literary giant). In the novel's pathetic ending, we see the sentimental imprint of nineteenth-century morality: in Flaubert's time, the myth of monogamy was widespread, at least in the case of women. A sexual double standard was firmly ensconced culturally but based equally firmly on the biological asymmetries between men and women. As we've seen earlier, this comes down to who makes sperm and who makes eggs, which sex gets pregnant, and which lacks confidence of parentage. Moreover, it was assumed that although men— even married men—would have multiple lovers, women's libido was essentially nonexistent. Their yearning for quiet, monogamous domesticity was supposed to be the flip side of men's randiness. Now we know the universality of what Flaubert described a century ago: women, too, are sexual creatures, influenced no less than men by their own biology.

"*Madame Bovary, c'est moi*," wrote Flaubert. He might have written, more accurately, "*Madame Bovary, c'est nous*."

Madame Bovary's ovaries weren't really hyperactive (although her romantic imagination may have been regrettably stuck in overdrive). Certainly she isn't the only sexually unfaithful woman in literature.

The American writer Kate Chopin (pronounced like the renowned composer) is often described as a "regionalist," and yet she has of late been acclaimed as nothing less than a universalist, especially in her masterpiece account of female adultery, *The Awakening*. This short novel, published in 1899, was considered so scandalous that it effectively terminated Chopin's career as a publishable author. Today, she is revered as a feminist icon, someone ahead of her time in depicting womanly independence from male-dominated society, and one of the first to probe the hidden secrets of the (sometimes adulterous) female heart.

It is unclear whether Guinevere underwent a particular sexual awakening with Lancelot, beyond whatever she experienced with Arthur. But it is pretty obvious that in Chopin's novella, Edna Pontellier—attractive, young, frustrated spouse of the older, benevolent, but tiresomely traditional Léonce Pontellier—is due for her own awakening:

> The acme of bliss . . . was not for her in this world. As the devoted wife of a man who worshipped her, she felt she would take her place with a certain dignity in the world of reality, closing the portals forever behind her upon the realm of romance and dreams. . . . She grew fond of her husband, realizing with some unaccountable satisfaction that no trace of passion or excessive and fictitious warmth colored her affection.

Edna is needy and unfulfilled: she goes swimming in the heat of the day (itself a shocking violation of turn-of-the-century norms), lies languorously in her hammock refusing her husband's demands that she come inside, defies the rigid social conventions of New Orleans society, becomes increasingly interested in Robert Lebrun—who flirts with married women but can't deal with a serious relationship—and, finally, has an affair with Alcée Arobin, like Emma Bovary's Rodolphe an accomplished Don Juan:

He stayed and dined with Edna. He stayed and sat beside the wood fire. They laughed and talked; and before it was time to go he was telling her how different life might have been if he had known her years before. With ingenuous frankness he spoke of what a wicked, ill-disciplined boy he had been, and impulsively drew up his cuff to exhibit upon his wrist the scar from a saber cut which he had received in a duel outside of Paris when he was nineteen. She touched his hand as she scanned the red cicatrice on the inside of his white wrist. A quick impulse that was somewhat spasmodic impelled her fingers to close in a sort of clutch upon his hand. He felt the pressure of her pointed nails in the flesh of his palm.

Edna doesn't love Alcée. But he satisfies a sexual passion that had been dormant within her and was, ironically, aroused by another man, Lebrun, who returns her feelings but ultimately flees from the prospect of an illicit affair.

Other women in Chopin's novel exemplify alternative routes to personal gratification: one of Edna's friends is the embodiment of maternal virtue; another is a serious pianist, exclusively committed to her art; an old woman (encountered only briefly) signifies religious satisfaction; but Edna's awakening is a matter of social independence combined with pure sexual fulfillment. At one point, the benevolent family doctor, consulted by her worried husband because Edna had been acting so strangely,

> noted a subtle change which had transformed her from the listless woman he had known into a being who, for the moment, seemed palpitant with the forces of life. Her speech was warm and energetic. There was no repression in her glance or gesture. She reminded him of some beautiful, sleek animal waking up in the sun.

Although *The Awakening* includes no account of physical intimacy between Edna and her husband, and even its description of Edna Pontellier's "waking up" with Alcée is notably delicate by current standards, there is no question that with her lover, Edna experiences something exciting, compelling, and new: "It was the first kiss of her life to which her nature had really responded. It was a flaming torch that kindled desire." Later, after she and Alcée make love,

> she felt as if a mist had been lifted from her eyes, enabling her to look upon and comprehend the significance of life, that monster made up of beauty and brutality. But among the conflicting sensations which assailed her, there was neither shame nor remorse. There was a dull pang of regret because it was not the kiss of love which had inflamed her, because it was not love which had held this cup of life to her lips.

Edna's affair with Alcée is all about sex, and little else:

> He did not answer, except to continue to caress her. He did not say good night until she had become supple to his gentle, seductive entreaties. . . . [She] unfolded under his delicate sense of her nature's requirements like a torpid, torrid, sensitive blossom.

So let's talk a bit about what Kate Chopin is implying but is too delicate to state explicitly: female orgasm. It had been widely thought until recently that female animals didn't experience orgasm; even now, with clear evidence for female climax in a variety of species, its adaptive significance remains a biological mystery, since clearly it is not necessary in order for females to reproduce. A number of theories have been put forth, suggesting ways in which orgasm might aid a woman's chance of conceiving, but none of them is terribly convincing. There is the "knockout" hypothesis, which suggests that a postorgasmic woman is likely to remain lying down longer, thereby facilitating conception. Another is that female orgasm may be something that is just along for the evolutionary ride, a mere by-product of ejaculation in men. Like nipples, which are nonfunctional in men but biologically useful in women, perhaps orgasm in women persisted simply because it is closely tied to ejaculation in men, although among women it may be physiologically and behaviorally inconsequential.

Another possibility is that female orgasm provides what psychologists call "positive reinforcement," which is to say, a mechanism whereby individuals are internally prodded to continue what they are doing when what they are doing is somehow good for them. Thus, maybe female orgasm, tied as it is to "good sex," is how a woman's body tells her that she is with a desirable sexual partner. Consider, for example, this observation of sex in grizzly bears. When subordinate males copulate, they spend their time looking around, heads swiveling for possible sight of an approaching dominant bear. By contrast, dominant grizzlies are more leisurely when they have mounted a female. It isn't clear whether grizzly sows experience orgasm, but if so, they are probably more likely to do so under the "gentle, seductive entreaties" of a successful, dominant, and unhurried male, whereupon they might well "unfold" "like a torpid, torrid, sensitive blossom," which is to say, like Edna Pontellier with her lover. But, sad to relate, not with her husband.

Among animals, perhaps the major risk that females run when they engage in an EPC is that their mates, if they find out, might abandon them and their offspring. It is interesting that although both Emma Bovary and Edna Pontellier are mothers, the two are presented as lacking any deep maternal inclinations, the absence of which facilitated their adulteries. Edna, unlike her friend Adèle Ratignolle, wasn't a "mother-woman," and Emma Bovary treated her child as a dress-up doll.

By contrast, both Hester Prynne, the key figure in Nathaniel Hawthorne's *The Scarlet Letter* (of which more later), and Anna Karenina, eponymous heroine of Tolstoy's great novel, are devoted mothers, such that the possible loss of their children emerges as a major threat to their happiness—in fact, *the* major threat. Hester struggles with the Puritan authorities to be allowed to keep Pearl, her child by the Reverend Arthur Dimmesdale (and Dimmesdale, in turn, shows a degree of paternal solicitude by arguing success-fully in support of this desperate request). Karenin, on the other hand, is, we might say, paternally challenged, and when he threat-ens Anna with the loss of her child if she persists in demanding a divorce, he is clearly seeking advantage rather than responding out of fatherly solicitude. Indeed, Anna's deceived husband makes it clear that one consequence of Anna's affair is that he has begun to question his paternity itself: "I doubt everything, I cannot bear my son, sometimes I do not believe he is my son."

Anna, meanwhile, has no such doubts. After all, she is a per-fectly good mammal, with all the consequences of internal fertiliza-tion:

> No matter what happened to her, she could not give up her son. Let her husband put her to shame and turn her out, let Vronsky grow cold towards her . . . she could not leave her son. She had an aim in life. And she must act; act to secure this relation to her son, so that he might not be taken away from her.

Anna becomes pregnant by Vronsky, gives birth to a daughter, and the three go off together, while Karenin makes good on his threat to take control of Anna's son, Seriozha. This is an unen-durable blow, and the forced separation contributes greatly to her eventual suicide.

Suicide is transgressive in that it violates the prevailing social code. So, of course, is marital infidelity. Moreover, adultery is also—from the perspective of the cuckolded husband—a transgres-sion against an even deeper, biological code. This is probably why it is universally considered such a serious offense, especially when done by women. "The difference [between the consequences of a man's and a woman's infidelity] is boundless," noted Samuel Johnson. "The man imposes no bastards upon his wife." It is tempt-ing to interpret Anna's fate as the punishment for such a potential imposition, meted out—not coincidentally—by a male writer, except that Kate Chopin exacts similar punishment upon Edna Pontellier. Maybe Ms. Chopin, although remarkably liberated for her time, was nonetheless swayed by the same powerful antiadultery sentiment that prevails even today, under which a sexually unfaithful *woman*, in particular, must suffer for her actions. Or maybe she was simply reflecting the bias of her day, according to which adulterers—especially if female—must come to a bad end.

In *Anna Karenina*, a liberal-minded gentleman named Pestov comments that the real inequality between husband and wife is the fact that infidelity by each is punished differently, to which Karenin responds, "I think the foundations of this attitude are rooted in the very nature of things." Here, at least, Anna's husband is sensitive indeed. Asymmetric punishment for adultery—in effect, the sexual double standard—hardly exhausts the catalog of husband-wife social inequality. Nonetheless, both Pestov and Karenin are correct: adultery by a wife is indeed punished differently than is adultery by a husband. And Karenin is even more correct: this difference is indeed rooted in the "very nature" of things.

Moreover, a man is *expected* to react intolerantly to his wife's adultery. In many countries, men are even legally excused for murdering an unfaithful spouse and her consort. Lest you assume that we're talking only about third world countries or those practicing an extreme form of Islam, until 1974 homicide was fully legal in the state of Texas "when committed by the husband upon the person of anyone taken in the act of adultery with the wife, provided the killing takes place before the parties to the act have separated" (Texas Penal Code 1925, article 1220). What was meant by "in the act" isn't entirely clear, and one has to wonder whether this particular brand of Texas justice required that a homicidal husband slay his rival while sexual intercourse was literally in progress. But the basic idea is clear enough: adultery—especially on the part of a wife—is assumed to be such an immense provocation to a husband that violence is anticipated and even "justified."

Literature gives us many cases of the wronged—"outraged"—husband as avenging angel. In Leo Tolstoy's novella *The Kreutzer Sonata*, a man named Pozdnyshev brags how he killed his wife, thinking her guilty of adultery. She was a pianist who evidently had an affair with a violinist with whom she had played Beethoven's passionate sonata. Pozdnyshev blames the romantic music: "An awakening of energy and feeling unsuited both to the time and place, to which no outlet is given, cannot but act harmfully." We blame biology.

For another icon of literature in which biology looms far larger than most critics have allowed, and which features a paradigmatic "wronged" husband, consider Hawthorne's *The Scarlet Letter*, which isn't so much about adultery as about society's response to it. That response is both vengeful and—albeit indirectly—violent as well, on the part of one Roger Chillingworth. Hester Prynne, young and alone in the Massachusetts Bay Colony, has reason to think that Chillingworth, her husband, has died, whereupon she has an illicit sexual relationship, as evidenced by the incontrovertibly biological fact that she bears a child, and for which she is condemned to wear the famous scarlet letter: an *A* for adultery.

It turns out, however, that Hester's husband, the not-very-jolly Roger, isn't dead after all. He returns in time to witness Hester's (and, incognito, his own) humiliation, whereupon Chillingworth commits himself to discovering and revenging himself on the man who cuckolded him. It turns out to have been the community's straitlaced minister, the Reverend Arthur Dimmesdale. Chillingworth proceeds to destroy Dimmesdale physically as well as psychologically, referring to himself along the way as a "fiend." Roger Chillingworth is old, deformed, and likely wasn't an especially loving or appealing husband even when he and Hester lived as a (presumably faithful) couple: "Hadst thou met earlier with a better love than mine," he admits to

Hester, "this evil [i.e., her adultery] had not been." But following Hester's infidelity—which produced the "love child," Pearl—Chillingworth is chilling indeed in his single-minded pursuit of vengeance:

> There came a glare of red light out of his eyes; as if the old man's soul were on fire. . . . old Roger Chillingworth was a striking evidence of man's faculty of transforming himself into a devil . . . devoting himself, for seven years, to the constant analysis of a heart full of torture, and deriving his enjoyment thence, and adding fuel to those fiery tortures which he analyzed and gloated over. . . . "A mortal man, with once a human heart, has become a fiend for his [Dimmesdale's] especial torment!"

Chillingworth angrily rejects Hester's plea that he leave off persecuting Dimmesdale: "By thy first step awry, thou didst plant the germ of evil; but, since that moment, it has been a dark necessity. . . . Let the black flower blossom as it may!" Chillingworth's pursuit is so violent, persistent, and consuming that he could as well have killed the minister directly. *The Scarlet Letter* is unusual in the annals of literature in that the male participant, rather than the married woman, ends up suffering the most. Another example of male comeuppance—played this time for laughs rather than tragedy—occurs in a more contemporary novel, John Irving's *The World According to Garp*. Here, the transgressing man gets his penis amputated when Garp, the cuckolded husband, accidentally drives his automobile into a parked car within which Mrs. Garp is performing fellatio on her extramarital lover.

Whether lethally violent (as in *The Kreutzer Sonata*), indirectly so (*The Scarlet Letter*), or comically and unintentionally retributive (*The World According to Garp*), biology nonetheless underpins a predictable male response to female infidelity. For most behaviors, evolutionary inclinations whisper within us. But when it comes to certain things—notably, male response to a spouse's adultery—

those whispers fairly rise to a shout. Indeed, the expectation of such a response is so great that when it is *not* met, when a cuckolded husband reacts meekly or not at all, this may be considered evidence for his inadequacy, and even a kind of justification for the wife's adultery in the first place. For example, after Anna Karenina's adultery has been revealed to him, Karenin makes it clear that he values propriety above all else, that his outrage is limited to the embarrassment caused by her behavior, and that he will not grant Anna a divorce because of the social awkwardness it would entail:

> "My decision is as follows. Whatever your conduct may have been, I do not consider myself justified in severing the ties with which a Higher Power has bound us. The family cannot be broken up at the caprice, discretion, or even the sin of one of the partners of that marriage, and our life must continue as before."

Karenin is only concerned with sparing himself the social consequences of acknowledging his wife's affair. His unflappable indifference to the emotional consequences of his wife's behavior, itself so counter to biological expectations, helps illuminate his own character, which in turn sheds light on why Anna was so dissatisfied with Karenin in the first place and why she turned to Vronsky: Karenin's coldness, his valuing of social appearances over the warmth of love and the promptings—sometimes unruly and even violent—of life itself.

> He [Karenin] went on coldly and calmly. . . . "As you know, I look upon jealousy as a humiliating and degrading emotion and I shall never allow myself to be influenced by it; but there are certain laws of propriety which one cannot disregard with impunity."

And here is Anna talking with her lover, Vronsky, about Karenin's response to their adultery:

"In general terms, he [Karenin] will say in his official manner, with all distinctness and precision, that he cannot let me go but will take all measures in his power to prevent a scandal. And he will quietly and punctiliously do what he says. That is what will happen. He's not a human being but a machine, and a cruel machine when he's angry . . . He's not a man, not a human being—he's a . . . puppet! No one knows him but I do. Oh, if I'd been in his place, if anyone else had been in his place, I should long ago have murdered and torn in pieces a wife like me. I shouldn't be calling her 'ma chère'! He's not a man, he's an automaton."

Throughout this book, we point to cases in which behavior parallels the expectations of biology. Equally revealing, however, are those unusual depictions of people whose actions run *contrary* to prediction. When this happens, it is likely to throw light on what is special about them, whether their abiologia reveals them to be especially cold and thus undesirable (like Karenin) or especially saintly (such as Jesus or the Buddha, whose renunciation of earthly pleasures and selfish pursuits marked them as notable in their own way). In other words, departures from expectation can themselves be meaningful, but only if we begin with an expectation of what human beings "naturally" are like. It is also significant that even Karenin, for all his protestations of propriety, eventually shows some jealousy toward Vronsky and anger toward Anna that go beyond the frozen "disappointment" that he expresses; a cold fish, indeed, but still a fish.

Even when, for whatever reason, the husband doesn't exact physical vengeance as such, a philandering wife is nearly always punished (especially, we might add, in stories written by men). Emma dies. Anna dies. Even the liberated Edna Pontellier dies. In Stendhal's *The Red and the Black*, the social-climbing opportunist Julien Sorel has an ongoing affair with Madame de Rênal, who is married to the local mayor. She dies a few days after Julien is executed (for having tried, earlier, to kill her), embracing her children but still loving

Julien hopelessly and helplessly, driven to religious distraction by her guilt but, by the laws of social and biological propriety, not permitted to recover emotionally from her adulterous affair.

Of course, there is no one-size-fits-all response to adultery. In *The Golden Bowl*, Henry James depicts a situation that in anyone else's hands would have been worthy of Jerry Springer–type fireworks yet is notable for its apparent mildness. At the same time, *The Golden Bowl* shows biology lurking just offstage, fluttering the curtain of social rules and cultural guidelines. Maggie Verver, a wealthy young American living in Europe (most of James's characters, it seems, are wealthy young Americans living in Europe), discovers that her best friend, whom she had encouraged to marry her widower father, previously had an affair with Maggie's current husband, the urbane Prince Amerigo. Moreover, they are still at it! But no suicides in this case, no murder à la Pozdnyshev nor fiendish pursuit à la Chillingworth; rather, sensitivity and delicacy.

Above all, James's sophisticated upper-crust characters are careful not to upset the matrimonial applecart as they strive— successfully—to keep up appearances and the code of upper-crust respectability: make one's life a work of art. Fake it till you make it? Perhaps. At the same time, anyone reading *The Golden Bowl* cannot help but notice the coiled tension generated by the various revelations of past and present infidelity and how this energy suffuses the outwardly unruffled response of the various protagonists. Indeed, it is the power of their evolutionary heritage that drives much of the action, just as the characters' refusal to act upon its dictates highlights the social restraints and sophistication that James so successfully conveys. Like a tornado that races through a museum, miraculously sparing the precious artifacts, adultery slashes through the Verver/ Amerigo family, and the reader is left breathless, wondering how so much energy can have done so little apparent damage.

Perhaps the finest literary account of postadultery reconciliation, however, comes from James Joyce's *Ulysses*, widely seen as the greatest novel of the twentieth century. In it, the author parallels the mythic, elevated adventures of the Homeric superhero, Odysseus, with the genuine, down-to-earth, quotidian experiences of a very ordinary guy, Leopold Bloom, during a very ordinary day in early-twentieth-century Dublin. While Bloom goes to work, attends a funeral, eats, and has various quintessentially normal and earthy encounters, his wife, Molly, has a steamy afternoon extramarital dalliance (also all too normal) with the aptly named Blazes Boylan. Our hero knows of this, is greatly disturbed by it, but comes to a kind of peace nonetheless, emphasizing in this reverie the fundamental "naturalness" of Molly's rendezvous by contrasting it with other provocations:

> As natural as any and every natural act of a nature expressed or understood executed in natured nature by natural creatures in accordance with his, her and their natured natures, of dissimilar similarity. As not as calamitous as a cataclysmic annihilation of the planet in consequence of collision with a dark sun. As less reprehensible than theft, highway robbery, cruelty to children and animals, obtaining money under false pretenses, forgery, embezzlement, misappropriation of public money, betrayal of public trust, malingering, mayhem, corruption of minors, criminal libel, blackmail, contempt of court, arson, treason, felony, mutiny on the high seas, trespass, burglary, jailbreaking, practice of unnatural vice, desertion from armed forces in the field, perjury, poaching, usury, intelligence with the king's enemies, impersonation, criminal assault, manslaughter, willful and premeditated murder. As not more abnormal than all other altered processes of adaptation to altered conditions of existence, resulting in a reciprocal equilibrium between the bodily organism and its attendant circumstances, foods, beverages, acquired habits, indulged inclinations, and significant disease.

Molly Bloom is no Penelope, whose legendary faithfulness to Odysseus—despite a slew of suitors—can be contrasted with the wily hero's dalliances with Circe and Calypso. Similarly, Leopold

Bloom is no Odysseus; his sexual conquest during "Bloomsday" consists of masturbating while surreptitiously watching a young woman who, leaning backward, reveals her underwear.

But Molly's adultery doesn't itself demonstrate that Leopold is a loser. Rather, the telling thing would appear to be his lethargic response to her infidelity, verging on nonresponse. But wait! Things are more complex than this; indeed, great literature is made great, in part, by its complexity. To be sure, it would have been possible for Joyce to portray Leopold Bloom as murderously enraged by his wife's adultery, like Tolstoy's Pozdnyshev. But throughout *Ulysses*, Joyce is after bigger game; he portrays Bloom as a modern-day Odysseus, not the legendary, hormonally predictable hero of yore and of straightforward biology. He is, for one thing, a pacifist. But at the same time, Bloom is wonderfully believable as an embodied male animal. Thus, he is hardly indifferent to Molly's affair with Boylan. For much of the novel, in fact, our hero is preoccupied with it, terribly agitated and driven, if not to distraction, then certainly to a high level of guilt, anger, and—especially in the phantasmagorical Circe ("night-town") chapter—to a remarkable and prolonged bout of obsessive erotic imaginings.

Here is yet another layer of complexity: in writing *Ulysses*, Joyce was concerned to show how daily life can rise to its own version of grandeur, with Bloom the pacifist emerging as a memorable counterpart to the homicidal suitor-slaying fury of Homer's Odysseus. In this sense, Leopold's overt tolerance of Molly's behavior elevates him, just as Molly's famous monologue at the novel's end elevates us all, concluding as it does with an affirmation of love and of affirmation itself:

> I asked him with my eyes to ask again yes and then he asked me would I yes to say yes my mountain flower and first I put my arms around him yes and drew him down to me so he could feel my breasts all perfume yes and his heart was going like mad and yes I said yes I will Yes.

6

WISDOM FROM *THE* GODFATHER

Kin Selection, or the Enduring Importance of Being Family

———————

The Godfather may not have been an evolutionary geneticist, but he knew a thing or two about life. "How do I love you?" Don Corleone might have written. "Let me count your genes."

Genes, not bodies, are where the evolutionary action is. It may be hard to believe, since superficially the organic world is filled with trees, flowers, birds, fish, mammals, insects, and people—not a speck of DNA to be seen. And yet the genes are there. It is genes, not bodies, that persevere through the trajectory of life, and they do so by hitchhiking (or hijacking) a ride in one body or another. After all, bodies are mortal; not so genes. Bodies come and go; genes can, at least in theory, go on forever. And of course, those that succeed in "going on"—if not forever, at least into those generations that have persevered thus far—are the ones responsible for all of the life around us.

So while the "family" that Mario Puzo wrote about was literally a family—a congregation of distant, individual bodies—shared genes made up the mortar that held the Corleones together; similarly for the Tataglias and the other Mafia clans. The importance of being family, however, isn't limited to criminal enterprises or godfathers. It is the earnest enterprise of life.

In his poem "Heredity," Thomas Hardy had a premonition of modern evolutionary biology and the endurance of genes:

I am the family face
Flesh perishes, I live on
Projecting trait and trace
Through time to times anon,
And leaping from place to place
Over oblivion.

The years-heired feature that can
In curve and voice and eye
Despise the human span
Of durance—that is I;
The eternal thing in man,
That heeds no call to die.

When people refer to evolution with the verbal shorthand "survival of the fittest," only rarely do they understand just what they are talking about. Ever since Herbert Spencer coined this phrase in the nineteenth century, it has been misused to justify one group's domination over another: stronger over weaker, smarter over less intelligent, less scrupulous over more restrained, "pure" races over "mixed," and so forth. Yet, aside from the egregious immorality of such abuse, it is also scientifically wrongheaded. "Fittest" means none of these things, nor does it imply any ethical justification for what is found in nature. The living world simply is what it is. If human beings were to derive ethical guidelines from the natural world, we should probably refrain from walking upright; after all, gravity would dictate crawling on our bellies! And in deference to entropy, rooms should never be tidied. As to "fitness," this biological concept simply indicates a living thing's capacity to pass on genes, in a given environment. Thus, being "fit" may mean being big and strong, or perhaps smart and cunning, or it might be the weak and suitably frightened or the sneaky and unprincipled who reproduce successfully.

The "fittest," as biologists use the term, are, as we've seen, those who outcompete their rivals for whatever reason; more precisely, those most successful in projecting copies *of their genes* into the future. Evolutionary success—that is, fitness—is what genes strive for; bodies are how they do it, and reproducing is the most direct route, but, as we shall see, it isn't the only one. Physical fitness often helps, but the bottom line isn't bodily strength, or even overall health. Rather, what matters to evolution is the ability to stay in the game, for genes to prosper as self-promoters over long stretches of time. And the usual way for genes to benefit themselves is to package themselves in creatures known as offspring. The issue isn't health, happiness, strength, or even longevity (that is, a long-lived body), since even a Methuselah will eventually fall by the evolutionary wayside, to be replaced by genetic lineages that somehow manage to persevere longer than the most elderly individual.

So, survival of the fittest? Certainly. But the fittest *what*?

It can't be the fittest body, since most individuals of most species are actually rather short-lived. In the billions of years that evolution has had to work with, natural selection has perfected all sorts of highly sophisticated, complex adaptations, absolute marvels of effective design: mammals that fly and that use sonar to hunt moths on the wing, caterpillars that look like snakes and vice versa, bacteria that can prosper in superheated seawater, eagles that can make out the face of a dime while hovering a hundred feet in the air. Amid all these marvels, if there had been a significant evolutionary advantage for individuals to live for centuries, it seems very likely that this could have been done, too. After all, in some cases it has. Redwood trees and bristlecone pines survive for literally *thousands* of years. And yet, they are notable exceptions. Most creatures, plant or animal, are ephemeral.

Turning to the vertebrates, where natural selection has shown itself *capable* of producing long-lived bodies (for example, giant tortoises or sturgeon), the sad reality is that most of the time, it doesn't bother. This is because mere survival of the individual is not very high on the evolutionary agenda. In fact, the overwhelming majority of living things have a life span of less than a year. So what *does* matter? What is evolution all about? Not the individual, and not the species (which, after all, is merely the sum total of all individuals), but rather the survival of the "family face." The Corleone line and blood. In short, the gene.

This gene's-eye view of evolution emphasizes the most important quality of DNA: its ability to copy itself. (Second in importance would be its ability to construct bodies and equip those bodies with instructions as to how to grow and develop, as well as how to behave under various circumstances.) In his book *The Selfish Gene*, Richard Dawkins emphasized that what are known as bodies or organisms—that is, individual plants or animals—are really "survival machines" manufactured by genes for their own selfish benefit. This captures not only what life is at present but how it started.

In the beginning was the gene. Or rather, an array of organic molecules, some of which were capable of copying themselves. Most of their fellow molecules likely broke apart over time, but some were self-replicating, perhaps like crystals mechanically repeating their structure. In any event, even copycatting genes wouldn't have left an indelible imprint on the natural world, especially once they found themselves competing with other replicators that happened to blunder into the world's second greatest discovery (after replication itself): building bodies. Here is Dawkins's account, which we quote at length since not only is it suitably dramatic, but the story it tells is laden with meaning and even beauty.

> Replicators began not merely to exist, but to construct for themselves containers, vehicles for their continued existence. The replicators that survived were the ones that built survival machines for them to live in. The first survival machines probably consisted of nothing more than a protective coat. But making a living got steadily harder as new rivals arose with better and more effective survival machines. Survival machines got bigger and more elaborate, and the process was cumulative and progressive.

Was there to be any end to the gradual improvement in the techniques and artifices used by the replicators to ensure their own continuation in the world? There would be plenty of time for improvement. What weird engines of self-preservation would the millennia bring forth? Four thousand million years on, what was to be the fate of the ancient replicators? They did not die out, for they are past masters of the survival arts.

But do not look for them floating loose in the sea; they gave up that cavalier freedom long ago. Now they swarm in huge colonies, safe inside gigantic lumbering robots, sealed off from the outside world, communicating with it by tortuous indirect routes, manipulating it by remote control. They are in you and in me; they created us, body and mind; and their preservation is the ultimate rationale for our existence. They have come a long way, those replicators. Now they go by the name of genes, and we are their survival machines.

Genes are the ultimate survivors.

In his novel *The Sound and the Fury*, William Faulkner pronounces this judgment upon his seemingly doomed yet stubbornly persistent characters: "They endured." The same can be said of genes. As Faulkner relates it, the Compson family of Mississippi endured through lust and violence, madness and incest, thievery and the heavy hand of history. Ditto for genes. Genes also endured through drought and flood, predators and parasites, friends and foes, good times and bad. And unlike Faulkner's fictional inhabitants of Yoknapatawpha County, genes are real.

How, then, did they survive?

Certainly not by giving up on themselves, nor by dropping the ball. Those genetic chunks of DNA that constitute every human— or hippo, halibut, or hyacinth—are directly continuous with similar genes in their ancestors, and theirs before that, and so on, back to the slimy, sloshy, organic soup from which we all have sprung (or swum, or crawled). Going back through evolutionary time, not a single one of your antecedents has failed to reproduce. Not one ever missed a beat. Otherwise, you wouldn't be reading this.

Those genes that "made it" did so by creating bodies that have proved successful when it comes to making it in their own lives and—most important—in helping project copies of themselves into the future. After all, imagine a gene that did a great job of creating a superb body but failed utterly at getting itself passed along to the next generation; it would perish eventually, along with that superb body. Bodies are merely slingshots, designed by their genes to shoot copies of themselves into the future. From a strictly biological perspective, in fact, this is *all* that bodies are. Of course, it isn't adaptive for naked genes to be catapulted about; they'd quickly be destroyed and devoured by the array of rapacious bodies, generated by other genes, that people our planet. And so genes are projected into the future enclosed in bodies of their own.

In Herman Melville's great novel, Captain Ahab strove mightily to "strike through the mask" beyond the outer appearance of his nemesis, Moby-Dick, to its deeper reality (evil, enmity, God?). It may require a similarly mighty act of the imagination to see through the superficial reality of organisms and acknowledge the deeper reality of genes that lies beneath the universal mask of fleshy bodies.

After all, looking around, we see bodies, not naked genes. Bodies, bodies everywhere: eating, sleeping, being eaten, growing, reproducing, laughing, lounging, walking, running, swimming, hopping, and slithering their way to . . . what? To either success or failure, as measured by how well they project their component genes into the future.

This gene's-eye view was first brought to the attention of biologists by William D. Hamilton, a British geneticist and perhaps the most innovative evolutionary thinker since Darwin. In a series of papers in the 1960s, Hamilton pointed out that the business of genes is to look out for identical copies of themselves, packaged in different bodies. In the most obvious cases, we call these particular bodies "children," and those individuals who share an above-average amount of genetic relatedness "families." A family—whether Compson, Corleone, yours, or ours—is thus a constellation of bodies, created by genes, providing the prospect of their own perpetuation.

Hamilton went further, showing mathematically as well as logically that even reproduction is a special case of the more general phenomenon of genetic self-promotion via promulgation. Seen through this gene-ial lens, parents care for their offspring "because" those offspring are the most direct route for parental genes to advance themselves. Parental love is, accordingly, an evolutionary mechanism assuring that all this caretaking actually takes place. Moreover, there is no reason why genes should limit themselves to merely caring for offspring, since children, after all, are merely a special case of the more general phenomenon of genes looking out for copies of themselves tucked into other bodies. Accordingly, these bodies, as particular "persons of interest," needn't be limited to one's children. To varying degrees, people also look after nieces and nephews, grandchildren, cousins, and so forth. And now we know why: because each genetic relative is biologically important in precisely the same sense that a child is, only somewhat less so because the relative is more distantly related. Hamilton was inspired to make a marvelous conceptual leap, one that allowed him to perceive what evolution had been up to all along: he was able, at last, to make sense of the previously puzzling phenomenon of altruism and, to some extent, of social behavior generally.

Here, in brief, is—or was—the conundrum: why does altruism exist? Technically, it shouldn't, since any gene or combination of genes that induces its body to do something that helps another at the expense of itself would by definition benefit other genes, while hurting itself. Why should any of the Corleones *ever* look out for each other? Dysfunctional, you say? Actually, the Godfather's clan differs from others only in the intensity of their self-sacrificial benevolence (not to mention their violent way of expressing it). Altruism, or benevolence toward others generally, seems to fly in the face of evolution's quintessential selfishness. "Mercy did not exist in the primordial life," according to Jack London in his best-known novel, *The Call of the Wild*. "It was misunderstood for fear, and such misunderstanding made for death. Kill or be killed, eat or be eaten, was the law." We are very fond of *The Call of the Wild* and, like generations of readers, have thrilled to the adventures of Buck, the great dog who, at the story's end, answers the wild's call.

And we have been equally entranced by the protagonist of Jack London's other great animal story, *White Fang*, who "became quicker of movement than the other dogs, swifter of foot, craftier, deadlier, more lithe, more lean with iron-like muscle and sinew, more enduring, more cruel, more ferocious, and more intelligent." According to the ostensibly omniscient narrator, Mr. Fang "had to become all these things, else he would not have held his own nor survived the hostile environment in which he found himself."

But Jack London's sense of the "primordial life" was more than a little overheated. Here is a corrective dose of biological reality: cooperation is as genuine, and often as necessary, as competition. It is also perplexing. Thus, animals frequently give alarm calls when a predator shows up, thereby helping alert others to the danger . . . but in the process exposing themselves to greater risk. Similarly, they frequently share food, and Vito Corleone, among others, always seems to be urging his family members to sacrifice for each other. How can evolution arrange for the perpetuation of genes that promote this sort of thing, that appear to be self-sacrificing, if their effect is to *reduce* their own abundance?

Here is Hamilton's in-gene-ious solution: altruism is actually selfishness in disguise. Genes can enhance—not reduce—their fitness by prodding their bodies to help other bodies within which there reside identical copies of themselves. So when an altruist helps a family member—whether an offspring or some other genetic relative—even at some cost to himself, the benefactor can actually be benefiting himself at the gene level. (More precisely, genes for such altruism are helping themselves.) This holds if there is a sufficient probability that genes underlying the altruism are present in the beneficiary, which is to say, so long as the beneficiary is a genetic relative. The "paradox" of altruism, then, is resolved by realizing that what appear to be altruistic bodies are, at the same time, the manifestation of selfish genes. Looking out for a relative, even at personal cost, can be, accordingly, a case of selfish genes looking after themselves. The closer the relative, the greater the probability of shared, identical genes, and hence the more we should expect to see such altruism.

Inspired by Hamilton's insight, students of animal behavior have found that the alarm calling of prairie dogs, for example, is more likely when the alarmist is genetically related to the beneficiaries. Similarly, whenever food is being shared, genes are often shared as well. Here is another seeming incongruity, resolved by a dose of gene-oriented thinking: when zebras are attacked by lions, other zebras often come to their aid; not so, however, for wildebeest. The resolution? Zebras generally live in family groups; accordingly, aid rendered to a zebra in distress is more parsimoniously viewed as gene selfishness than as inexplicable altruism. And as for the selfish disregard of one wildebeest for another, it is significant that wildebeest live in anonymous crowds of nonrelatives, so the evolutionary geneticist expects them to be indifferent to each other's fate.

The list of examples goes on, but probably the most dramatic was recognized and explained by Hamilton himself. This is the case of the social insects (bees, wasps, and ants), in which workers typically do not even attempt to reproduce. Rather, they labor selflessly for the success of someone else, namely, the queen. Such altruistic restraint puzzled biologists since Darwin. Hamilton helpfully pointed out that those insect species with a uniquely intense form of altruism have an equally unique genetic system, known as haplodiploidy. As a result, worker bees, wasps, and ants are actually more closely related to their sisters (by a factor of three-quarters) than they would be to their own offspring (half), were they to reproduce. In short, genes within each worker do more to promote their own success by staying home and caring for their siblings, who are also offspring of the queen, than by seeking to rear their own offspring.

The point is not that because something is true of ants (or bees, or zebras, or prairie dogs) it is also true of people. Rather, it is that evolutionary genetics has revealed a powerful general rule, something to which a remarkably wide range of living things adhere. It takes extraordinary hubris—not to mention a willful denial of the basic facts of life—to claim that we are qualitatively different from the rest of the living world. To be sure, human beings are many things to themselves and others. But, no less than our fellow creatures, people are *also* the way their genes act out their goals.

Think, for example, of this universal human trait: nepotism. It means favoritism toward relatives or, more specifically, treating relatives more kindly than nonrelatives and closer relatives better than more distant ones. And think as well of this secret passcode learned by the feral child, Mowgli, in Rudyard Kipling's *The Jungle Book*: "We be of one blood, thee and I." By it, Mowgli gained the allegiance of all creatures of the tropical Indian jungle. He is literally correct. We really *are* of one blood: frogs, fishes, fowl, and folks. Birds of a feather, all of us, sharing an evolutionary history. More to the point, we share genes right here and now, those who are genetic relatives more so than others. And so, not surprisingly, those who are genetic relatives are more likely than others to share acts of kindness.

Back in the Corleone clan, we have Michael (memorably played in the movie by a youthful Al Pacino) telling his girlfriend, somewhat apologetically, how his father (played even more memorably by Marlon Brando) had once gotten his way by suggesting that a particular gentleman would put either his signature or his brains on a disputed contract. "That's my family," explained Michael. "It's not me." Seeing—or reading—this exchange, we all know that reality will prove otherwise, and not just because such is the foreshadowed narrative arc of the story. Rather, because of the nature of biological reality, it *is* the story, a tale of genes looking out for themselves: our families, our genes, ourselves, how it is that being in the same family means that we are of one blood.

He was not a biologist, but in his letters, nearly two hundred years ago, the English romantic poet John Keats anticipated what would become one of the cornerstones of the newfangled "revolutionary biology." It is a prescient recognition of what life is all about. "I go amongst the fields and catch a glimpse of a stoat or a fieldmouse peeping out of the withered grass," wrote Keats. "The creature hath a purpose and its eyes are bright with it. I go amongst the buildings of a city and I see a man hurrying along—to what? The creature hath a purpose and its eyes are bright with it."

Fifty years before Darwin, Keats realized that animals have a purpose of some sort. And furthermore, he sensed that human beings, too, have a purpose. Although Keats didn't state unequivocally that human bodies and animal bodies share the same purpose, (r)evolutionary biologists are now prepared to do just that. Furthermore, we can even identify that purpose: achieving the greatest possible success of their genes. (Whether it brightens their eyes is another question.)

People can, and do, go about their lives in pursuit of their biological "purpose," even if they don't know what that purpose *is*, or if—like those stoats, field mice, or the first gene molecules of the early soup—they don't realize they are doing so. If we eat when hungry, sleep when tired, engage in sex when the right opportunity presents itself, run from enemies (or overpower them or hide from them, depending on what is called for), we are behaving purposefully, with that purpose going beyond the immediate and obvious motivation of filling our bellies, slaking our desires, saving our skins, and so forth. Behind the superficial facade of satisfying one's needs or responding to one's fears lies the deeper purpose of satisfying the ever-present, bottom-line requirement of evolutionary success.

When this purpose is thwarted, something is awry. This is why Don Vito Corleone, Michael's father, responds as follows to a feature in *Life* magazine describing the exploits of his son, a war hero in World War II: "A friend had shown Don Corleone the magazine (his family did not dare), and the Don had grunted disdainfully and said, 'He performs those miracles for *strangers*.' " Genes are supposed to look after each other, not strangers.

Of course, the Corleone clan is not unique in this regard. The Mafia, fictional as well as real, is constructed around nepotism: in a family, the various members are more firmly committed to each other than to the outside world of laws and customs. Speaking of a competing clan, we learn from author Mario Puzo that "the Bocchichios' one asset was a closely knit structure of blood relationships, a family loyalty severe even for a society where family loyalty came before loyalty to a wife." (Ironic, isn't it, that an enterprise synonymous with violence and brutality is also founded on altruism.)

The Corleone family gets its power by appealing to friendship, duty, and—most crucially—family loyalty, rather than mere threats and extortions; that's why it is so successful. Don Vito Corleone will go out of his way to assist a friend, appealing to his honor and pride, getting him to trust the family, and then expecting similar favors in return. At one point, when singer Johnny Fontane, whom Don Vito Corleone considers his godson, requests assistance in getting a movie contract, the Godfather responds: "Friendship is everything. Friendship is more than talent. It is more than government. *It is almost the equal of family* [our emphasis]. Never forget that." (The theme of reciprocity, essentially the exchange of favors—what biologists call "reciprocal altruism"—looms large in both the animal and human worlds, as we'll see in Chapter 9; for now, we emphasize that despite the special place of friendship in the don's world, it is clear from his advice to Johnny Fontane that even this takes a backseat to family.)

Within the immediate family, the expectation of such loyalty is even more important and even more evident. It goes without saying that the family is very close: Sonny Corleone—Michael's brother—is enraged when his sister Connie is beaten up by Carlo, her husband; members of the family are expected to rely on each other for their lives and mutual protection, and so, Sonny rushes over to "get" Carlo . . . and is then killed en route by a rival clan. And not surprisingly, what eventually lures Michael Corleone back into the family is a series of attempts on the life of his father. Not only is Don Vito the symbol of the family, he is integral to its flesh and blood, progenitor of (half) of its genes. Michael may have claimed otherwise, but to say that it is his family is also to say that it is him.

One of the most powerful incentives that Don Corleone offers to prospective "friends" is that he will always look out for their family in the event of their death; the Godfather guarantees that the children and wife of anyone who gets injured during his service will always be looked after. (A chilling analogy can be found among those indirect sponsors of Middle East terror who reimburse the families of suicidal "martyrs.")

The potency of shared genes (biologists call it "kin selection") is so great that even nonkin can readily be sucked in. People have developed ways of tapping into its gravitational force by alleging kinship even when it doesn't occur. Sociologists and anthropologists use the term "fictive kinship," and we see it operating whenever appeals are made to "brothers" and "sisters" who are neither, in the myriad nationalistic claims about "fatherland" or "motherland," and in supranationalistic appeals to the human "family," and even in the Black Power movement of the 1960s and 1970s.

Interestingly, the very notion of a godparent—even without the Mafia implication—suggests just such a fictive relationship, a pseudo-blood connection between individuals (typically, recipients of favors, the kind of altruism that one expects from a blood relative). The expectation of powerful bonding between Don Vito Corleone and numerous others is precisely why the Godfather became such a powerful man. He successfully expanded his family, fictive as well as genuine, and then reaped the benefit of equally immense family loyalty (underscored, of course, by fear).

An especially interesting case of fictive kinship is played out in the story of Tom Hagen, brought up by the Corleone family since he was orphaned at about the age of ten. Distrusted by other families because he is of Irish descent, rather than Sicilian, Tom's situation emphasizes a further expansion of blood loyalty, since only Sicilians are to be trusted and respected. However, the Don knows how clever and wily Tom is, and therefore welcomes him despite his biological liabilities, eventually even making him *consigliore*, second in command. Tom is pleased, and the narrator is in no doubt as to the conflation of family with loyalty: " 'I would work for you like your sons,' Hagen said, meaning with complete loyalty, with complete acceptance of the Don's parental divinity."

Later, after an attack on the Godfather's life, Tom is discussing with Don Corleone's biological offspring, Sonny and Michael, what to do. Tom advises caution; Sonny, the impatient son, is upset and wants to do something right away. Furthermore, when push comes to shove, all three recognize the compelling power of genetic connection:

> "If your father dies, make the deal. Then wait and see." [said Tom Hagen] Sonny was white-faced with anger. "That's easy for you to say, it's not your father they killed." Hagen said quickly and proudly, "I was as good a son to him as you or Mike, maybe better. I'm giving you a professional opinion. Personally I want to kill those bastards." The emotion in his voice shamed Sonny, who said, "Oh, Christ, Tom, I didn't mean it that way." But he had, really. Blood was blood and nothing else was its equal.

It is all too easy, incidentally, to take it for granted that people love and care for family members, and to ask "What's new or surprising about that?" We would bet that Isaac Newton may well have been met with a similar response when he announced the existence of gravity: "Of course things fall. What's new or surprising about that?" To be sure, objects fell long before Newton recognized that there was something at work, gravity, that was worth exploring and explaining. Similarly, pointing out that relatives look out for each other seems too obvious to mention. But because something is so much a part of our daily existence that we take it for granted doesn't mean that we necessarily understand it. Everyone knows blood is thicker than water; now, thanks to William Hamilton, we know why.

Ever true to life, literature has long assumed that genetic ties are genuine ones, almost gravitational in their force. Sophocles' tragic play *Antigone* gives us the affecting story of how Antigone (daughter of Oedipus) ultimately goes to her death for insisting that her brother Polyneices receive a decent burial. (The tyrant Creon had decreed that Polyneices's body must remain unburied and thus defiled, because he had led a revolt against the duly constituted authorities.) In *The Charterhouse of Parma*, by Stendhal, we get to observe the numerous machinations of Gina Pietranera, aunt of the adventurer Fabrizio del Dongo, during the young man's exploits in wild-and-wooly Napoleonic Italy and France. Aunt Gina gets her nephew released from prison, sets him up as a student in Naples, sponsors a jailbreak when he is imprisoned once again, and even arranges for the poisoning of Fabrizio's mortal enemy. Families, we learn from literature—as well as from life—are likely to stick together.

Fabrizio's father was a domineering, miserly fanatic to whom his mother was altogether subservient. And so Aunt Gina stood up for him. In another wartime tale, from yet another generation, Louis Begley's *Wartime Lies* recounts the experiences of Maciek, a twelve-year-old Polish Jew, and his aunt Tania as they (barely) survive the German invasion of Poland during World War II. In this case, Maciek's mother died in childbirth, and Aunt Tania has been raising him ever since. Having no children of her own, she "settled for being the perfect aunt."

To Antigone, the dutiful sister, or Gina and Tania, both perfect aunts, we could add any number of brothers, sons, daughters, fathers, mothers, grandparents, nieces and nephews, cousins, and so forth, nearly always with their nepotistic beneficence varying inversely with the probability of genes held in common . . . that is, with the degree of genetic closeness. Blood is blood and nothing else is its equal.

In a perceptive discussion of Ralph Waldo Emerson, Mark Van Doren once wrote that "he was at his best . . . not when he was trying to understand the man he was, but when he was being that man." Literature, similarly, is at its best not when it is self-consciously trying to understand the human condition but when it is demonstrating that condition. There may be nothing more emblematic of human nature than those primordial family-based patterns whereby our bodies/genes interact with other bodies composed, in part, of copies of our own genes.

If you were to interview an intelligent fish and ask her to describe her environment, probably the last thing you would hear from your hypothetical piscine interlocutor is "It's mighty wet down here!" Some things—especially those all around us—are taken for granted. They constitute the ocean in which we swim. Kin selection and its corollaries altruism and nepotism are like that. Every story in the human repertoire takes place within the context of shared genes (with our relatives) cooperating and competing with not-so-shared genes (everyone else). This is because every human life takes place in this same context, immersed in that familiar, familial ocean.

We have all been swimming in it for a very long time, even before we literally crawled onto the land up into the trees and then down again to become recognizably human, and doubtless ever since. It is nearly impossible to cite, or even to imagine, a literary creation in which kin selection of one sort or another does *not* feature prominently. A revealing exception: William Golding's dark tale *Pincher Martin*, which recounts the solitary exploits of a pilot shot down during World War II, who crawls up on a tiny oceanic outcropping and survives by eating sea urchins, sea cucumbers, and starfish . . . until he dies, alone. Even such tales—including those featuring shipwrecked survivors—rarely lack sociality altogether; *The Swiss Family Robinson*, of course, involved a *family*.

The assumptions of kin selection run so deep that they are more likely to be noticed when breached than when followed, just as we take the normal functioning of our bodies for granted and pay attention only when something goes wrong. Take when Cain killed Abel—brothers share 50 percent of their genes and aren't supposed to do this sort of thing! That's precisely the point. Biologically, we *are* expected to be our brother's keeper, or at least not his murderer.

Thus, when Shakespeare's Richard III arranges to have his brother Clarence imprisoned in the Tower of London and then killed, and similarly when Richard contrives to murder his two young nephews (both of whom stand between him and the throne of England), it simply italicizes his monstrous, inhuman nature. It might, of course, be pointed out that human beings are by definition incapable of behaving inhumanly: "Nothing human is foreign to me," wrote the Roman poet Terence. Nevertheless, it also remains that some acts—because they seem unnaturally cruel as well as unexpected—are simply beyond the pale, thereby conveying a powerful message about the perpetrator. The killing of a close relative ranks high among these.

Accordingly, there is something riveting and revealing about fratricide because it so thoroughly defies the expectations of kin selection. By the same token, the most memorable scene in William Styron's novel *Sophie's Choice* occurs when Sophie must choose which of her children is to die in a Nazi concentration camp. And there may be no more powerful indictment of slavery than the shocking realization that Sethe, central figure of Toni Morrison's *Beloved*, has killed her child rather than allow her to grow up in bondage.

Few things, however, are as simple as we might wish, and as we shall see in Chapter 8, there are even exceptions to the seemingly straightforward genetic logic that tells close kin not to harm each other. Cain had one-half of his genes in common with Abel, just as Richard did with Clarence. But at the same time, neither Cain nor Abel was genetically identical to his sibling/victim. They had, in addition to their shared evolutionary interest, their own biological fish to fry, emphasized, perhaps, by high-stakes competition for limited resources (God's approval, the crown of England). Nonetheless, in most cases kin selection generates benevolence toward relatives, such that when close kin do serious harm to one another, our attention is immediately engaged.

Although fratricide and infanticide (and, for that matter, matricide and patricide) are especially chilling crimes, the killing of any family member is generally perceived as highly agitating to the survivors and is therefore especially likely to generate murderous tit-for-tat feuds. Huck Finn, for example, finds himself involved in precisely such a nightmare of lethal retaliation between the Grangerfords and the Shepherdsons, and it may well be noteworthy that shortly after Romeo and Juliet were secretly married— leading to a brief hope that their union might finally dissolve the enmity between Montague and Capulet—Romeo gets embroiled in a fight and ends up killing Juliet's cousin, Tybalt. After this, there is no hope for reconciliation between the two clans. Just as genes promote altruism among relatives, they aren't very forgiving when it comes to its opposite. Fortunately, however, we are most likely to see and to celebrate the beneficent side of shared genes.

For decades, biologists were intrigued by the extent to which certain individuals would run risks, sometimes even laying down their lives, for others. Armed at last with the insights of kin-based altruism, these actions now make sense: whether it is the self-sacrificial stinging of a worker bee or the willingness of adult zebras—being "perfect aunts"—to defend a colt attacked by lions, we now see genes caring for themselves. Armed with those same insights, it is also possible to make sense of those fictional tales in which people reveal desires and connections that had previously seemed incongruous until later, when it is shown that shared genes have been involved after all, which is to say that kin selection has been pulling the strings backstage.

For example, in Henry James's *Portrait of a Lady*, we encounter the machinations of one Madame Merle, who, we eventually discover, is the former mistress of the effete Gilbert Osmond. All along, Madame Merle had been contriving to get the very wealthy Isabel Archer (the lady of the book's title) to marry Gilbert. Why? To promote the success of Pansy, ultimately revealed to be Madame Merle's child by Gilbert. "Aha!" says the reader: a mother helping out her own offspring. ("Aha!" says the evolutionary biologist: genes helping themselves.) The novels of Charles Dickens are similarly filled with cases in which individuals behave with incomprehensible concern for another's welfare until it is revealed that the beneficiary is actually a relative—son, daughter, brother, sister, and so forth—of the "altruist," whereupon the altruism is instantly comprehensible, even if the plot itself defies realism.

Like gravity, kin selection surrounds us. Granted, kin selection is not often made manifest in the many novels in which it figures. But by the same token, neither does imaginative writing (this side of the *Annals of Physics*) bother to discuss why apples fall or why Marcel Proust's teacup, once placed on the table, remained there! At the same time, it is clear that kin selection exerts a kind of gravitational pull upon family members, often bringing them satisfyingly together after circumstances have cruelly pulled them apart. And the closer the kin, the greater the efforts at mutual assistance; moreover, the greater the satisfaction when bonding is achieved. We are thinking, for instance, of Alice Walker's *The Color Purple*, which concludes with the gratifying reunion of separated sisters Celie and Nettie (an important theme in the novel, which, by the way, received short shrift in the otherwise excellent motion picture based on the book).

We don't want to push the gravity metaphor too far, but let's stick with it a bit longer: just as earthly gravity isn't universal (objects float in space), so parental love isn't universal in nature. Some animals simply squirt sperm or pop out their eggs, after which they let success or failure take its course. But just as gravity is stronger when the distance between two objects decreases, altruism among living things is stronger when those relatives are genetically closer.

In one of his least satisfying attempts at scientific explanation, Aristotle once claimed that objects accelerate as they fall because they become increasingly "jubilant" as they approach the earth. Readers can relate to the visceral satisfaction of separated kin who are finally reunited. Thus, the reunion of separated sisters emerges as a cheery bookend theme at the beginning and end of Amy Tan's *The Joy Luck Club*. In this case, the gradually revealed story of Jing-mei Woo provides the thread that binds the book together. At the novel's onset, Jing-mei's mother, Suyuan, has just died. Gradually, we learn her story: how Suyuan, daughter of a Chinese officer in the early days of World War II, had been forced to abandon her twin daughters while fleeing the advancing Japanese. (Another version of *Sophie's Choice*, that is, an agonizing kin selection conundrum.) As we progress through the numerous personal narratives of *The Joy Luck Club*—all, incidentally, involving family ties and the sacrifices various women had been forced to make on their behalf—the novel concludes with a return to the story of Jing-mei. Fulfilling her mother's long-cherished wish, Jing-mei returns to China to meet her two half-sisters, so reluctantly abandoned by their mother decades earlier and now adult, who welcome her warmly.

A warm welcome for wayward relatives: the theme recurs regularly in the literary mind, and although one needn't be familiar with evolutionary genetics to share the feeling of satisfaction it evokes, there is additional satisfaction (if not jubilation) to be had in understanding *why*. There is nothing like a sudden—even if implausible—revelation that so-and-so is actually the son or daughter of such-and-such to neatly tie up the loose ends of a sentimental narrative. The implausibility in such cases resides in the coincidence that people who have encountered each other outside a recognized family context are—typically unknown to themselves—actually genetic relatives as well. There is nothing at all implausible, however, about the warmth and benevolence that results; it is pure biology.

For example, Esther Summerson, the admirable young heroine of Dickens's *Bleak House*, turns out to be the illegitimate daughter of the formidable Lady Dedlock. The two are joyously united and their relationship acknowledged when Esther is deathly ill with smallpox (don't worry: she recovers; Lady Dedlock, however, is unable to survive her shame). Henry Fielding's *Tom Jones*, one of the earliest English novels—published in 1749—recounts the bawdy adventures of the tale's namesake, thought to have been the bastard child of one Jenny Jones, a serving girl in the wealthy Allworthy household. Tom was accordingly brought up as a foundling alongside a spoiled and rather dastardly young man, known as Master Blifil, who in turn was the acknowledged son of Bridget Allworthy, sister of the all-worthy squire. As it happens, Tom became the apple of Allworthy's eye (Bridget having died and young Blifil being a spoiled brat), although because of his low birth, Tom always played second fiddle. When things look bleakest for our hero, however, Tom is revealed to be not the son of Jenny Jones after all—which is just as well, since he had previously enjoyed a sportive one-night stand with Ms. Jenny—but yet another son of the secretly prolific Bridget. Thus, Tom isn't merely a foundling but Squire Allworthy's altogether genetically worthy, fully related nephew after all. The squire gets to be a "perfect uncle."

What a relief!

And why is it such a relief? Quite possibly because the affirmation of a genetic bond reassures nervous males that in fact they may well be the biological progenitors they assume themselves to be . . . but sometimes aren't. (More of this in Chapter 7.)

When biologists speak of the "literature on kin selection," they are referring to various technical accounts of how the process works in nature. And there is in fact an immense literature of this sort. At the same time, it should by now be apparent that there is an even larger body of literature on kin selection within literature itself. Much of it examines the agony of how genes respond when their own best interests are thwarted. Here, for obvious reasons, the death of a child looms especially large, as in Alice Sebold's *The Lovely Bones*, Barbara Kingsolver's *The Poisonwood Bible*, or Louisa May Alcott's *Little Women*. Let's take a closer look at this perennial favorite, with its bittersweet mix of desolation and gratification.

Little Women tells of the March family: a mother and her four daughters while the husband/father is away dealing with lesser matters than attending to the demands of kin selection (i.e., fighting the Civil War). Back in Massachusetts, Beth—who eventually dies—is ever the paragon of family devotion. When her sisters complain about one thing or another, Beth points out, "We've got Father and Mother and each other." Moreover, she says this "contentedly." Discussing their future plans at a later point, Beth reveals, "Mine is to stay at home safe with Father and Mother, and help take care of the family. . . . I only wish we may all keep well and be together; nothing else."

Beth may be exceptional but not unique. The Marches are a tightly bound genetic unit, unflaggingly devoted to each other, even when this means they must stay poor as a result. At one point, when the family is particularly destitute, a rich aunt offers to adopt one of the sisters. The response is immediate: "We can't give up our girls for a dozen fortunes. Rich or poor, we will keep together and be happy in one another." If there is something saccharine about all this mutual devotion—and there is—there have also been hundreds of thousands of readers who have basked in its genuine, biological sweetness. It takes a hard heart indeed, one inured to suffering, perhaps, to remain unwarmed by the benevolent caretaking shown by the March sisters toward each other:

> Meg was Amy's confidant and monitor, and, by some strange attraction of opposites, Jo was gentle Beth's. . . . The two older

girls were a great deal to one another, but each took one of the younger into her keeping, and watched over her in her own way; "playing mother" they called it, . . . with the maternal instinct of little women.

At one point, after a teacher has been cruel to young Amy, the entire family offers support:

> Mrs. March did not say much, but looked disturbed, and comforted her afflicted little daughter in her tenderest manner. Meg bathed the insulted hand with glycerine and tears; Beth felt that even her beloved kittens would fail as a balm for griefs like this; Jo wrathfully proposed that Mr. David be arrested without delay; and Hannah shook her fist at the "villain" and pounded potatoes for dinner as if she had him under her pestle.

When Jo finally receives some payment for her writing, her immediate inclination is to give it to her family. Similarly, toward the end—of the book, and of Beth's life—Jo and Beth remain devoted to each other, even at the cost of becoming nearly oblivious to others:

> It was not a fashionable place, but, even among the pleasant people there, the girls made few friends, preferring to live for one another. Beth was too shy to enjoy society, and Jo too wrapped up in her to care for anyone else; so they were all in all to each other, and came and went, quite unconscious of the interest they excited in those about them, who watched with sympathetic eyes the strong sister and the feeble one, always together.

It is said that there is no such thing as a single ant. Similarly, there is no such thing as a solitary human being. Even when people aren't doling out benefits as a function of their genetic relatedness, they are looking ahead to their lineage.

Take *The Aeneid*, a classic example—in both senses of the word—of kin selection. This epic, two-thousand-year-old poem has been interpreted as many things: a history/allegory of Rome's founding, an effort by its author to ingratiate himself with the emperor Augustus, the greatest surviving example of Latin verse, a prefiguration of Christianity, even a work of divine inspiration. Whatever one's take on *The Aeneid*, Virgil's masterpiece also reflects our shared human biology.

Homer's earlier tale, *The Iliad*, concludes with the coming end of the Trojan War. According to legend, the task of founding Rome as a glorious successor to Troy fell to Aeneas, son of Venus, whose divine parentage doubtless bolstered Roman pride. (It can only be an added evolutionary plus if those shared genes are also divine.)

The Aeneid is divided into twelve books, the first six of which describe the tribulations of Aeneas and his men at sea as they recount the fall of Troy, travel to their promised land, and pause for a time in Carthage, where Aeneas famously dallies with Queen Dido. The second half of the poem details the war between Aeneas and his rival, Turnus, for control of Italy.

Throughout, Aeneas has a mission: to establish a new city, modeled after Troy, and—not coincidentally—to initiate a genetic line that will come to rule much of the known world. Aeneas has been promised that his children, grandchildren, and great-grandchildren will become great rulers. For the pre-Romans, as for most people today, posterity was a prime objective. So even though the genetics of kin selection and fitness maximization were not consciously acknowledged, the iconic image of Aeneas fleeing Troy has the renowned progenitor carrying Anchises, his father, on his shoulders, and leading his son, Ascanius, by the hand.

But what of Aeneas's sojourn with Dido in Carthage? It seems a perfect deal, at least for many contemporary men: to have the resources of an entire city and the love and affection of a beautiful queen, no strings attached. Why, then, does he leave for uncharted waters? What, furthermore, can one say about Aeneas's personal qualities if he abandons his lover, thereby causing her suicide? Such coldheartedness seems counter to Aeneas's heroic reputation, and indeed, it has divided students of the poem for ages: was he right to leave, or an inexcusable bounder? Whatever else he was doing, Aeneas was following human, biological impulses, conveniently projected onto the gods, who scold him for impeding his posterity.

Informed of Aeneas's initial dalliance with Dido, Jupiter sends his messenger Mercury to remonstrate with the errant hero. Mercury asks Aeneas, "Are you forgetful of what is your own kingdom, your own fate?" The message is clear: he must depart and settle eventually in Italy. The final blow comes with Jupiter's insinuation that were he to remain in Carthage, Aeneas would be not only reneging on his duty to found Rome but begrudging his son, and subsequent descendants-to-be, their rightful inheritance.

If Aeneas's genes could spell out their reckoning, it would go somewhat like this: although staying with Dido is great fun, you—and, more important, your genes—have bigger fish to fry. When the alternative is founding a dynasty to rule the world and establish an eternal city and way of life, a sterile dalliance with a middle-aged woman just doesn't cut it. Given the option of maximizing your inclusive fitness—the sum total of your success in projecting your genes into the future[1]—by founding a dynasty, the calculation is self-evident, even for nonbiologists. So Aeneas sets sail once again, revealing, as he departs, an intuitive comprehension of his actions. (Of course, it probably helps to know that the success of your endeavors is divinely ensured.) As he pleads for Dido's understanding, Aeneas explains, "It is not my own free will that leads me to Italy." In his conscious mind, it is the gods who drive Aeneas's actions, but deep down, it is his biological impulses that compel him to leave. Indeed, it is biology—the yet-to-be established lineage of Rome—that lies behind the gods' dictate. It would have

---

[1] Or, more accurately, the success of one's genes in projecting copies of themselves into the future.

been more than a bit unliterary, as well as ahead of his time scientifically, for Virgil to have Aeneas announce, "My genes made me do it," but in fact, for much Greek and Roman literature, the gods serve as a personification of Darwinian desires and needs, the embodiment of otherwise shadowy genetic imperatives.

Genes—or the Roman equivalent, "blood"—are at work throughout The Aeneid. Toward the end of Book VIII, Venus, Aeneas's mother, gives him a great shield upon which is engraved the fate of Rome and, thus, of Aeneas's descendants. In wonder, Aeneas surveys this future and then, not entirely understanding what he sees, he puts the shield to his shoulder, "lifting up the fame and fate of his sons' sons." The biological metaphor should be clear: Aeneas carries the burden of starting this new line. No one but he can father those descendants engraved on his shield. The pressure is enormous, yet he must shoulder the burden—risk his and his friends' lives—to provide for his progeny and ensure success for the generations to come. His genes work like a Trojan.

The ancient Romans evidently understood evolutionary genetics nearly as well as the Godfather, since additional manifestations of kin selection abound throughout The Aeneid. For example, after Aeneas and his men leave the burning Troy (and before they arrive at Carthage), they come upon an island, where our stalwart hero encounters a large dogwood that drips blood. Understandably, Aeneas is less than delighted at this discovery, especially when an unearthly moan rises from the plant. But then it beseeches, "Spare my body. . . . I am no stranger to you; I am Trojan." It turns out that Polydorus, a Trojan, was murdered here by the Greeks. Aeneas's fear is immediately quenched. Trojans—even when turned into a tree—aren't a threat to other Trojans, which also explains why Polydorus first refers to their common ancestry when speaking to Aeneas. Polydorus expects that Aeneas will honor their shared genetic tie and follow his wishes. In fact, the Trojans hold a proper funeral for poor Polydorus, an act that takes considerable time and resources, but one deemed appropriate for a blood relative.

The connection between kinship and altruism also appears notably at the beginning of Book V, after Aeneas has left Carthage. While at sea, with a great storm brewing, the helmsman, Palinurus, suggests that the Trojans take shelter on land. He recalls that "the faithful shores of Eryx, your [Aeneas's] brother, are not far off," to which Aeneas agrees: "Can any country . . . offer me more welcome harbor than the land that holds my Dardan [Trojan] friend?" When in doubt, go to a friend and fellow countryman who is, moreover, also one's brother. Sure enough, when the Trojans reach land, Aeneas's kin responds as expected to this internal genetic reckoning: "not forgetting his old parentage, he welcomes their return with joy."

Consider two initial greetings between Aeneas and Evander, a petty king in Italy. In theory, Aeneas should be wary of Evander, who came from Arcadia, a district of Greece. But Aeneas points to an ancient biological connection between their two lineages, explaining, "I was not afraid because you were a Danaan [Greek] . . . our related ancestors join me to you." He then launches into a detailed description of how the two chieftains are genetically related: the mother of Dardanus, the ancestor of the Trojans, was Electra, whose father was Atlas. Evander's father is Mercury, whose mother was Maia. And by lucky chance, Maia was Atlas's daughter. After rattling off their shared genealogy, Aeneas finally concludes that "both our races branch out of one blood. Trusting to this, I shunned ambassadors or sly approaches."

When people struggle—or simply work—on behalf of their children and other relatives, when they concern themselves with the "family name" in any of a variety of manifestations, they are also, whether consciously or not, carrying out a deep-seated biological mandate. Not uncommonly, this involves competing with other, parallel lineages.

Shakespeare's history plays give us a panorama of two such squabbling genetic lines, the Yorks and the Lancasters, each struggling to bestow benefits on their own kin, and *not* someone else's.

Beginning with *Richard II*, we witness the replacement of a York with a Lancaster (Henry IV), whose offspring—Prince Hal—and associated cohorts struggle against those affiliated with the competing lineage. On goes the tumult, through *Henry IV* parts I and II, *Henry V*, *Henry VI* parts I, II, and III, and concluding with *Richard III*, which recounts the return to power, and subsequent overthrow, of the Yorks. In evolutionary terms: York genes are supplanted by Lancaster genes, to be defeated for a time by Yorks, after which the Lancaster lineage emerges once more on top. It's a very old story, but a startlingly new perspective, in which people are proxies for their DNA.

Such tales of dynastic succession, whether from ancient Rome or late medieval England, are tales of kin selection, writ in equal parts kindness and blood. Why is blood thicker than water? Not simply because of its various formed elements (red blood cells, white blood cells, and so forth), but because it is chock-full of human genes, which stands as a literal fact no less than a metaphor. Insofar as our greatest storytellers take this thickness of blood and blood relations for granted, they are using their personal genius to build upon the thick, firm foundations of life itself.

Who better to close a chapter on family ties than William Faulkner, the master of southern gothic relations in all their wayward intricacies?

Faulkner is the great American portraitist of pain, specifically the South's anguish over its bitter legacy of slavery and the Civil War, of hatred, fear of miscegenation, the rancidity of racism, and the aftermath of lust, typically focused through multiple points of view. But nearly always, the different viewpoints and even the oft-confusing shifts of time and narrative style that Faulkner serves up are united in their concern with various members of a family: the Bundrens in *As I Lay Dying*, the Compsons in *The Sound and the Fury*, the Sutpens in *Absalom, Absalom!*

There isn't a whole lot of overt altruism to be found among Faulkner's people, but no one has ever said that this writer—probably the greatest American novelist—was straightforward in any respect! Yet it is the family ties, however pained and stressed, that literally tie his narratives together, providing coherence to a body of work that is often devilishly fractured in all other respects. Kin are the glue of Faulkner's greatest masterpieces: confused kin, incestuous kin, angry and agitated kin, rebellious and resentful kin, morose and murderous kin . . . but kin nonetheless. And so, when the Bundrens, Compsons, and Sutpens begin to fall apart, we know that things are bad indeed.

Even as Faulkner's folks undergo their familial decline, they also struggle and scratch and strain against each other, closely bound by their blood ties while also undergoing the push and pull of history, racism, and plain old-fashioned individual idiosyncrasy. They are like escaped convicts, shackled together by their genetic legacy while simultaneously yearning for personal freedom. To some extent, whereas the March family, depicted by Louisa May Alcott, shows us the glass of kin selection half full, the denizens of Faulkner's Yoknapatawpha County show us that glass half empty. After all—as we'll investigate more fully in Chapter 8—although the genetic interests of relatives are similar, they are not identical. So if you find *Little Women* too treacly and sweet, concerning itself so unrelentingly with the positive kin-selected ties among the March sisters, you might well find in Faulkner's families either a bracing corrective or a painful minefield. His people struggle against each other, yet they also suffer *together*, within the context—both bitter and better—of shared genes.

As I Lay Dying gives us the tragicomic tale of how the Bundren family endeavors to bury Addie, wife and mother, dragging her corpse through biblical travails of flood and fire, losing many of their most treasured possessions on the way, suffering pain, fracture, infection, and sexual betrayal. They finally bury Addie a full nine days after her death, by which time the coffin is followed by ominous circling vultures and resented by anyone with the ill luck to be downwind . . . except for her kinfolk.

In the only chapter narrated from Addie's viewpoint, the dying woman recalls her father's advice: "the reason for living was to get ready to stay dead a long time." Bleak words, to be sure. Yet the Darwinian reader cannot help seeing the natural wisdom in them: you won't be around for long, so do well by your progeny, the only entities that can persevere. And the same reader can't help but wonder about the role of kin: to assist in the process and, along the way, to assist each other, sometimes in spite of themselves and the awful burdens those Bundrens bear.

Another Faulkner masterpiece, *The Sound and the Fury*, recalls Macbeth's famed soliloquy, the one that describes life as "a tale told by an idiot, full of sound and fury, signifying nothing." Sure enough, *The Sound and the Fury* begins as just that: a tale told by a genuine idiot, thirty-three-year-old Benjy Compson, who is mentally retarded. But it signifies plenty.

The Compson family, once a part of the southern aristocracy, is—like so many of Faulkner's families—in serious decline. Daughter Candace ("Caddy") is loving, and even loyal in her own way, but also libidinous; her promiscuity was an intolerable burden to her brother, Quentin, who, we learn, committed suicide several decades earlier, shortly after his sister married someone other than the father of the child she was then carrying. Quentin had somehow managed to convince himself that he had committed incest with Caddy—although he hadn't—and he "identified family with his sister's membrane." Presumably, a rupture of one was therefore a rupture of the other.

Quentin Compson clearly is in bad straits, as his suicide makes clear, but strangely, it seems to have been missed by most critics that Quentin's despair—like the struggles of the Bundrens—is almost entirely family-based, the consequence of ill-satisfied kin concerns. Quentin despairs over his brother Benjy's feeblemindedness and over the Compson clan's deterioration due to the weight of pride, history, and a seemingly ineluctable biological degeneration.

Quentin is also contorted with guilt that the last of his family's land was sold to finance his Harvard education. But most of all, he is obsessed with Caddy: the loss of her honor as well as the fact that it was a stranger—and not himself—who impregnated her.

Brother Benjy, meanwhile, also harbors a persistent yearning for sister Caddy that, unlike Quentin's, isn't sexual but filial: she was the only one who offered him love and protection. With her gone, brother Benjy hangs out at the former Compson pasture (now a golf course, since being sold), and in his uncomprehending way is emotionally lacerated whenever he hears the golfers shout "Caddy!" Once more, it is a special strength of Faulkner's stories that his characters mix anguish about family members with an unspoken, but pervasive and often obsessive, involvement with them.

Jason Compson, another Compson brother, is no great shakes, either: mean-spirited, petulant, bitter, and deceitful. His most creative act is to have his feebleminded brother, Benjy, castrated, and to vow eternal bachelorhood. It is an understatement to note that the Compson family is fraying. Quentin is dead, Benjy is castrated, Jason is sworn to bachelorhood, and Caddy's offspring is illegitimate (and no less prone to promiscuity than her mother). At the same time, it is also an understatement to note that family, dilapidated as it may be, is all that the Compsons can cling to.

The most admirable figure in *The Sound and the Fury* is Dilsey, the black "mammy" who is the only consistently present, loving, and reliable character. A modern-day Greek chorus, she intones, "I've seed de first en de last. . . . I seed de beginnin, en now I sees de endin." Still, Faulkner's focus on family—even decaying and fractured families such as the Compsons—implies that the end isn't yet in sight. It was Faulkner, after all, who proudly noted that whatever else can be said about the families he described, "they endured." We, in turn, point out that the endurance of families means the endurance of genes, just as it was Faulkner who demonstrated more clearly than any other writer that the network of shared genes can be both supportive and ensnaring.

7

THE CINDERELLA SYNDROME

Regarding the Struggles of Stepchildren

These days, more Americans have seen the musical *Les Miz* than have read Victor Hugo's novel *Les Misérables*. In both versions, however, Jean Valjean adopts the young and vulnerable Cosette, who had been living as the fosterling of Monsieur and Madame Thénardier. In both versions, Cosette's situation under the roof of the innkeeper is less than enviable, although unlike the musical's presentation of the Thénardiers as lovable scoundrels, Hugo's account is much grimmer and their treatment of Cosette sinister and downright abusive:

> Cosette was in her usual place, seated on the cross-bar under the kitchen table near the hearth. Clad in rags, her bare feet in wooden clogs, she was knitting woolen stockings for the Thénardier children by the light of the fire. . . . Two fresh childish voices could be heard laughing and chattering in the next room, those of Éponine and Azelma [the Thénardiers' biological offspring; in the musical version, Azelma was deleted]. A leather strap hung from a nail in the wall near the hearth.

As to the condition of Cosette herself:

> She was thin and pale, and so small that although she was eight years old she looked no more than six. Her big eyes in their

shadowed sockets seemed almost extinguished by the many tears they had shed. Her lips were drawn in the curve of habitual suffering that is to be seen on the faces of the condemned and the incurably sick. Her hands . . . were smothered with chilblains . . . she was always shivering. . . . Her clothes were a collection of rags which would have been lamentable in summer and in winter were disgraceful—torn garments of cotton, with no wool anywhere. Here and there her skin was visible, and her many bruises bore witness to her mistress's [Madame Thénardier's] attentions. Her bare legs were rough and red, and the hollow between her shoulder-blades was pathetic.

By contrast, note the state of the Thénardiers' own children, Éponine and Azelma:

They were two very pretty little girls with a look of the town rather than of the country, very charming, the one with glossy chestnut curls and the other with long dark plaits down her back, both of them lively and plump and clean with a glow of freshness and health that was pleasant to see. They were warmly clad but with a maternal skill which ensured that the thickness of the materials did not detract from their elegance. Winter was provided for but spring was not forgotten. They brought brightness with them, and they entered like reigning beauties. There was assurance in their looks and gaiety, and in the noise they made.

Next, jump ahead from a nineteenth-century French bestseller to a publishing phenomenon of the late twentieth and early twenty-first century: Harry Potter. Any child can confirm that Harry's early days, growing up as a stepchild within—but not part of—the Dursley family, were more like the experience of Cosette than like that of Éponine and Azelma. The Dursleys' own son, the despicable Dudley, is ugly, stupid, and spoiled beyond comprehension. Photos of the young brat adorn the

Dursley walls, which reveal "no sign at all that another boy lived in the house, too."[1]

Contrasted with the overindulged Dudley, Harry never gets enough to eat, never gets new clothes, never gets toys, never gets a birthday celebration, sleeps in a cupboard under the stairs, does menial labor, and is yelled at constantly. Moreover—and for many children, perhaps the unkindest cut of all—Dudley gets to have birthday parties and presents, but not Harry:

> Harry got slowly out of bed and started looking for socks. He found a pair under his bed and, after pulling a spider off one of them, put them on. Harry was used to spiders, because the cupboard under the stairs was full of them, and that was where he slept. When he was dressed he went down the hall into the kitchen. The table was almost hidden beneath all Dudley's birthday presents. . . . Every year on Dudley's birthday, his parents took him and a friend out for the day, to adventure parks, hamburger restaurants, or the movies. Every year, Harry was left behind with Mrs. Figg, a mad old lady who lived two streets away. Harry hated it there. The whole house smelled of cabbage and Mrs. Figg made him look at photographs of all the cats she'd ever owned.

Harry is also expected to wear the equivalent of Cosette's rags:

> One day in July, Aunt Petunia took Dudley to London to buy his Smeltings uniform, leaving Harry at Mrs. Figg's. . . . There was a horrible smell in the kitchen the next morning when Harry went in for breakfast. It seemed to be coming from a large metal tub in the sink. He went to have a look. The tub was full of what looked like dirty rags swimming in gray water. "What's this?" he asked Aunt Petunia. Her lips tightened as they always did if he dared to

---

[1] Granted, Harry is nephew to Dudley's mother, so presumably a bit of kin selection ameliorates his rotten treatment, but our point is that compared to the overindulged Dudley, Harry is a stepchild indeed.

ask a question. "Your new school uniform . . . I'm dyeing some of Dudley's old things gray for you."

Shades of Cinderella? Indeed. But Cosette and Harry aren't the only cases of abused stepchildren depicted via story. In fact, Cinderella herself, unlike Mickey Mouse or Donald Duck, did not spring fully formed out of the Walt Disney studios, or even out of the fertile forehead of Uncle Walt himself. She exists, in various forms, in many cultures, but always with the same recognizable tale of woe.

In an ancient Japanese folktale, a kind, gentle, and honest young lady named Benizara was much put-upon by her stepmother. Benizara was so virtuous (and also—a lovely Japanese touch—so good at extemporizing a poem) that she wins the heart of a noble-man. Her wicked stepmother, however, tries to substitute her own daughter—Cinderella's (sorry, Benizara's) stepsister, Kakezara—at the wedding, but stepmom screws up and Kakezara ends up dead. Which is probably just as well for Benizara: there is a broad-leaved and fiendishly sharp-spined plant, similar to the devil's club found in the Pacific Northwest, known in Japan as *mamako-no-shiri-nugui*, or stepchild's bottom wiper!

And that's not all. According to evolutionary psychologists Martin Daly and Margo Wilson, the Russian folktale of Baba Yaga begins as follows:

> Once upon a time there was an old couple. The husband lost his wife and married again. But he had a daughter by his first mar-riage, a young girl, and she found no favour in the eyes of her evil stepmother, who used to beat her, and consider how she could get her killed outright.[2]

The stepmother urges the girl to go to her "aunt," sister of the stepmother, who is a witch, a cannibal, and, moreover, not very

---

[2] M. Daly and M. Wilson, *The Truth About Cinderella* (New Haven: Yale University Press, 1998).

nice, but our Slavic Cindy cleverly consults her real aunt first and thereby learns how to elude the snare. "As soon as her father heard all about it, he became wroth with his wife, and shot her. But he and his daughter lived on and flourished." Living and flourishing is precisely what Cinderellas around the world have had a hard time doing, especially if their welfare is left to the not-so-tender mercies of stepparents. In this regard, the Grimm brothers' fairy tales are especially grim as well as consistent: in addition to Cindy herself, there is also Snow White, Hansel and Gretel, and The Juniper Tree. Whenever a deserving child is mistreated, cherchez la stepmother.

From Cinderella and her fellow sufferers to *Les Misérables* and Harry Potter, and lots more in between: what in Darwin's name is going on?

Biology, that's what. Evolution frowns on taking care of someone else's kids because there is no payoff in offering parental assistance when you aren't really the parent, when the genes thus promoted are not your own. From the dawn of human existence to the present day, people have lived in an amazing variety of different social systems, from capitalism to communism, feudalism to democracy, hunting and gathering to high-tech lifestyles of the rich, famous, and forgettable; we can be industrialists, serfs, monarchists, democrats, subsistence farmers, computer programmers. Yet for all this diversity, there is not now and has never been a single society in which people routinely give up their reproduction to someone else. Sure, we may delegate child care (typically for pay), but actual reproduction? No way. People indulge in all sorts of specialization and division of labor, but propelling genes into the future is something nearly everyone chooses to do for him- or herself. As we saw in Chapter 6, this can be achieved by promoting the success of relatives; the most obvious and direct route to genetic advancement, however, is to package your own genes in your own child. (More accurately, for genes to package copies of themselves in bodies known as children.)

The clear-cut biological significance of reproduction is why altruism is so interesting: when we first encounter it, altruism appears to go against this most basic principle of the living world. Being a parent, by contrast, is so obvious, so appropriate, so biologically de rigueur that up until recently it has largely escaped the scrutiny it deserves.

The obviousness of reproduction and parenting derives from the simple fact that it is the most straightforward way for genes to enhance their evolutionary success. If you want something done right, goes the saying, do it yourself. And nowhere in the living world is this more true than when it comes to parenting. Whenever offspring are being produced, fed, trained, kept warm or cool or wet or dry, protected from enemies or introduced to friends, something fundamental is going on: genes are nurturing copies of themselves.

"He that hath wife and children," wrote the sixteenth-century English philosopher Francis Bacon, "hath given hostages to fortune, for they are impediments to great enterprise, either of virtue or mischief." Bacon, one of the great architects of modern science and philosophy, lived too early to understand this important finding of evolution: children may be impediments to some things, but they are also passports to the most pressing enterprise—indeed, the only persistent enterprise—of life itself. In this respect, all living things are hostages, not to fortune but to natural selection.

"We had lots of kids, and trouble and pain," goes the folk song "Kisses Sweeter than Wine," "but oh Lord, we'd do it again." Why would they do it again, given that having kids involves so much trouble and pain? And why did they do it the first time? Hint: not simply because of those oh-so-sweet kisses. In fact, natural selection has only contrived to make love and sex and kisses sweet in the first place because this is how biology gets us to do it.

Try asking spiders of the African species *Stegodyphus mimosarum* about trouble and pain. Comfortably housed within silken nest chambers woven by the mother just for this purpose, baby spider-lings perch on her arachnid abdomen and cheerfully fill their own bellies with their mother's flesh (or whatever passes for flesh among spiders), eventually killing her in the process.

Why does Mommy *Stegodyphus mimosarum* permit such an out-rage? Because they are so irresistibly cute. Or because it feels so wonderfully good, perhaps like having an itch scratched. Or maybe because she simply feels no alternative, like the mammalian need to breathe or circulate blood. Whatever the immediate mecha-nism, the end result is that her spiderlings are sent off into the world with a full stomach at their mother's expense. This is some-what more extreme than the suburban parent making sure Junior goes off to school with a freshly made peanut butter and jelly sandwich, but at the most basic biological level it's not altogether different.

By contrast, picture a sleek, plump female elephant seal, mater-nally nursing her baby. Along comes an interloper, someone else's pup, who attempts to sneak-suckle. This youngster already has a mother, of course, but is trying to cadge an additional meal. (In the immortal phrase coined by elephant seal guru Burney Le Boeuf of the University of California at Santa Cruz, it is seeking to become a "double mother sucker.") What happens? Sometimes the sneaky little tyke succeeds, but most often the seal cow is outraged, and sometimes murderously so: she bites the little thief, occasionally killing him for his larcenous presumption.

Undoubtedly much of the difference between a self-sacrificial spider mom and a milk-withholding momma seal can be chalked up to differences between spiders and elephant seals. But you can still be sure that Spiderwoman wouldn't cheerfully offer herself for dinner to the arachnid equivalent of a swarm of double mother suckers, hatchlings of some *other* reproducing female, just as even the most puppicidal pinniped behaves quite benevolently toward her own offspring. Parenthood matters. Parental benevolence in the natural world is not broadcast indiscriminately.

And so we come to a tiny, abundant, and intriguing animal, the Mexican free-tailed bat. Although each female produces only one young at a time, these creatures congregate in immense gatherings, hundreds of thousands and more in a single cave. While the adults are out cruising for insects, the young crowd together in "crèches," with population densities as high as two pups per square inch. Utter chaos appears to reign, especially when females return from foraging and the nurslings swarm all over them. Consistent with good-of-the-species thinking, instead of its good-of-the-gene alternative, batologists had long thought that the babies were fed indiscriminately and rather communistically: from each lactating female according to her ability, to each according to his or her need. Looking at the melee, it is difficult even for a modern biologist to imagine how parent-offspring pairs are ever sorted out.

But when Gary F. McCracken of the University of Tennessee studied these nurseries, he found that female Mexican free-tailed bats were not at all free when it came to dispensing milk. Mothers recognized their own young 83 percent of the time, apparently by sound and smell. Whenever a female suckled young not her own, it was evidently a result of error (on her part) and/or milk stealing (by the little batling). Stepbats need not apply.

Next, a bird, specifically the mountain bluebird. Birds are especially interesting when it comes to parental care because unlike mammals, whose females are uniquely adapted to nurse their offspring, both males and females contribute about equally in the avian world. Rutgers University ornithologist Harry Power asked whether male mountain bluebirds who were manipulated into being stepparents rather than biological parents would behave differently as a result. In one experiment, mountain bluebirds were provided with nest boxes designed to be especially attractive to them. Bluebird pairs quickly moved in and started families, after which the males were removed, leaving the females single parents. They did not remain single for long, however. In what passes for bluebird society, they were "wealthy widows," since good nests are hard to find, and, thanks to the researchers, each of these females now owned a valuable piece of property. They and their dependent offspring were soon joined by fortune-hunting males. Significantly, these new arrivals—stepfathers of the nestlings—did *not* participate in feeding the youngsters, and only one in twenty-five gave alarm calls in response to possible predators (biological fathers sound an alarm nearly 100 percent of the time).

Similar examples can be multiplied almost indefinitely. Indeed, it is now a commonplace among biologists that parenting in any species means caring for one's own children. Not for other living things the blithe assumption that parental solicitude is a mere social convention, as in this dialog from Bernard Malamud's novel *The Fixer* between Yakov Bok, falsely imprisoned in a Russian jail, and his estranged wife:

> "I've come to say I've given birth to a child."
>
> "So what do you want from me? . . ."
>
> ". . . it might make things easier if you wouldn't mind saying you are my son's father. . . ."
>
> "Who's the father . . . ?"
>
> ". . . He came, he went, I forgot him. . . . Whoever acts the father is the father."

It may seem perverse to cite the above, which points *away* from biology; after all, our basic argument is that most literature makes sense in the light of biology rather than contradicting it. But those few cases that go against evolutionary wisdom stand out because of their rarity. When it comes to parenting, the truth is more often the precise opposite of Mrs. Bok's wishful thinking: whoever *is* the father acts the father. (The same applies, of course, to mothers, although they are less likely to be deceived.)

Whether bat or bird, seal or spider, living things reproduce because this is the major way their genes propagate themselves. It is also the major reason for love, including love of adults for each other and of parents for children. And it goes a long way toward telling us why stepparenting is so often a conflicted and difficult business.

In the extreme case, stepparenting among animals leads to outright murder. The paradigmatic example was first reported by anthropologist Sarah Blaffer Hrdy, who studied langur monkeys in India. In this harem-forming species, one male monopolizes a number of adult females and breeds with them, while a corresponding bunch of langur bachelors languish resentfully in the background. Every now and then, a revolution takes place in langurland, whereupon the dominant male is ousted and one of the bachelors takes over the troop of females. In such cases, the newly ascendant male is likely to methodically pursue and kill the nursing infants, who are offspring of the previous male. Without suckling infants, the newly bereaved mothers stop lactating, their ovaries begin cycling once again, and they mate with their offspring's murderer. So, because nursing females are less likely to ovulate, by killing their infants a male not only eliminates the offspring of his predecessor but also improves his own reproductive prospects.

When Hrdy first presented her findings in the late 1970s, anthropologists and even some biologists were disbelieving. How could a behavior that is so hurtful to the species have evolved? (At that time, many scientists were still in thrall to species-level benefit.) It must be some sort of pathology, they insisted, or perhaps a result of overcrowding or malnutrition, or maybe just some weird anecdotal rarity. But subsequent decades have supported Hrdy's interpretation; moreover, a similar pattern of infanticide on the part of animal stepparents has been documented for lions, chimpanzees, and various species of rodents, almost wherever biologists have looked. The evidence is overwhelming: infanticide—and nearly always by nonbiological "parents"—is distressingly commonplace. It may well be downright terrible for the species, but so long as it's a net plus for the infanticidal individual, there it is.

What about people?

The Canadian husband-and-wife team of psychologists Martin Daly and Margo Wilson, professors at McMaster University in Hamilton, Ontario, have pioneered the evolutionary underpinnings of stepparenting as a risk factor for child neglect and abuse. Since child rearing is difficult, costly, and prolonged in our species, they reasoned, natural selection is unlikely to have produced indiscriminate parenting. (If even the Mexican free-tailed bat can be fussy about dispensing parental care, so can human beings.) In fact, parental feelings are expected to vary with the evolutionary interest that children hold for the adults in question: the greater the genetic return, the greater the inclination to invest time, energy, and love. And similarly, the greater the disinclination to mistreat them.

To summarize two decades of research on human beings: youngsters living with a stepparent are from forty to sixty times more at risk of neglect, abuse, and infanticide than are comparable children living with their biological parents. This is true even when other factors such as income, education level, and ethnicity are taken into account. Like it or not—and, given the high frequency of stepparenting and blended families, many people don't like it—the step relationship is by far the highest predictor of a child's maltreatment.

These numbers are staggering, and once again we must ask, what is going on here? Does this mean that all stepparents are abusive? Of course not. Neither does it imply that biological parents are necessarily doting. Nor that biologists have it in for nonbiological parents (one of the present authors, as a stepparent as well as a biologist, can testify on both accounts). But these startling findings do mean that in daily life, stepfamilies—because they are out of step with biology—are liable to be stressful places, demanding the best within us and sometimes bringing out the worst, leading in some cases to reduced caretaking, increased intolerance, and even, in extreme situations, violence. This is where langurs, lions, and chimpanzees come in, contributing to an understanding of child abuse, neglect, and even, on occasion, murder in human beings.

Despite its many rewards, child rearing can, after all, be stressful, even for the most well-balanced and devoted parents. It is understandable—if not pardonable—that without genetic connection to ameliorate the rough edges, there would be a lower threshold for adults' ability to tolerate infant crying, children's interrupting, and the normal demands of even the most well-behaved youngsters, not to mention the predictable requirements of food, clothing, education, and so forth, which often can only be satisfied at some cost to the stepparents' own biological children. Moreover, for unstable adults already teetering on the edge of self-control, stepparenthood could well make a tragic difference.

Earlier, we visited with *Jane Eyre* as an example of the girl-chooses-boy theme among Gothic novels. This romantic classic also tells several stepparent tales. Start with Jane and her aunt Reed, who, it must be noted, is her aunt through marriage and not blood. As the story begins, Mrs. Reed has assumed responsibility for the orphaned Jane, though not out of any altruistic feelings on her part, but rather because while on his deathbed, her husband (who had a genetic tie to Jane) admonished her to do so. Jane describes the case as follows:

> I knew that he was my own uncle—my mother's brother—that he had taken me when a parentless infant to his house; and that in his last moments he had required a promise of Mrs. Reed that she would rear and maintain me as one of her own children. Mrs. Reed probably considered she had kept this promise; and so she had, I dare say, as well as her nature would permit her; but how could she really like an interloper not of her race [i.e., a nonrelative], and unconnected with her, after her husband's death, by any tie? It must have been irksome to find herself bound by a hard-wrung pledge to stand in the stead of a parent to a strange child she could not love, and to see an uncongenial alien permanently intruded on her own family group.

Although Aunt Reed kept her promise, she did so only half-heartedly, after having first "entreated him [her husband, Jane's uncle] rather to put it [Jane] out to nurse and pay for its maintenance." And so Aunt Reed proceeds to abuse our young heroine—psychologically for the most part—including a famous incident in which the girl is locked in the spooky room where her uncle died. Jane is then sent to an even more abusive school (in loco stepparentis) before eventually encountering Mr. Rochester of Thornfield Hall. It is not that Aunt Reed didn't understand her role as stepparent or that, as sociologists like to claim these days, she lacked role models, but rather that she didn't want to lavish the same solicitude on Jane that she made readily available to her own offspring.

As Daly and Wilson point out,

> There is a commonsense alternative hypothesis about why some "roles" seem easy and "well-defined" while others are difficult and "ambiguous." It is simply that the former match our inclinations while the latter defy them. Stepparents do not find their roles less satisfying and more conflictual than natural parents because they don't *know* what they are supposed to do. Their problem is that they don't *want* to do what they feel obliged to do, namely to make a substantial investment of "parental" effort without receiving the usual emotional rewards. The "ambiguity" of the stepparent's situation does not reside in society's failure to define his role, but in genuine conflicts of interest within the stepfamily.

To this, we add that those "genuine conflicts of interest" are genuine because they are, at heart, genetic.

Consider now another classic English novel, *Oliver Twist*. We first meet young Oliver when he is a famously abused orphan who outrages the establishment by asking, among other things, for more porridge. As punishment, he is sent away to an abusive stepfamily of undertakers and thence circuitously to the underworld of London crime, where his newest "stepfather," Fagin, is interested only in how Oliver's small, deft hands can contribute, by picking pockets, to Fagin's own material advancement. Obviously, Oliver isn't nurtured in this environment; rather, he is provided with just enough food to keep him alive and functioning, albeit unwillingly, as a participant in the gang's nefarious activities. Things end well, however, for our young waif precisely when his waifhood ends, that is, when he connects with his own biological relatives, the Maylies, and with a nonbiological protector, Mr. Brownlow (who eventually recognizes Oliver as the offspring of a dear friend's child).

Oliver Twist is unusual not only in turning out well but also in ending up remarkably sweet and good-natured, given his very difficult upbringing. More commonly, the stepchild—often a bastard child as well—is portrayed as angry at being dispossessed and ill-treated. To some extent, bastardy has thus been equated with nastiness (just think of the epithet), which provides a way for the biologically unsophisticated to understand what might otherwise be inexplicable. Consider Mordred, bastard child of King Arthur, who is ultimately responsible for nothing less than the fall of Camelot; the murderous Smerdyakov in Dostoyevsky's *The Brothers Karamazov*; or the violent and vengeful Edmund, the illegitimate child of Gloucester in *King Lear*, whose machinations result in his father's blinding and the deaths of all three of Lear's (biological) daughters.

As we've seen already, the evolutionarily optimal male strategy is to make as many children as possible but to invest preferentially only in those that are legitimate. Nonetheless, there are many stories of bastard children inheriting large amounts of money upon the father's death, especially if there are no natural children with a competing claim. (Despite his illegitimacy, Pierre Bezuhov, one of the central characters of Tolstoy's *War and Peace*, inherits a large fortune when his father dies; notably, Pierre has no siblings.)

Denial of the bastard seems counter-Darwinian, since parents should presumably want the best for their children, regardless of whether those children derived from a legally consecrated marriage.

But a parent's solicitude toward his or her illegitimate children is often complicated by conflict with a current spouse, particularly if other children have been produced legitimately (Smerdyakov had to deal with the three acknowledged brothers Karamazov, Dmitri, Ivan, and Alyosha, just as Edmund competed with Edgar, Gloucester's acknowledged son). Moreover, it is typically a *father* who has to deal with a bastard child, and fathers, as we have already seen, cannot be entirely confident that they are in fact fathers.

Uncertain paternity cuts both ways, from father to child and back again. Thus, referring to Odysseus, young Telemachus remonstrates, "My mother saith he is my father. Yet for myself I know it not. For no man knoweth who hath begotten him." If this is true of the offspring of the famously faithful Penelope, how much more true must it be of everyone else!

Whether coincidentally or not, this issue—who is whose issue?—reappears in James Joyce's *Ulysses*, developed by none other than Stephen Dedalus, who in fact represents a twentieth-century Telemachus, (re)united at the novel's end with his pseudofather, Leopold Bloom. In the "Scylla and Charybdis" chapter of *Ulysses*, Stephen expounds on the unknowability of fatherhood:

> Fatherhood, in the sense of conscious begetting, is unknown to man. It is a mystical estate, an apostolic succession, from only begetter to only begotten. On that mystery and not on the madonna which the cunning Italian intellect flung to the mob of Europe the church is founded and founded irremovably because founded, like the world, macro- and microcosm, upon the void. Upon the incertitude, upon unlikelihood. Amor matris, subjective and objective genitive, may be the only true thing in life. Paternity may be a legal fiction. Who is the father of any son that any son should love him or he any son?

As Stephen notes, Telemachus's lament also works the other way: no man knoweth for certain whom he hath begot. And this, in turn, leads to a painful but prominent literary theme. In his mordant play *The Father*, the Swedish writer August Strindberg describes the dilemma of a husband tormented by whether he is the biological parent of his child:

> I know of nothing so ludicrous as to see a father talking about his children. "My wife's children," he should say. Did you never feel the falseness of your position, had you never had any pinpricks of doubt?

It is a good guess that by and large, fathers also find it easier to let go than do mothers, not necessarily because of any conscious doubt, but rather because of a biologically inspired diminution in confidence. In "Walking Away," the poet C. Day Lewis gives a predictably male view when he describes his eldest son going away to school, and the poet's awareness of "how selfhood begins with a walking away / And love is proved in the letting go."

Letting go is especially likely when there is doubt as to paternity. And not surprisingly, the phenomenon is cross-cultural. Take, for example, *The Tale of Genji*, written one thousand years ago by Murasaki Shikibu, and believed to be the first novel written in Asia, perhaps the first of all time. It tells of the picaresque adventures of Genji, offspring of the emperor and a concubine. Genji is exceptionally handsome and aristocratic, possessing a definite "way with the ladies." He has many lovers, including his own stepmother, Fujitsubo, with whom he has a child. He is also cuckolded: his favorite wife, the Third Princess, dawdles with Kashiwagi, the son of Genji's longtime political and sexual competitor, To no Chujo. Accordingly, when the Third Princess gave birth, Genji was deeply distressed: "How vast and unconditional his joy would be, he thought, were it not for his doubts about the child." And later, "It would not be easy to guard the secret [that the Third Princess had dallied with Kashiwagi] if the resemblance to the father was strong." The princess eventually abdicates and becomes a nun.

Anyone who still needs persuading that paternity matters should take a good look at Thomas Hardy's dark masterpiece *The Mayor of*

Casterbridge. A significant part of this novel examines how the relationship of the protagonist, Michael Henchard, with his purported daughter, Elizabeth-Jane, changes as Michael realizes that the girl he had thought to be his child turns out to be someone else's.

The book begins with a much younger Michael arriving at the English equivalent of a county fair with his wife and baby daughter, Elizabeth-Jane; in a drunken stupor, he sells them both—for five guineas—to a passing sailor. Eighteen years later, after Michael Henchard has reformed and made a name for himself as the highly respected mayor of Casterbridge, who should show up but his long-abandoned wife, with Elizabeth-Jane in tow, claiming that the sailor died and left them penniless. Elizabeth-Jane believes the sailor to be her father, and Henchard, seeking to avoid the obloquy of owning up to his despicable behavior eighteen years previously, but also wanting to make good on his obligations, suggests that he (re)marry his wife, after which their daughter will consider Michael her stepfather.

Henchard describes the scheme as follows:

> "I meet you, court you, and marry you, Elizabeth-Jane coming to my house as my step-daughter. . . . the secret would be yours and mine only; and I should have the pleasure of seeing my own only child under my roof, as well as my wife."

He believes Elizabeth-Jane to be the daughter he sold eighteen years ago, an assumption that is shown by his benevolent concern for her upbringing: "The freedom [Elizabeth-Jane] experienced, the indulgence with which she was treated, went beyond her expectations." Although hints abound, it never crosses Michael Henchard's conscious mind that this child might not be his after all, even when the answer is literally staring him in the face, as in the following discourse:

> "I thought Elizabeth-Jane's hair promised to be black when she was a baby?" [Henchard] said to his wife.

"It did; but they alter so," replied Susan.

"Their hair gets darker, I know—but I wasn't aware it lightened ever?"

"O yes." And the same uneasy expression came out on her face, to which the future held the key.

Later, after his wife's death, Michael discovers that Elizabeth-Jane is not in fact his child, the original Elizabeth-Jane having died soon after the sale to the sailor and been replaced by the present girl, who is of course the sailor's daughter. When this becomes clear, Michael rethinks the troubling matter of Elizabeth-Jane's lack of resemblance to himself, acknowledging that he and his now-identified stepdaughter look nothing alike:

> He steadfastly regarded her features. . . . They were fair: his were dark. . . . In the present statuesque repose of the young girl's countenance [the sailor] Richard Newson's was unmistakably reflected.

And how did Michael Henchard respond to that newly perceived reflection? As follows: "He could not endure the sight of her."

From this point on, Michael changes from being a secretly doting daddy merely pretending to be a stepparent into a predictable, withholding, and resentful stepparent trying unsuccessfully to act like a parent. Ironically, just as he tells Elizabeth-Jane the truth of their situation, Henchard notes that it has changed drastically: "The mockery was, that he should have no sooner taught a girl to claim the shelter of his paternity than he discovered her to have no kinship with him." And so he disowns and rejects her, further compounding the tragedy all around.

T. S. Eliot once noted that there was so much in Shakespeare—and, we would add, so much in Shakespearean criticism—that the best one could hope for is to be wrong about Shakespeare in a new way. Well, here is a new way to look at *Hamlet:* as a stepparent story. It is clear that for all Hamlet's complexity and depth, he wasn't happy with Claudius, his stepfather, even before he got the unwelcome news from the ghost of dear old departed Dad that Claudius had done him in. In any event, Hamlet isn't shy about berating his mother, Gertrude, for her "o'er-hasty marriage" and urging her to refrain from sex with her new husband. Forget about Freud: should Gertrude become pregnant, this would further cloud Hamlet's future and give him a likely unwelcome competitor.

There is a French proverb, dating from about the same era as Shakespeare, that speaks not only to Hamlet and his uncle/stepfather Claudius, but also to many others:

> *The mother of babes who decides to rewed*
> *Has taken their enemy into her bed.*

David Copperfield would have to agree. As Dickens presents it, young David is a male version of Cinderella. Cindy's life went rapidly downhill after her father remarried. David's took a dive when his father died and his mother took Mr. Murdstone—who quickly revealed himself to be David's enemy—into her bed. Earlier, when courting Clara Copperfield, Murdstone had gone out of his way to seem well disposed toward young David, bringing him gifts, taking him for pleasant daily outings, and allowing him to ride on the saddle in front of him, never seeming the least offended when David was predictably cold toward him.

Almost immediately after the marriage, however, Mr. Murdstone begins to reveal himself for who he really is: cold, domineering, and cruelly indifferent to David's needs. He moves quickly to separate David from Clara, first emotionally, by, as David puts it, "preventing [Clara] from ever being alone with [him] or talking lovingly to [him]," and then physically, by packing him off to boarding school. By the time David Copperfield returns for the holidays, his little brother—Murdstone's child by Clara—has been born. Mr. Murdstone is not literally a male langur monkey, killing an infant so as to breed with the mother, but the parallel is strikingly close.

Once Clara dies, Murdstone's true relationship with David becomes clear: young David is sent to work in Murdstone's factory at age ten, where he is ill-fed and overworked. When the boy runs away to the safety of his great-aunt, Murdstone is quick to give up on him altogether. Here is that great-aunt, Betsy Trotwood, confronting the stepfather with his behavior:

> "Do you think I don't know what kind of life you must have led that poor unworldly, misdirected baby? First you come along smirking and making great eyes at her [David's mother], all soft and silky. . . . Yes, you worshipped her. You doted on her boy, too. You would be another father to him. And the poor deluded innocent believed you. She had never seen such a man. Yes, you were all to live together in a garden of roses. . . . And when you had caught the poor little fool you must begin to make a caged bird of her and try to teach her your own ugly notes. So it was, Mr. Murdstone, that you eventually succeeded in breaking her heart. And if that were not enough you have done your best to break her boy's spirit."

For her part, Clara Copperfield had been clueless and perhaps somewhat desperate, not unlike Hamlet's mother, Gertrude, who evidently assumed that Claudius would treat young Hamlet in a benevolent, fully paternal manner and that the prince, similarly, would promptly accept Claudius as a replacement father. Instead, Hamlet persisted in his view that something was rotten, not only in Denmark generally but in his personal situation as well. But at least Hamlet was a young adult; David Copperfield, by contrast, is langurlike in his helplessness.

Parentless waifs tug at our heartstrings; we cannot help recognizing their need for family. But Oliver Twist and David

Copperfield are exceptions, at least in retaining their own good humor: stories often suggest that once they become someone's stepchild, waifs who have been sinned against ere long become sinners in their own right. Joe Christmas, protagonist of William Faulkner's *Light in August*, starts life in an orphanage, where he has the bad fortune to accidentally eavesdrop on a sexual encounter involving two of the adult employees. In punishment—and fear that he will expose the couple—he is sent to become the foster child of Mr. McEachern, a willful, violent Christian fundamentalist who regularly beats young Joe for stubbornly refusing to memorize the catechism. As his life unfolds, Joe grows up tough, resentful, and violent, eventually killing a woman who sought to befriend and help him (and who also became his lover). Joe Christmas—everybody's stepchild, forced by a violent and rejecting world to become violent and rejecting in turn—is soon captured, castrated, and killed by a pursuing mob of vigilantes.

A century earlier, Heathcliff grew up the disfavored stepchild of *Wuthering Heights*. Wild (as bespeaks the gusty implications of the book's title), abandoned (in both senses of the word), and fiercely in love with Catherine Earnshaw but deemed unsuitable to marry her because of his unknown background and lowly step status, Heathcliff wreaks revenge on both the Earnshaw family, which denied his legitimacy, and the Linton family, into which his beloved Catherine eventually marries. Heathcliff's retaliation involves destroying the offspring of both lineages in a passionate quest to compensate, somehow, for his intolerable outsider situation.

The stepchild or fosterling as violent outsider isn't a characterization limited to Joe Christmas and Heathcliff. In fact, it is difficult to identify an imaginative literary depiction of the stepchild as a happy, well-adjusted, wholly accepted member of either family or society.

When it comes to stepparenting stories, one need only consult the immense, six-volume compendium *Motif-Index of Folk Literature* to see just how universal is the idea of the wicked stepparent. Tale after tale features evil stepmothers, but nary a case in which stepmothers are benevolent or well-intended. As for stepfathers, the *Motif-Index* identifies two categories: "cruel" and "lustful."

It is fruitless to deny the ubiquity of the negative stepparent image. But maybe the very myth itself of the malevolent stepparent is the cause of the problem. Maybe it is because stepparents are widely seen to be so difficult that they in fact are difficult. However, this begs the question of *why* stepparents are so widely viewed in a negative light. Most likely, stepparents are perceived as potentially dangerous and liable to treat their stepchildren badly because—all over the world—they occasionally do so, and, more to the point, they are on average more prone to do so than are biological parents. Whereas most stepparents are decent, humane, and loving—and some genetic parents are truly despicable—the fact remains that on balance, the former are significantly more liable to be "bad parents" than are their genetically connected counterparts. And nonbiological children—although perhaps less dramatically than Heathcliff, Joe Christmas, or even Cinderella—are liable to suffer the consequences.

Parenting is an extreme form of kin selection. To be a parent is to participate in a one-directional flow of benefits, a disparity that is necessitated by the fact that parents are so much older, larger, wiser, and more powerful than their children. Parents are biologically (and therefore psychologically as well as socially) expected to conform to these expectations and to accept an asymmetrical relationship with their children. With some notable exceptions, discussed in the next chapter, it is an arrangement that works well for all parties.

Stepparents, on the other hand, often struggle to mimic genetic parents, in their behavior as well as their feelings. And yet it is a difficult undertaking, even for the best of them. The most well-intended advice, anecdotes, and pop psychology—even when utterly non-Darwinian—acknowledge that stepparenting is difficult, as is being a stepchild. By contrast with its widespread if unintentional depiction in literature, the evolutionary biology of stepparenting has not made impressive headway into the traditional wisdom of social science, which, as we have said, still tends to attribute its near-universal stress to problems of "role definition" and "social expectations." It is far more likely that the fault lies not in our stars and not in society but in ourselves, that is, in the fact that we are biological creatures, carrying on a long-standing tradition by which genes struggle with other genes and favor copies of themselves.

Such struggles aren't hopeless, however. Indeed, we would argue that they are much of what being human is all about. Think of the scene in *The African Queen* (based, incidentally, on a novel by C. S. Forester), in which Katharine Hepburn's character sternly points out to a grimy, boozy Humphrey Bogart, who has sought to excuse his alcoholic excess with the claim that somehow his nature made him do it: "Nature, Mr. Allnut, is what we are put on earth to rise above."

When it comes to rising above nature, what about adoption? Doesn't its success show the inadequacy of biology as an interpreter of family function and dysfunction? Quite the opposite. What adoption really demonstrates is how easy it is, in certain cases, for us to fool Mother Nature.

To understand how this can happen, we must first emphasize an important rule: natural selection doesn't do more than is needed. This is because it takes "selection pressure" to create something out of nothing. No pressure, no adaptation. This is relevant in the case of adoption because would-be adopting parents must somehow fool themselves into feeling that their adopted child is "theirs." As it happens, evolution strongly promotes mechanisms that enable parents to recognize their children—and which therefore work against adoption—but only if there is a threat that otherwise parents would waste their precious care on someone else's offspring.

In other words, parent-offspring recognition should be acutely developed when mixups are likely and absent when they aren't. People aren't biologically prone to such errors, and so we lack mechanisms to prevent them. For a good case of this notion, Mike Beecher of the University of Washington turned to a pair of bird species, the bank swallow and the rough-winged swallow. Bank swallows nest in burrows dug in clay banks and are colonial, with many nesting pairs closely associated. Hence, breeding members of this species run the risk that their parental care might be misdirected to someone else's young. Rough-winged swallows, on the other hand, although closely related, are essentially solitary, each pair maintaining a nest that is isolated from other rough-winged swallows. So there is very little chance that a rough-wing will accidentally proffer food to nestlings other than its own.

Beecher found that the vocalizations of young bank swallows (the colonial species, vulnerable to mixups) are much more distinctive than those of rough-wings (the go-it-alone guys). Having a unique vocal fingerprint makes it easy for bank swallow parents to learn the distinctive vocal traits of their offspring. As a result, when bank swallow youngsters land at the wrong nest—which they often do, since in this colonial species, nest entrances are typically close to each other—the adults shoo them away, reserving food and protection for their own offspring. By contrast, rough-winged swallows can afford to be undiscriminating, since under normal conditions they run no risk of being importuned by strangers. There are no rough-winged swallow equivalents of double mother suckers, as among elephant seals. Interestingly, rough-winged swallows can be fooled by an experimenter, duped to accept strangers introduced into their nest, something that bank swallows never do. Rough-wing parents will even feed bank swallow babies; bank swallow parents reject any babies not their own.

To recapitulate: rough-winged swallows (the species that, because of its solitary lifestyle, doesn't possess offspring-recognition mechanisms) can essentially be induced to adopt, whereas bank swallows (whose social tendencies put them at risk of misdirecting their parental efforts) are equipped with a built-in tendency to recognize their offspring, and to reject nestlings that aren't their own.

Although people are more social than solitary, when it comes to offspring recognition, we are rough-wings rather than bank swallows. After a woman gives birth, there is simply no question whether the baby is hers. Switching newborns may take place in Gilbert and Sullivan operettas or—very rarely—in a modern, crowded metropolitan hospital, but not among a small band of early hominids trudging around the Pleistocene savannah. There is simply no way an African Eve could find herself *accidentally* nursing someone else's child. Lacking the threat of misidentifying our babies, our ancestors would almost certainly have also lacked any automatic, lock-and-key recognition mechanisms. (Recall the minimalism of evolutionary adaptations.) As a result, we have a wonderfully open program when it comes to identifying children as our own.

Granted that our evolutionary past gives us leeway to fool ourselves, in a sense, into responding as though someone else's offspring is actually our own, but why do so? After all, to adopt is to expend time and resources on behalf of someone *unrelated* to the adopter. Accordingly, it would appear to be an evolutionary blunder, comparable to genuine altruism (that is, beneficence toward another without any genetic compensation). Yet human beings can be quite insistent upon adopting, often struggling against heavy odds and bureaucratic red tape to do so. Adopted children, moreover, are typically well loved and cared for, and about as successful as biological children.

To start with, let's point out the obvious: adoption, overwhelmingly, is *not* most people's first choice. When it comes to children, the vast majority prefer to make their own. Only if this is not an option are most people inclined to satisfy their desire to be a parent—a desire that is almost certainly a highly adaptive legacy of evolution—by parenting someone else's kids. In addition, bear in mind that for perhaps 99.99 percent of its evolutionary past, *Homo sapiens* lived in small hunter-gatherer bands that almost certainly numbered fewer than a hundred. Within such groups, most individuals were related. As a result, anyone who adopted a child was likely to be caring for a genetic relative (say hello once again to our old friend kin selection). Even individuals who cared for an unrelated child may well have positioned themselves to receive a return benefit from the child's genetic relatives as well as becoming a possible recipient of social approval, and hence biological benefit, from within the local group.

Note once more that stepparenting and adoption are not the same, the former being a much darker and more troubled phenomenon. To be sure, stepparenting is similar to adoption in that non-genetic "parents" end up taking care of someone else's children. But whereas adoption involves a specific commitment to the adopted child (typically on the part of *both* adopting adults), stepparenting nearly always comes about as a side effect of two adults' commitment *toward each other*. Stepchildren, if any, are generally thrown in as an unavoidable—and, if the truth be acknowledged, often unwanted—part of the deal.[3] Adoption, moreover, typically takes place when the child is an infant, thereby enhancing the prospects that adopting parents can fool their unconscious selves into responding as though the adopted child is genetically their own. On the other hand, it usually isn't until they are older that stepchildren enter the stepparent's life, which is a further obstacle to parental devotion.

Put it all together, and whereas stepparenting and adoption are both clearly part of the human behavioral repertoire, the latter is likely to be much less conflictual and—at the biological level, at least—downright easy. Not surprisingly, literary depictions of adop-

---

[3] Technically, fostering is yet another category, which applies when a child is taken into the house of adults, neither of whom is the biological parent. It pertains to the situations of Cosette and Oliver Twist, and especially in the past meant virtual slavery. For our purposes, it is essentially equivalent to stepparenting, but with two stepparents and no biological parent to leaven the child's plight.

tion tend to be correspondingly comfortable as well as comforting. Barbara Kingsolver's first novel, *The Bean Trees*, was a heartwarming, thought-provoking, yet thoroughly genuine depiction of the adventures of Taylor Greer, a delightful, headstrong, and impulsive young woman who adopts Turtle when the young child is deposited into the front seat of her car. The connection between adoptive parent and child constitutes the core of the book, and it is one that the reader never doubts, despite the fact that Taylor and Turtle are not genetic relatives. Although they don't share genes, they do share needs, and the affiliation is one that Taylor enters into of her own free will, not carried along in the slipstream of a higher-priority adult relationship.

Earlier, we looked at how Monsieur and Madame Thénardier treated Cosette very differently than their own daughters. Now it's time to consider another relationship depicted in *Les Misérables*, that between Jean Valjean and Cosette. The middle-aged Valjean didn't find himself stuck with the young girl because of a sought-for union with her mother, Fantine; rather, he adopted Cosette, because, as Hugo makes clear, she met his need for a child just as he met her need for a parent:

> The gulf that nature had created between Valjean and Cosette, the gap of fifty years, was bridged by circumstance. The overriding force of destiny united these two beings so sundered by the years and so akin in what they lacked. Each fulfilled the other, Cosette with her instinctive need of a father, Valjean with his instinctive need of a child. For them to meet was to find, and in the moment when their hands first touched, they joined. Seeing the other, each perceived the other's need. In the deepest sense of the words it may be said that in their isolation Jean Valjean had been a widower, as Cosette was an orphan; and in this sense he became her father.

Another example of adoption, and to our mind the most suitable and heartwarming account, is George Eliot's *Silas Marner*. A lonely, reclusive miser, Silas is a painfully nearsighted weaver whose only pleasure comes from counting his accumulated gold pieces. One day his trove is plundered, plunging him into despair.

> Formerly, his heart had been as a locked casket with its treasure inside; but now the casket was empty, and the lock was broken. Left groping in darkness, with his prop utterly gone, Silas had inevitably a sense, though a dull and half-despairing one, that if any help came to him it must come from without.

Shortly thereafter, upon entering his isolated cottage, Silas sees a golden gleam in front of his fireplace; it isn't his gold, but a tiny, yellow-haired girl who somehow managed to reach safety after her destitute mother died in the snow nearby.

Silas adopts Eppie, and she transforms him in return, helping the old man regain his life just as he saved hers. The once-bare windows of chez Marner are soon festooned with lacy curtains, and Silas, for his part, finds himself opened as never before to joy and fulfillment. Eppie is a replacement, and more, for the former miser's lost gold:

> He could only have said that the child was come instead of the gold—that the gold had turned into the child. . . . The gold had kept his thoughts in an ever-repeated circle, leading to nothing beyond itself; but Eppie was an object compacted of changes and hopes that forced his thoughts onward, and carried them far away from their old eager pacing towards the same blank limit— carried them away to the new things that would come with the coming years, when Eppie would have learned to understand how her father Silas cared for her.

But there is trouble in paradise, arriving in the person of Godfrey Cass, the biological father of Eppie and the sole surviving son of Squire Cass, the town's wealthiest man. It seems that eighteen years previously, in a fit of drunken foolishness, Godfrey had failed to rise above "nature" and had impulsively and secretly married a coarse and common woman, who became Eppie's mother. Mortified by his earlier error, Godfrey had kept secret not only his marital indiscretion but also his fatherhood until, many years into a childless marriage, he revealed the truth to his wife, Nancy. (Godfrey's truth-telling was also stimulated by the discovery of the body of his good-for-nothing brother, along with Silas's gold, which he had stolen.)

Godfrey and Nancy Cass go to Silas and Eppie, demanding custody of the now budding young lady, pointing out that they can offer her wealth and a "suitable upbringing" far beyond anything available from the rustic weaver. Eppie, however, elects to remain with her adoptive father, and also marries a fine young chap, thereby concluding our tale.

There is nothing demeaning about adoption being a win-win proposition, benefiting Jean Valjean as well as Cosette, Silas Marner as well as Eppie. And it is neither surprising nor disreputable that the childless Casses cast a longing parental eye on Eppie as well. Nor is it irrelevant that by their action, adopters are often seen to demonstrate their good character and even, on occasion, their marriageability: don't forget the importance of "good behavior" (Chapter 3) in demonstrating one's suitability as a mate.

Also, keep in mind Jane Eyre and her eventual encounter with the lordly, and also secretly married, Rochester. Jane was initially hired as governess to Rochester's young ward, a girl named Adèle who was the offspring of a French prostitute and maybe, just maybe, Rochester's natural child as well. He denies it, however, claiming that he adopted Adèle out of disinterested altruism:

> "I see no proofs of such grim paternity written in her countenance. . . . I acknowledged no natural claim on Adèle's part to be supported by me; nor do I now acknowledge any, for I am not her father; but hearing that she was quite destitute, I e'en took the poor thing out of the slime and mud of Paris, and transplanted her here, to grow up clean in the wholesome soil of an English country garden."

If you were Jane Eyre, wouldn't you, too, be moved by the kindliness of such a man, however forbidding and distant he appears in other respects? And wouldn't his benevolent adoption of Adèle go a long way toward modulating any sense you might have of him as cold and unfeeling? Isn't it interesting as well that the villagewide reputation of Silas Marner, who spent decades trying unsuccessfully to live down an unjust accusation of thievery in his youth, was finally rehabilitated when his devotion to baby Eppie, his adopted child, became public?

"All happy families are happy in the same way," wrote Leo Tolstoy in the famous opening sentence of *Anna Karenina*. "Every unhappy family is unhappy in its own way." As to happy families, there is room for debate, but when it comes to unhappiness, Tolstoy was certainly onto something: people have devised—or blundered into—innumerable ways of being unhappy. Even this diversity, however, resolves itself into some recognizable patterns, many of which involve the struggles of stepparenting.

8

On the Complaints of Portnoy, Caulfield, Huck Finn, and the Brothers Karamazov Everywhere

Parent-Offspring Conflict

Portnoy has a complaint. Holden Caulfield is pissed off. And let's face it, even that all-American boy Huck Finn has a hard time with adults. Nor are these three alone. In literature, as in life, children and parents don't always get along. In fact, one might say that they never do—at least, not without genuine friction—even though in the long run things have a habit of working out.

No one is shocked when men struggle over status, dominance, or money, not to mention direct one-on-one duels over mates. Similarly for comparatively toned-down conflict among women. There is even a powerful biological rationale to battles *between* the sexes, insofar as men and women are different genetically as well as in their reproductive tactics and strategies, despite the fact that their interests converge in reproduction. (As George Burns once pointed out, no wonder there's trouble between the sexes. After all, they want different things: men want women and women want men!) Yet it may seem surprising that parents and offspring are so often at odds, especially when we look through evolutionary spectacles.

The genetic interests of parents and their offspring would seem to coincide perfectly, if only because parents want their children to succeed, as do the children themselves. And so, as Portnoy's put-upon parents would no doubt observe, what's to complain about? Even a hard-eyed biological perspective, by which children are merely vehicles enabling parental genes to replicate themselves, leads to the suggestion that the latter achieve their goals via the former (think Little League). So little or no conflict might be expected (think *Little Women*).

Years of Walt Disney's *True Life Adventures*, combined with animated films from *Dumbo* to *The Lion King*, have both reflected and generated the presumption that parent and child—especially mother and child—are the epitome of shared goals and perfect amiability. The image among human beings is, if anything, even more clearly established: madonna and child convey a sense of peace and contentment that transcends the merely theological.

When rough spots emerge in the parent-child nexus, the traditional view has long been that the culprit is mutual misunderstanding, with its attendant failures of communication: everyone is supposed to mean well. The conventional wisdom is that in the course of conveying heartfelt parental assistance, advice, and information to the child, sometimes there are problems, largely because the child is necessarily inexperienced, and also liable to be headstrong and uninformed as to where its true interests lie. According to this view, the well-socialized and gradually more mature youngster eventually recognizes that it is best served by going along with parental inclinations, at which point conflict ceases and socialization has been achieved. Thus when conflict arises between parent and offspring, the traditional explanation is that children are primitive, even barbaric little creatures who need time to become incorporated into the society of responsible adults. And so we indulge Huck and his buddy Tom Sawyer, their boys-will-be-boyhood, in the comfortable assurance that eventually, they will grow up and shape up.

Then there is the psychoanalytic tradition, which focuses on sexual rivalry, especially between sons and fathers. As a result of presumed Oedipal conflict, boys are supposed to be terrified that their fathers will castrate them, while girls resent not having a penis; trouble therefore ensues until eventually things quiet down when the

child gets older and less obstreperous, reconciling its primitive conflicts by assuming the social role appropriate to its gender.

The view from evolutionary biology is quite different, rather
darker . . . and much more persuasive. It is closer to that expressed
in Shakespeare's A *Midsummer Night's Dream*: "The course of true
love never did run smooth." Which is not to deny the love of parent and offspring, but simply to point out their interests. The point
at issue, now known to biologists as "parent-offspring conflict," was
developed in a brilliant paper published in 1974 by the evolutionary theorist Robert Trivers. The following discussion owes much
to his insights (many of which now seem obvious, but only after
Trivers first pointed them out).

One of Trivers's most basic insights is that there is no genetic
identity between parent and offspring; rather, there is simply a 50
percent probability that any gene present in a parent is also present
in the child. Nonetheless, prior to recognizing the consequences of
this simple fact, biologists—and to an even greater extent most
psychologists and sociologists—tended to treat the child as an appendage to the parent, rather than a separate being with its own
strengths as well as weaknesses and, even more important, its own
agenda. It needs to be emphasized that there is a parent-offspring
genetic glass of DNA that is half empty: the 50 percent of parental
genome *not* shared between parent and child.

When we looked at the biology and literature of kin selection
(Chapter 6), the point was that when genes look out for themselves, the result, ironically, is altruism. But just as shared genes
result in shared interests, unshared genes result in conflicting agendas and even outright conflict.

So it isn't really surprising after all that Holden Caulfield, in *The
Catcher in the Rye*, becomes disgusted with his parents and with adults
in general, mortified at the "phoniness" that he sees around him,
suspicious of the grown-up world. After all, the biological interests of
a parent are limited to making the most of the *parent's* prospects, not
necessarily those of the parent's offspring. Remember, while the

parent does have a strong genetic interest in his or her child, the only biological reason for creating offspring in the first place is as a means of advancing the *parent's* fitness and not someone else's! Although it's in each parent's interest—or rather that of parental genes—to invest in offspring, they may not be well served by putting all their genetic eggs in one basket (just to mix the metaphor up even further). As a result, investing in any individual offspring must be balanced against maintaining the ability to invest in others, later on or simultaneously. Hence a potential clash of interests.

Among species with a short life span and not much to contribute to their offspring, such as most insects and many fish, adults typically reproduce in a single, gung-ho burst of enthusiasm, known rather indelicately to biologists as a "big bang." On the other hand, in the case of birds and mammals—including *Homo sapiens*—parents are selected to hold back a bit, rather than spend all their time and energy on behalf of any one offspring.

Accordingly, parents make unconscious calculations about how best to invest their reproductive resources, including the need to hedge their bets and keep enough in reserve for additional children. Insofar as parents hold back, it isn't simply because they have a 50 percent genetic overlap with their children, but because they need to remain capable of rearing other offspring, as well as to assist with additional kin such as nieces, nephews, grandchildren, and so forth.

At the same time, every child is ultimately interested in making the most of *its* fitness, not necessarily that of its parent. Another way of looking at it: a child is 100 percent related to itself but only 50 percent related to any parent. As a result, the child devalues its parents' interests by a factor of one-half, as parents do for each child. Children and parents can, in a sense, feel only one-half of each other's pain, just as they enjoy only one-half of each other's genetic gain. No wonder there's conflict. (As George Burns might have added: parents and children each want different things, namely, their own fitness, not each other's.)

The upshot has been an important new understanding in evolutionary psychology, one that makes sense of precisely those parent-offspring rough spots that literature has recognized for centuries, although without benefit of current genetic wisdom: despite their profound bonds, parent and child are also profoundly disconnected from each other. Thus, they are locked in a battle of evolutionary wills, with each party biologically primed to demand more than the other is inclined to give. Parents want grandchildren; once they reach a certain age, children want sex but not necessarily their own children. Parents want their offspring to be self-sufficient; children want their parents to be financially and emotionally generous. Parents want the chores to be done; children want freedom to live their own lives. Parents want to see themselves in their children; children want to see themselves in themselves. King Lear wants his daughters to vie with each other in expressing undying love for him; two of the three are brutally interested only in themselves.

At last, transgenerational conflict—so much a fixture of human life, and providing so much grist for the literary mill—is open to be examined, predicted, and understood.

Among animals, including human beings, some of the conflict between parents and offspring reveals itself during weaning, with offspring often seeking to obtain more milk than parents are inclined to provide. Lactating mothers who had been the epitome of maternal devotion become increasingly short-tempered with their nurslings. One can almost hear them complaining, like Portnoy's mother, "Enough already!" It is almost unheard of for a nursing cat, dog, lion, or chimpanzee to snarl at one of her babies—until, that is, those babies have gotten big enough and able to make it on their own, while at the same time remaining so demanding that they are beginning to impinge on the mother's future options.

How much milk should a mommy mammal provide? It depends who you ask. From the offspring's perspective, enough to guarantee the child's maximum growth and eventual success, with a small adjustment to make sure that Mom doesn't overdo it and so deplete herself that she cannot breed again; after all, given the exigencies of kin selection, it is often in the interest of each offspring to be provided with siblings. And Mom is the one to do so. From the mother's perspective, she should endow each child with enough milk to give it a good start, but with a much larger allowance for her own well-being and especially, granting her sufficient strength to breed again, or at least, to provide milk for any other siblings. Again, as Trivers emphasized, the mother and the offspring are each entirely related to itself and only one-half related to the other. The stage is set for trouble.

Something similar to the mammal pattern of weaning conflict even takes place among birds. Large nestlings—big enough to fly, hence known as fledglings—can often be found pursuing their harried parents, importuning them for food. In late spring throughout North America, it is common to see fledglings of many different species quivering their wings and uttering incessant begging calls while the parents back away, look far into the distance (as though trying to ignore what is in front of them), and often literally take wing, pursued by their nearly grown but indefatigably demanding offspring.

Conflict over weaning, or its equivalent in birds, does not exhaust the potential for parents and offspring to disagree. In this new evolutionary way of looking at parent-offspring relations, the root of all evils is conflict over parental investment, anything that parents provide to their offspring that contributes to the offspring's success but which carries with it a cost as measured by the parent's ability to produce and invest similarly in additional offspring. Among human beings, parental investment includes money but is not limited to it. It also goes on longer, and is more intense, than in any other species. Many a harried parent, struggling to provide for even the most loved and rewarding child, will answer the question "What do you want your child to be?" with an immediate reply:

"Self-supporting!" And many a put-upon child yearns for its parents to back off . . . but keep sending money.

And so we return to *Portnoy's Complaint*. How great a leap is it from a demanding fledgling to a complaining Alexander Portnoy? Not that far. The evolutionary theory of parent-offspring conflict tells us that parents seek to manipulate children in their own ways and for their own ends, whereas children can be expected to resist. And not surprisingly, it also predicts that many of these conflicts revolve around sex and reproduction, in which a youngster's developing sexual urges are more disruptive than reproductive.

In one notable scene from that antic, comic, iconic tale of generational conflict, Portnoy's father waits in constipated agony outside the bathroom door while young Alexander Portnoy masturbates within, after which our temporarily depleted hero must endure his mother's insistence on searching his nonexistent feces (after all, he was supposed to be pooping) for evidence of nonkosher hamburgers. It is more than a little challenging, as Portnoy complains, "being a nice Jewish boy, publicly pleasing my parents while privately pulling my putz!"

Nor is Alexander Portnoy's incessant masturbation the only indication that he and his parents aren't quite on the same wavelength. With all its hilarious, ribald, offbeat humor, *Portnoy's Complaint* is filled with parent-offspring conflict, notably his mother's "ubiquity," his father's blockheaded insistence as to how young Alexander should behave, and constant demands that he "capitulate," punctuated by his own occasional, if irresolute, efforts at self-assertion:

> "I'm sorry," I mumble . . . "but just because it's your religion doesn't mean it's mine."
>
> "What did you say? Turn around, Mister. I want the courtesy of a reply from your mouth."
>
> "I don't have a religion," I say. . . .

"You don't, eh?"

"I can't."

"And why not? You're something special? Look at me! You're somebody too special?"

"I don't believe in God."

"Get out of those dungarees, Alex, and put on some decent clothes."

"They're not dungarees, they're Levi's."

"It's Rosh Hashanah, Alex, and to me you're wearing overalls! Get in there and put a tie on and a jacket and a pair of trousers and a clean shirt, and come out looking like a human being. And shoes, Mister, hard shoes."

"My shirt is clean—"

"Oh, you're riding for a fall, Mr. Big. You're fourteen years old, and believe me, you don't know everything there is to know. Get out of those moccasins! What the hell are you supposed to be, some kind of Indian?"

What, then, is Portnoy's complaint? Basically, this: how hard it is to be yourself when your parents are constantly breathing down your neck, unendingly exhorting, complaining, warning, demanding, insisting, and—of course, this being a Jewish tale—guilt-mongering, all the while loving, to be sure:

"Call, Alex. Visit, Alex. Alex, keep us informed. Don't go away without telling us, please, not again. Last time you went away you didn't tell us, your father was ready to phone the police. You know how many times a day he called and got no answer? Take a guess, how many?"

It may be significant that the traditional view of parent-offspring relations, which assumes that father and mother know best, and which has never taken the perspective of offspring very seriously, is one that has been promulgated by adults. Similarly, we can expect that parents would be likely to present their teachings, manipulations, guilt-mongering, and arm-twisting as "for your own good," or even accompanied by protestations that "this hurts me more than it hurts you," emphasizing, in short, the value of their opinions and advice as well as the degree to which the parental perspective is solely in the best interest of the child. (Nonetheless, sometimes parents do have something worthwhile to offer their children, and not all interactions are hurtfully self-serving. Mark Twain once noted that when he was a teenager, his parents knew nothing; as a young man in his early twenties, he was astounded how much they had learned in just a few years!)

Philip Roth's novel is an extended comic monologue, with the adult Alexander (the not-so-great) telling his tale of developmental woe to an analyst. Included is this memorable recitation of Momma Portnoy's appeal to her son, followed by an added prod from Poppa Portnoy:

"Do you remember Seymour Schmuck, Alex?" she asks me. . . . "Well, I met his mother on the street today, and she told me that Seymour is now the biggest brain surgeon in the entire Western Hemisphere. He owns six different split-level ranch-type houses . . . and last year [he took] his wife and his two little daughters . . . to Europe for an eighty-million-dollar tour of seven thousand countries, some of them you never even heard of . . . and that's how big your friend Seymour is today! *And how happy he makes his parents!*"

And you, the implication is, when are you going to get married already? In Newark and the surrounding suburbs this apparently is the question on everybody's lips: WHEN IS ALEXANDER PORTNOY GOING TO STOP BEING SELFISH AND GIVE HIS PARENTS, WHO ARE SUCH WONDERFUL PEOPLE, GRANDCHILDREN? "Well," says my father, the tears brimming up in his eyes, "well," he asks, *every single time I see him*, "is there a serious girl in the picture, Big Shot? Excuse me for asking, I'm only your father, but since I'm not going to be alive forever, and you in case you forgot carry the family name, I wonder if maybe you could let me in on the secret."

Classic parental guilt-mongering (whether Jewish or otherwise) involves urging a child to make its *parents* happy, never mind him. Ironically, as in Alexander Portnoy's case, this can even involve parental desires for grandchildren, resisted by the child, now a young adult. The younger Portnoy is plenty interested in girls, lots of them; his parents, on the other hand, want to know if there is a "serious girl" in his future. They want grandchildren, not Alexander Portnoy's personal sexual satisfaction. There is abundant biological research—much of it involving sophisticated mathematical models—on the optimal timing of reproduction in animals; suffice it to note that what is optimal for a would-be grandparent isn't necessarily the best option for a future parent. A postadolescent oyster has few opportunities to argue with its parents over the perfect time to start making little oysterlings. Human beings aren't so lucky.

Which leads us to Caulfield's complaint. In J. D. Salinger's modern classic, the hero isn't especially hung up on sex (at least not like Portnoy) or on his "parental unit." Nonetheless, there is plenty of parent-offspring conflict: over Holden's failure in school, his yearning for a lost innocence, and the fact that he is at great pains to avoid encountering the elder Caulfields, who, he is convinced, couldn't possibly understand him. He's probably right. From the story's outset, Holden Caulfield is vigorously dismissive of his parents:

> If you really want to hear about it, the first thing you'll probably want to know is where I was born, and what my lousy childhood was like, and how my parents were occupied and all before they had me, and all that David Copperfield kind of crap, but I don't feel like going into it, if you want to know the truth.

Insofar as parents are often predisposed to push, pull, and prod their children to meet the parents' needs, it makes perfect sense that adolescents in particular are prone to fight back, and also that they are likely to respond favorably to depictions of their peers doing just that. (This helps explain the spectacular popularity of *The Catcher in the Rye*, which almost certainly exceeds its literary merit.) Furthermore, given that children are smaller, weaker, poorer, and less experienced than their parents, it also makes sense that in their case, parent-offspring conflict often involves a series of strategic retreats and more of a guerrilla conflict than out-and-out warfare.

Holden Caulfield impulsively runs away from the boarding school from which he is about to be dismissed—the fourth one—after failing in his halfhearted efforts to explain his dissatisfactions to a fellow student, and resenting his roommate's selfish (but successful) relationship with girls. Significantly, the only people to whom he relates positively are his two siblings: a brother, now dead, and his younger sister, Phoebe (whom he hopes to save from adults).

As to the adult world, it is a continuing source of conflict for young Master Caulfield, leaving him alienated, misunderstood, and profoundly alone: keeping away from his parents, he wanders lonely and alienated through deserted city streets, an empty and brooding hotel lobby, a silent dormitory. Here are his final words as he leaves school:

> When I was all set to go, when I had my bags and all, I stood for a while next to the stairs and took a last look down the goddam corridor. I was sort of crying. I don't know why. I put my red hunting hat on, and turned the peak around to the back, the way I liked it, and then I yelled at the top of my goddam voice, "*Sleep tight, ya morons!*"

No one understands him and, to be fair, he doesn't understand anyone else, either. Holden's attempts to connect with the world are all pathetic failures: he goes to crowded bars where he feels painfully isolated; he looks up an old girlfriend only to find her unable to relate to his concerns; he tries to make a date with someone he had heard described as "loose" but doesn't follow through; he spends time with one of his former teachers only to flee in terror when the man appears to make a homosexual advance; he invites an unresponsive taxicab driver to have a drink with him; he even, at the instigation of a hotel elevator operator, has a prostitute to his room, only to spend the time talking and then being beaten by the hotel man.

In some ways, the biology of parent-offspring conflict is really about a wider kind of conflict: between every young individual and the adult world that he or she must learn to negotiate. We have seen that doing so often requires performing a delicate dance with/against one's own parents, who have their own agendas. It also involves an even more dangerous dance with/against the rest of the adult world, which, after all, is often primed to view the newly emerging individual as a competitor and/or someone to be exploited. No wonder youngsters, being vulnerable, are often both alienated and wary.

Holden is appalled when the adult world intrudes on his sister's life in the form of obscene graffiti scrawled on the walls of her school. The demands and preoccupations of adult reality fall short of his hopes, leaving him convinced that everyone is a "jerk," "phony," a "moron," "corny," "crummy," "lousy," or "dopey." He idealizes himself as a protector of children, a defender of offspring in their conflict with the grown-up world, dreaming idealistically that he might some-day be the "catcher in the rye" who rescues little children as they play in a field of rye and keeps them from falling off a cliff:

> Anyway, I keep picturing all these little kids playing some game in this big field of rye and all. Thousands of little kids, and no-body's around—nobody big, I mean—except me. And I'm stand-ing on the edge of some crazy cliff. What I have to do, I have to catch everybody if they start to go over the cliff—I mean if they're running and they don't look where they're going I have to come out from somewhere and *catch* them. That's all I'd do all day. I'd just be the catcher in the rye and all.

Holden Caulfield probably wants to be caught and protected himself, hence his fantasy about catching and protecting younger children. Yet, ironically, he is misquoting the Robert Burns song, which asks whether there is anything wrong "if a body *meet* [not *catch*] a body comin' thro' the rye," and if that meeting results in casual sex between them. Holden's fantasy involves catching children before they plunge over a cliff into the adult world, with its demands, its insistent "phoniness," and of course its knowledge of sex. Meanwhile, Holden falls off his own cliff, leading to a "victory" of sorts by adult society, since he tells his story while incarcerated in a mental institution.

For a half century, *The Catcher in the Rye* has had a firm grip on the imaginations of millions of readers, most of them teenage, despite the fact that Holden Caulfield is an absolute jerk: he lies to everyone, cannot complete anything or connect with anyone, and is unrelentingly critical of those around him. Most likely, this is why Holden Caulfield speaks so convincingly to adolescents: as he says to one of his teachers, he feels trapped on "the other side" of life, and his story is one of nearly frantic and continually unsuccessful attempts to find companionship, to satisfy E. M. Forster's dictum, "Only connect." He has, of course, his red hunting hat (worn backward long before this became popular) as an enduring symbol of his individuality. It's about all that he has.

Holden Caulfield sought desperately to freeze childhood innocence, thereby protecting it from the polluting effects of the adult world, while at the same time, not coincidentally, shielding children—including himself—from the conflicts that the adult world unavoidably generates. Nonetheless, parent-offspring conflict, like shit, happens. Nearly every story of growing up therefore involves some degree of rebellion, dissatisfaction, and disputation with parents and other "authority figures." Earlier, we wrote about kin relationships as an ocean in which we swim. There are other natural bodies of water so pervasive that they are largely taken for granted. Conflict between parent and offspring are prominent among them.

Long-lasting tales of young people owe much of their enduring appeal to varying degrees of immersion in this enduring theme. *Huckleberry Finn* is a perfect example. Admittedly, Huck's mother is dead and his biological father is of no great consequence in his story except as an abusive alcoholic. But significantly, Huck has numerous substitute parents: Judge Thatcher, the Widow Douglas, Tom Sawyer's Aunt Polly, Aunt Sally, Miss Watson, the Grangerfield family, Jim, the rather sinister Duke and King. Some are helpful, some hurtful, some admirable, some despicable, but in all cases they constitute the adult background against which our young hero must struggle to find himself.

By contrast to the wealthy Holden Caulfield, Huckleberry Finn—that quintessential, mythic American boy—is utterly impoverished when it comes to money but infinitely richer in relationships with adults, with whom he has no dearth of conflicts. As Mark Twain's novel begins, the Widow Douglas and Miss Watson, her sister, are determined to civilize Huck; they want him to stop swearing and smoking, to wear clean clothes, go to school and sleep in a bed. Listen to Huck's account:

> The widow rang a bell for supper, and you had to come to time. When you got to the table you couldn't go right to eating, but you had to wait for the widow to tuck down her head and brumble a little over the victuals, though there warn't really anything the matter with them—that is nothing only everything was cooked by itself. In a barrel of odds and ends it is different; things get mixed up, and the juice kind of swaps around, and the things go better.
>
> After supper she got out her book and learned me about Moses and the Bulrushes, and I was in a sweat to find out all about him; but by she let it out that Moses had been dead a considerable long time; so then I didn't care no more about him, because I don't take no stock in dead people.

The old ladies are well-meaning but annoyingly self-righteous, and Huck certainly notices:

Pretty soon I wanted to smoke, and asked the widow to let me. But she wouldn't. She said it was a mean practice and wasn't clean, and I must try to not do it any more. That is just the way with some people. They get down on a thing when they don't know nothing about it. Here she was a-bothering about Moses, which was no kin to her, and no use to anybody, being gone, you see, yet finding a power of fault with me for doing a thing that had some good in it. And she took snuff, too; of course that was all right, because she done it herself.

Children are notoriously sensitive to adult hypocrisy, especially when it emanates from parents or—in Huck's case—parent substitutes. Perhaps this is part of our specieswide legacy of such conflict: an acute awareness of who is doing what, and who is trying to get whom to do what, and why.

Huck rises above the mean, low people he encounters, and even above the expectations of a society and of his elders, by eventually repudiating the slave-owning culture in which he had been raised. Thus Huck initially decides to write a letter telling where Jim, an escaped slave, can be found and returned to slavery. But then, in his signal crisis of conscience, Huck reconsiders:

[G]ot to thinking over our trip down the river; and I see Jim before me, all the time, in the day, and in the night-time, sometimes moonlight, sometimes storms, and we a floating along, talking, and singing, and laughing. But somehow I couldn't seem to strike no places to harden me against him, but only the other kind. I'd see him standing my watch on top of his'n, stead of calling me, so I could go on sleeping, and see him how glad he was when I come back out of the fog; and when I come to him again in the swamp, up there where the feud was, and such-like times . . . and how good he always was; and at last I struck time I saved him by telling the men we had small-pox aboard, and he was so grateful, and said I was the best friend old Jim ever had in the world, and the only one he's got now; and then I happened to look around, and see that paper.

It was a close place. I took it up, and held it in my hand. I was a-trembling, because I'd got to decide, forever, betwixt two things, and I knowed it. I studied a minute, sort of holding my breath, and then says to myself: "All right, then, I'll go to hell"— and tore it up.

Finally, at the book's end, Huck rejects civilized, adult, faux-parental society once and for all, and we cheer: "But I reckon I got to light out for the Territory ahead of the rest, because Aunt Sally she's going to adopt me and sivilize me, and I can't stand it. I been there before."

It seems like a one-sided fight. After all, parents are bigger, older, stronger, wealthier, and presumably wiser than their children. The little tykes shouldn't stand a chance, at least so long as the parents in question are still young enough to remain vigorous. At the same time, however, offspring aren't altogether helpless: as Trivers emphasized, they can be expected especially to resort to psychological techniques. August Wilson's play *Fences* describes the struggles of family patriarch Troy Maxson as he confronts his children. Maxson's son Lyons, although thirty-four, keeps showing up and requesting money; as Trivers predicted, Lyons Maxson has ways of getting his way, in particular playing upon his father's guilt over the fact that the elder Maxson had not been substantially involved in his son's upbringing:

> "You can't change me, Pop. I'm thirty-four years old. If you wanted to change me, you should have been there when I was growing up. I come by to see you . . . ask for ten dollars and you want to talk about how I was raised. You don't know nothing about how I was raised."

Troy is also in conflict with his other son, Cory, who wants to go to college and play football instead of taking a more "reliable" job.

At the play's end, Troy ruthlessly and unsympathetically pushes Cory out of his house, in part to make room for Troy's infant daughter (by another woman), who is coming to live with them, and in part as a reenactment of Troy's own childhood experience. Thus at the age of fourteen, he was disowned by *his* father after it became clear that the two were fighting over the same woman:

> "Now I thought he was mad cause I ain't done my work. But I see where he was chasing me off so he could have the gal for himself. When I see what the matter of it was, I lost all fear of my daddy. Right there is where I become a man ... at fourteen years of age. ... The only thing I knew was the time had come for me to leave my daddy's house. And right there the world suddenly got big."

To be sure, a dose of tough love can sometimes be a worthwhile component of good parenting for human beings who—at some point—insist that their children pay their own way, or at least accept responsibility for their own actions. And there are things parents can and should do to help their children's world "get big." At the same time, a dose of evolutionary theory helps clarify how it is that in many cases such actions are more than a little self-serving.

King Lear is doubtless correct when he says that it is "sharper than a serpent's tooth to have a thankless child." The converse also holds, as biology helps make plain: it is a genuine pain in the ass to have a selfish, demanding parent!

Although parent-offspring conflict seems tailor-made for adolescence, no one is ever too old to participate. Parents and offspring can be expected to disagree over many things beyond the relatively simple question of how much parents should provide for a child or whether they should do so at all. They will predictably disagree, for instance, over the child's behavior toward a third party—in the most obvious and probably most frequent case, a brother or sister.

Here's how it works. For a parent, who is equally related to each child, every one is equally important. Parents come out ahead anytime one of their children acts altruistically toward a brother or sister, so long as the benefit to the recipient is greater than the cost to the altruist. But the child can be expected to see things differently, since he or she is related by only 50 percent to a sibling (as to a parent), but 100 percent to itself. The result is conflict, not only between siblings—sibling rivalry indeed—but also between parent and offspring.

Think of parents urging a child to play nicely with its brother or sister, typically more nicely than the child wants to do. Or pressuring a child to share when the youngster is inclined to be more selfish. Part of the power of the evolutionary approach comes from its recognition that such cases are not simply due to stubbornness or sheer perversity on the part of a rivalrous or selfish child. Rather, the key is that children are inclined to act in response to *their own* biological interests rather than those of their siblings, their parents, society, or anyone else, for that matter. In most such cases, the bottom line is that parents are expected to exhort, extort, or otherwise try to induce their offspring to act differently—toward each other as well as toward the parent—than the offspring would choose if left to themselves.

When extreme, sibling rivalry can become siblicide, and it is more frequent in the natural world than biologists used to think. Embryonic sharks, for example, begin their predatory lives with an early burst of sibling competition, devouring each other as they swim about in utero before they are born. And pronghorn antelope fetuses kill each other in the womb, presumably thereby increasing the amount of mother's milk that they will eventually obtain. Siblicide has even been reported for plants. The Dalbergia tree of India disperses its seeds via pods that float in the wind; lighter pods travel farther. The first Dalbergia seed to develop produces chemicals that kill its pod siblings before it leaves the tree, thereby giving this particular "bad seed" sole occupancy of the vehicle, and thus, the advantage of greater dispersal distance.

Fortunately, there is no evidence—as yet—that human beings partake of siblicide as an evolutionary strategy. But the story of Cain killing Abel (which has resonance, in one form or another, in a variety of cultures) suggests that brothers and sisters may be less mutually supportive than many, especially the parents, might wish. Such an insufficiency of brotherly love is exactly what John Steinbeck recognized in *East of Eden*, his dark tale of fratricidal competition, and its sisterly counterpart inspired Shakespeare when he wrote *King Lear*.

Ivan Turgenev's classic *Fathers and Sons* has long been seen as social criticism, representing the conflict between old and new, between traditional and "scientific" conceptions of society, and a novel in which the younger generation's fascination with nihilism foreshadows the forthcoming Russian Revolution. And so it is. Arkady and Bazarov are recent graduates of the university in St. Petersburg, filled with new and "nihilistic" ideas, critical of their families but also assuming that they will be taken care of by them. At the same time, it is worth noting that Turgenev chose parents and offspring to exemplify these issues. Indeed, *Fathers and Sons* is a textbook depiction of parent-offspring conflict, in which two sons (Arkady and Bazarov) struggle with their fathers (Nikolai and Vassily), to establish their own independent identities, complete with sexual pursuits and predictable concerns about inheritance.

There is even some overt sexual conflict across the generations, when Bazarov makes an advance on his friend's father's mistress and must fight a duel as a result. Parent-offspring conflict is real and troublesome enough, but add a hefty dose of plain old-fashioned male-male sexual competition and the dynamic becomes dynamite.

This explosive mix is dramatically portrayed in Dostoyevsky's *The Brothers Karamazov*. Here, we are given the panoramic tale of genetic and sexual conflict—ultimately lethal—between a father and his offspring.

Fyodor Karamazov is a philanderer, a brutal buffoon, a man of means, a drunkard, a "sensualist" (which is to say, a very horny and unrestrained SOB), and, least of all, a father. Old man Karamazov had abandoned all of his offspring, one by one, leaving each in turn to be cared for by Grigory, a devoted servant, and eventually placed with other relatives while the old ogre indulged in his orgies.

Dmitri, the eldest Karamazov son, and offspring of Fyodor's first wife, grew up believing that he was entitled to a substantial inheritance via his mother. Dmitri became a soldier and a sensualist like his father, a prodigal son whose life is wild, passionate, and violent. Fyodor's two other legitimate children, both via his second wife, are Ivan, an atheist and intellectual, and Alyosha, the youngest, a paragon of moral and religious probity and would-be man of God, follower of the saintly Father Zossima. Then there is Smerdyakov, Fyodor's illegitimate son by the town idiot, "stinking Lizaveta." (Fyodor Karamazov's previous wives are now dead, so in Dostoyevsky's novel, parent-offspring conflict is reduced to conflict between father and offspring.) Smerdyakov is kept on as a servant in the old rake's household, and it is he who murders Fyodor, a crime for which Dmitri is convicted.

Dmitri had plenty of motive. In addition to conflict over his inheritance—wanting more resources than the parent wants to provide—there is direct competition over the same woman: the lovely and seductive Grushenka, a luscious lady of ill repute. Imagine the struggles of McTeague and his erstwhile friend Marcus (see Chapter 2), this time taking place between father and son. Although shared genes may help soften the (literal) blows, such outright conflict within the context of kin is likely to be especially painful if only because of the ambivalence involved. Dmitri acknowledges the "hideous horror" of his struggle with "the old voluptuary" over Grushenka, a battle in which the hotheaded son had become increasingly enraged since his father and sexual competitor was also the holder of the purse strings, access to which he was unfairly—but understandably—denying his son. Things are more complicated yet. Dmitri is engaged, not to Grushenka but to Katerina, who in turn is loved by his brother Ivan! (Now sibling rivalry rears its unlovely head; moreover, as evolutionary theory would predict, it is especially intense among these two since they are half-brothers.) Ivan wants Dmitri to go ahead and marry Grushenka so that he can marry Katerina. But old man Karamazov also has hot pants for Grushenka, which is why he refuses to give any money to Dmitri. Fyodor's bankbook is all that he has with which to lure the gorgeous Gru.

Enter the saintly Father Zossima, patron and idealized father figure of the third brother, Alyosha, who tries to mediate an end to the family feuding, especially between Dmitri and his father, Fyodor, over Dmitri's inheritance. But to the embarrassment of all, the old rake simply acts like a buffoon, later insisting that he will hoard all the family money to use on young women. Specifically, Fyodor plans to offer the seductive Grushenka three thousand rubles in return for her sexual favors. Thus, the two men, father and son, literally do battle in competition over both resources and sex. Dmitri later beats his father, threatening to kill him if he in fact seduces Grushenka, so when Fyodor is murdered, the blame falls naturally enough on Dmitri. But actually Smerdyakov did it.

Freud claimed that *The Brothers Karamazov* was the greatest novel of all time, evidently because it "confirmed" his theory, developed in *Totem and Taboo*, that humankind began with a primal act of patricide, in which sons gathered together and killed the father (who, Fyodor Karamazov–like, had appropriated all the nubile women). Dostoyevsky's book is extraordinary, but its quality—or indeed that of any work of imaginative fiction—should emphatically not be judged by its consistency with any particular theory, even evolution. If biological accuracy made for great writing, then the next Nobel Prizes for literature should come from field and laboratory notebooks or the output of DNA sequencing machines. Indeed, writing that sets literary achievement second to any other goal is invariably second-rate. T. S. Eliot once noted, for example, that the problem with most religious poetry is that it is more religion than poetry.

Themes of violent sexual competition between fathers and sons are more widespread than one might think; moreover, the underlying biological reality of so-called Oedipal competition likely resides not at all in sexual competition for the mother, but for other women, with parent-offspring conflict thrown in for good measure. Take, for example, Eugene O'Neill's *Desire Under the Elms*, in which a son goes so far as to have sex with his stepmother, thereby cuckolding his father. In O'Neill's dark masterpiece of parent-offspring conflict set among stony people in equally stony, rural New England, old Ephraim Cabot had gained control of his second wife's farm, worked her to death, and brutalized his three sons. The youngest, Eben, stubbornly insists that the property is his birthright—shades of Dmitri Karamazov—and he proceeds to pay off his two older brothers, getting them to leave for California and forgo any claim to the farm in return. But flinty old Ephraim then shows up with his third wife, attractive Abbie Putnam, another tool in the contest between parent and child.

Not only does Eben resent the arrival of his young stepmother, he also recognizes that she threatens his inheritance. Abbie, in turn, wants to solidify her situation, and with unerring biological wisdom, she recognizes that producing a child is just the ticket. She proceeds to do so by seducing Eben, bearing his child, and announcing it as Ephraim's. It is as though Grushenka had married old Fyodor, then had a child by Dmitri so as to ensure herself the Karamazov kopeks. Good revenge for Dmitri—that is, Eben—as well, except for the fact that whoever cuckolds his father in this way also assures that he will be disinherited in favor of his biological son, the alleged child of the old man.

In O'Neill's version, Abbie comes to love Eben, who, in turn, is infuriated when he realizes how he has been used by her. Abbie then smothers her child, hoping thereby to prove that she really wanted Eben as a man and not just a sperm donor with whom to deceive her elderly husband into thinking she had borne him an heir.

The theme of parent-offspring conflict via sexual competition is not merely one for the nineteenth or twentieth century. It appears in Western literature as early as Euripides' ancient tragedy *Hippolytus*, which details the doomed passion of Phaedra, wife of Theseus, for her stepson, Hippolytus. Racine's seventeenth-century play continued the story into the beginning of modern times. In this tale, Hippolytus revered his father, the renowned monster slayer Theseus, but also had to deal with Theseus's darker side: his career as a womanizer who readily abandoned his conquests. Theseus's wife, Phaedra, was the sister of Ariadne, who had obligingly provided Theseus with the thread by which he found his way back out of the labyrinth after killing the notorious Minotaur. After this, Theseus ran off with both Ariadne *and* Phaedra, only to dump the previously helpful Ariadne in favor of her more nubile sister. Neither of these ladies, incidentally, gave birth to Hippolytus; that was a matter of Theseus hooking up—briefly, once again—with the queen of the Amazons. Theseus certainly got around.

Hippolytus is a perfect example of the lopsided playing field for children when battling with their parents, not only because of the obvious asymmetry in age, power, and psychological influence but also because of the latter's accumulated past. In Racine's play, considered one of the great cultural milestones of French literature, Hippolytus doesn't even make a pass at his stepmother; rather, Phaedra lusts unavailingly for him, then falsely accuses the youngster of rape, whereupon Theseus has him killed. And Phaedra kills herself.

The theme of cross-generational conflict, often with violent and sexual overtones, is alive and well in recent and contemporary literature, and we can be grateful that sometimes, at least, it stops short of murder. On occasion, it emerges as humorous, ironic, and even touching, as in John Millington Synge's finest work, *The Playboy of the Western World*. A young man named Christopher Mahon arrives one evening at a tavern on the wild Mayo coast, announcing that he has run away from home because he killed his father, Old Mahon, during a fight. This indication of manly independence greatly impresses the locals, especially Pegeen, the tavernkeeper's a-bit-too-easily-impressed daughter. (It is tempting to suggest that apparent victors in parent-offspring conflict are especially appealing to the opposite sex, because such victors are likely to be successful in turn; shades of the "sexy son hypothesis," described earlier. There is an added and ironic complication, however: insofar as success in parent-offspring conflict is inheritable, then offspring who emerge victorious over their parents are presumably prone to produce offspring who are, in turn, liable to best *them*.)

In any event, Christopher Mahon is prevailed upon to repeat, over and over, his tale: how he had always been a meek, obedient, put-upon son until Old Mahon insisted that he marry an elderly rich widow. Christopher's disobedience precipitated a battle between father and son, in the course of which the old man was struck lethally on the head. Young Chris becomes quite the local hero, admired by all the ladies, and as his fame spreads, he comes to believe his own tale and to relish his renown. This newly crowned playboy of the Western world is eventually accosted, however, by Old Mahon, who is not in the least dead after all and who humiliates Christopher in front of the village and demands that he return home. But at this point the son isn't so meek as before, and, energized by his status as young lord of filial defiance, he proceeds, much to the old man's amazement, to strike his father over the head once again; this time, moreover, it appears that he has finally, really, and truly killed his father. The townspeople—even Christopher's sweetheart, the pretty and impressionable Pegeen—now turn against him, being sensible of the difference between a rumored patricide in a distant county and the real thing, up close and personal. (As per our earlier suggestion, maybe Pegeen has second thoughts about possibly raising sons who are inclined to bash parental skulls.) But as Christopher Mahon, undutiful son in the extreme, is about to be hanged for his lethal lack of filial piety, his father comes to, for the second time—Old Mahon, we must conclude, has a hard head indeed—staggers over to his son, and unties him, whereupon the two leave arm in arm, reconciled at last and commenting contemptuously about how naive some country bumpkins can be.

Such cheerful foolishness aside, parent-offspring conflict generally assumes a more somber tone, one in which, as we have noted, the parents hold most of the cards. It dominates, for example, at least two of Tennessee Williams's plays: *Cat on a Hot Tin Roof* and *The Glass Menagerie*. In the former, generational conflict is played out most notably between Big Daddy Pollitt and his sons, once again, as in the Karamazov clan, over an inheritance. Big Daddy is the richest landowner in the Mississippi Delta, with two sons: Brick—his favorite—a bitter, alcoholic former football star (played in one film version by Paul Newman), and Gooper, a hypocritical, greedy father of five, with number six on the way. By contrast, Brick and his wife, Maggie (in which role Elizabeth Taylor sizzled opposite Newman), are childless. The stakes are huge, since Big Daddy is dying of cancer and, true to evolutionary expectations, no one expects the Pollitt plantation to go to a childless couple.

As the drama unfolds, we discover that Maggie is sexually (and financially) frustrated, describing herself as being "nervous as a cat on a hot tin roof," because Brick has no carnal interest in her, which makes it unlikely that either Brick or Maggie will produce the child necessary for them to get their share of Big Daddy's millions. The family's dirty laundry is revealed: Maggie had seduced Skipper, Brick's closest friend, in a peculiar effort to snap Brick out of his homosexual longings, and Skipper had subsequently committed suicide. As this lacerating play comes to an end, Maggie makes the lying announcement that she is, at last, carrying Brick's child, and then sets about trying to make it so.

While *Cat on a Hot Tin Roof* tells of parent-offspring estrangement, with parental expectations exceeding filial inclinations, in *The Glass Menagerie* Tennessee Williams presented his audience with a different side of parent-offspring conflict, this one proceeding via pathological enmeshment. It is the story of middle-aged Amanda, by turns infuriating and pathetic, who lives via the illusions of her youth, in the process stifling her children, one of whom eventually escapes while the other remains entrapped, surrounded by a menagerie of miniature glass statues. Parent-offspring conflict all right, in which a neurotic, controlling parent—whose pathology presumably precludes an accurate assessment of where her ultimate biological interest really lies—is unable to let go of her daughter; her son, meanwhile, must pry his way out of this particular menagerie.

Jonathan Franzen's *The Corrections* brings us yet another vision of conflicted parent-offspring interactions, a take that once again proves especially rewarding when subjected to an evolutionary perspective. In *The Corrections* we see a moderately dysfunctional but altogether recognizable family, the Lamberts, whose patriarch is slipping into dementia while the matriarch yearns for the perfect Midwest Christmas, which would meet parental needs but not those of her grown children. The younger Lamberts—Chip, Denise, and Gary—are pretty much making a mess of things, each failing to meet parental expectations in how they ply their own lives; at the same time, the siblings are unable or unwilling to support each other as the disappointed elder Lamberts would prefer. (Recall that the theory of parent-offspring conflict predicts conflict between parents and offspring not only over parental resources but also with regard to offspring behavior toward each other.) In Franzen's prize-winning novel, numerous "corrections" are attempted—and some even succeed, for a time—but underlying it all is a family dynamic that cannot be altogether corrected (because it derives from our human nature) and of which even the author was apparently unaware, even as he depicted it so faithfully.

Although growing up isn't a disease requiring correction, it evidently feels that way to many people. In the process, it's hard not to notice that when serious parent-offspring conflict is portrayed in literature, it is overwhelmingly a son (Holden Caulfield, Huck Finn,

Alexander Portnoy, and so forth) who does most of the conflicting. Why not daughters? There is nothing in the evolutionary origin of parent-offspring conflict that is sex-specific; certainly, daughters are no less endowed than sons with a 50 percent probability of *not* sharing genes with their parents. Perhaps the relative scarcity of depicted parent-daughter conflict is a result of the fact that, as we've seen, females are more likely to employ subtle styles of conflict, whereas males are more overt. But on the other hand, good literature is more than capable of revealing subtle interactions.

A notable—and notably gentle—portrayal of mother-daughter conflict comes from Laura Esquivel's magical re-creation of life in turn-of-the-century Mexico, *Like Water for Chocolate*. Tita, youngest daughter of the tyrannical Mama Elena, is required by her mother to remain unmarried, so as to be available to care for the aging matriarch. (It's a common practice in a number of cultures, analogous perhaps to those bird species in which the youngest offspring is often undersized and undernourished, essentially sacrificed for the benefit of other family members.) Tita must watch helplessly and miserably as her older sister gets to marry Pedro, the man of her dreams. Tita, however, succeeds via cooking, by which she imbues magnificent meals with her anger, grief, and longing. And, this being magical realism, Tita eventually triumphs.

In the less magical world of realistic biology, such triumphs are, sad to say, rare.

For an ominous and complex perspective on parent-offspring conflict (and another one in which sons are the centerpiece of conflict between parents and offspring), let's turn to William Faulkner's *Absalom, Absalom!*—the novel's title echoing the cry of grief and loss uttered by King David at the death of the son who had engaged in some no-nonsense parent-offspring obstreperousness. (Absalom had rebelled against his father and in the process killed one of his brothers.) In Faulkner's fictional Yoknapatawpha County, the reader gradually comes to understand the saga of Thomas Sutpen—a violent and dangerous Extra-Big Daddy—who is an even harder act to follow than is Theseus, less foolish than Fyodor Karamazov, less pathetic than Jack Portnoy, and a more potent presence than the parents of Huck Finn and Holden Caulfield put together. Sutpen is a larger-than-life figure (indeed, a larger than larger-than-life figure) who carves "Sutpen's hundred"—a hundred square miles of land—and a mansion out of the Mississippi wilderness by brutality and force of will. He is a genuine, genetic force of nature, a man whose vitality both defies and demands conflict from offspring and strangers alike.

From the onset, Sutpen has his "design," his plan for his own life and that of his posterity; all others are left to struggle in his wake. Sutpen, in Faulkner's hands, is history made flesh. His story and that of his descendants is reconstructed, piecemeal, by a southerner, Quentin Compson (who also figures prominently in *The Sound and the Fury*). The account is complex and multidimensional, and—as bespeaks true conflict—there is no single "correct" story line. Just as the "best" course of action varies depending on whether one is, for example, parent or offspring, and each gene and genetic lineage can rightly see itself as central to the process of life, everyone in *Absalom, Absalom!* has a different version of events. But despite the fractured and competing narratives, some things are clear: Thomas Sutpen was a fierce and driven progenitor who reveled in conflict and provoked more than his share. When not working on his land or building his mansion, he liked to relax by fighting hand-to-hand with his most powerful slaves. Once when his two children, Henry and Judith, observed this lurid scene, Henry fainted while Judith watched with fascination and delight. It doesn't take a literary genius to see that young Henry was somewhat unlike his father, whereas Judith was a chip off the old genetic block, yet Thomas Sutpen demands a *male* heir worthy, in his mind, of himself.

Henry attends college, where he befriends Charles Bon, an immensely seductive young man who is only later revealed to be Henry's half-brother, offspring of Thomas Sutpen by a Haitian woman many years ago, and who, because of his mixed blood, has been rejected by his father. Charles desperately seeks the elder Sutpen's acknowledgment but is continually denied. So he woos and wins his half-sister, Judith, without divulging their genetic relationship; when he arrives to marry her, he is murdered on the outskirts of the Sutpen plantation by Henry, his friend and half-brother, who evidently had learned of Charles's background and could not countenance the forthcoming incest. Having acted out his lethal share of half-sibling rivalry, Henry becomes a fugitive. Desperate to carry on his line, the aging but still "demonic" Sutpen proceeds to impregnate Milly Jones, young enough to be his granddaughter.

Milly is the granddaughter of Wash Jones, a squatter on Thomas Sutpen's land and Sutpen's occasional drinking companion. When Milly gives birth to a girl child instead of a boy, Sutpen brutally rejects her, which drives Wash to behead Sutpen with a scythe. As the curtain closes on several more Sutpen generations, each bedeviled by conflict, even Thomas Sutpen's brute strength and ferocious will are unable to carry the day against the destructive, divisive consequences of race hatred, brutality, and incest. Parent-offspring conflict pervades this story, just as the brooding and demanding presence of Sutpen himself weighs like a suffocating blanket on his offspring and, by extension, all children of the South. Their filial and sororal love eventually give way to fratricide as patterns of generational and individual conflict work their malignant and obsessive ends. Faulkner's plots are marinated in conflict—notably within as well as between families—and so is life.

Just as there is no single point of view that offers a unitary truth about Faulkner's South or its people, biological reality dictates that there is no unitary perspective when it comes to the process of living. Natural selection acts—not always successfully—to "maximize the fitness" of each individual, which means that even in the case of parents and offspring, personal agendas often clash and in the process, victory may be elusive, even impossible. Sutpen's grand design isn't necessarily shared by others, and this is why he fails. Here is Quentin Compson, meditating (in poetic stream of consciousness) on Thomas Sutpen in particular, but also on the demands of pushy parents more generally:

> Mad impotent old man who realized at last that there must be some limit even to the capabilities of a demon for doing harm, who . . . can deliver just one more fierce shot and crumble to dust in its own furious blast and recoil, who looked about upon the scene which was still within his scope and compass and saw son gone, vanished, more insuperable to him now than if the son were dead since now (if the son still lived) his name would be different and those to call him by it strangers and whatever dragon's outcropping of Sutpen blood the son might sow on the body of whatever strange woman would therefore carry on the tradition, accomplish the hereditary evil and harm under another name and upon and among people who will never have heard the right one.

A similar disconnect is central to the evolutionary concept of parent-offspring conflict: individuals, even close relatives such as parent and child, have their own distinct interests, since everyone occupies center stage in his or her own personal drama. Sutpen's design, and on a smaller scale the designs of all parents, are readily upended by historical realities, current situations, bad luck, and most of all by the stubborn but altogether understandable insistence of others—notably including, but not limited to, their own offspring—to pursue their own goals, their own designs, be they grand or petty. Whether the stuff of comedy, tragedy, or quotidian reality, such conflicts are part of evolution's bequeathal to us all.

Finally, for readers who crave yet more violence as well as those who may decry the lack of women in these accounts of parent-offspring conflict thus far, there is *The Oresteia*, the fall of the house of Atreus. If you think the Sutpen saga reveals that a house divided against itself cannot stand, the ancient Greek tragedy of Agamemnon and company shows just how divided and destructive such conflict can become. No one, it seems, outdid the Greeks.

Ten years before the action depicted in Aeschylus's classic tragedy, Agamemnon, commander of the Greek armies sailing for Troy, had sacrificed his own daughter, Iphigenia, in order to propitiate the gods and obtain a good wind for his fleet. He had lured Iphigenia to her doom, by the way, by falsely promising that she was there to be married to the Greek hero Achilles. Iphigenia wanted Achilles; Agamemnon wanted a favorable wind by which to pursue his own goals. How's that for conflicting interest between father and daughter? News of Agamemnon's deed generated no small amount of husband-wife conflict when it was reported to Mrs. Agamemnon, aka Clytemnestra. (It was not coincidental, incidentally, that Faulkner used this name—Clytie for short—in *Absalom, Absalom!*)

Generations before the killing of Iphigenia, the House of Atreus was not unfamiliar with lethal deeds. Indeed, it started out with a few skeletons in the family closet, notably the corpses of the children of Thyestes, who had been murdered by his competitor, Atreus, tyrant of Argos, and then served up as dinner to their father. (Parent-offspring consumption?) Actually, things are genetically more sinister yet: Atreus and Thyestes were brothers, whose sibling rivalry was such that the latter seduced the former's wife. This, in turn, is what had led Atreus to seek the culinary comeuppance of Thyestes, but by doing so via the shedding of kindred blood, Atreus contributed to a bad precedent.

Atreus, in turn, had two sons, Menelaus and Agamemnon, the former the cuckolded husband of Helen (she of Troy) and the latter chosen to lead the avenging Greek army against that city, and who, in the process, willingly presided over the killing of his own daughter. When Agamemnon returns to Argos after the Trojan War, he is murdered by the infuriated Clytemnestra—Helen's sister, by the way; the two brothers had married two sisters—who had been plotting her bloody retaliation while shacking up with a fellow named Aegisthus. All quite complicated, but it is about to get more so. Aegisthus is the sole surviving son of Thyestes, the one who had seduced Atreus's wife and was then unwittingly deceived into eating his own murdered children. Accordingly, Aegisthus has a bone or two to pick with the family of Atreus.

Agamemnon's ill-treatment of Iphigenia thus stands in a long tradition of the elders of the House of Atreus looking out for their own interests at the expense of their offspring. "It is bitter, bitter being the chief," complains Agamemnon in Aeschylus's play. "To slay my own little girl? With my hand to pour her virgin's blood on an altar to go to war? And yet, if I fail we never shall sail to Troy, as we have pledged to each other to do, and I shall dishonor myself and each of you." Murdering Iphigenia may well have been bitter, but as we suggested earlier, the Greek gods have often served as external excuses for the unpleasant but biologically influenced behavior of human beings. In Agamemnon's case, it is at least convenient that he is able to repackage the nastiness of especially intense parent-offspring conflict as divinely mandated: the gods made me do it.

True it is that by sacrificing Iphy, Aggy lost a daughter, but he gained immense prestige among his fellow Greeks and, with the ultimately successful war against Troy, his pick of their women. One of these was a daughter of King Priam, Cassandra, the one who famously warned in vain of Troy's coming fall and whose very presence added to Clytemnestra's fury . . . and whom Clytemnestra also slew. Part of the biology of parent-offspring conflict is that whereas each parent may be inclined to take advantage of his or her offspring, the other parent is likely to disagree vigorously, especially if, as in Agamemnon's case, the spouse's actions are asymmetric. Agamemnon's lopsided "conflict" with Iphigenia benefited only Agamemnon; not only was there no compensating benefit for Clytemnestra, there was even an additional loss beyond the death of her daughter, since Agamemnon ended up with a concubine whose success would in no way help Clytemnestra. No wonder she was annoyed.

So much for *Agamemnon*, the first of Aeschylus's three monumental tragedies. In part two, *The Libation Bearers*, Orestes—son of the murderess Clytemnestra and the murdered murderer Agamemnon—teams up with his sister, Electra, to kill Clytemnestra and Aegisthus. Killing Aegisthus is no big deal, but for a son to kill his mother is parent-offspring conflict with a vengeance, even when done with a substantial dose of vengeance in mind. And so, in part three, *The Furies*, Orestes is pursued by none other than the Furies themselves (representing his anguished guilt and society's demands for justice, or perhaps the agonized cries of overwrought genes whose interests have ultimately been betrayed because their possessors have overplayed their hand). In the course of the extended legal proceeding that follows, Apollo testifies on Orestes's behalf, making the biologically novel argument that matricide isn't as serious as it might seem, since mothers aren't really related to their children: only the father, who plants his seed in the mother's womb, is the true parent. Orestes beats the rap!

More likely, some things do matter, and one of them, whatever its biological origins, is the pain that comes from conflicts that evolutionary theory tells us may be modulated but not avoided altogether. Perhaps, however, they can at least be understood, and thereby rendered less hurtful, since unlike a lower mammal caught in the grip of weaning conflict or an adult bird bedeviled by a crew of insatiable fledglings, people are capable of wisdom (a capacity that is also part of our biology). Here is some of the wisdom of *Agamemnon*, reflecting the agony of parent-offspring conflict turned to murder, chanted by a Greek chorus and filtered through poetry that, although twenty-five-hundred years old, is transfixingly human:

> Even in our sleep, pain that cannot forget falls drop by drop upon the heart, and in our own despair, against our will, comes wisdom to us by the awful grace of God.

9

OF MUSKETEERS AND MICE AND MEN
AND WRATH AND RECIPROCITY
AND FRIENDSHIP

In Steinbeck Country and Elsewhere

"All for one," as the Three Musketeers were wont to say, "and one for all." Sounds good, but the biological reality is a bit more selfish and sobering, and so, for the most part, are its literary depictions. Even though virtue is reputed to be its own reward, the evolutionary process has a hard time rewarding virtuous behavior unless it is directed toward genetic relatives, either offspring (Chapter 8) or other kin (Chapter 6). In either case the reward comes from direct payoff to the genes in question, so altruism is revealed to be selfishness in disguise.

Yet altruism doesn't absolutely require shared genes; shared favors will do. The key is positive payback, or reciprocity: you scratch my back, I'll scratch yours. As a result, people—and other animals—can stick together through thick and thin, better or worse, so long as no one individual ends up with all the benefit and another with all the cost.

Buddy stories, which abound in literature as in life, offer models of seemingly selfless devotion. Scratch the surface, however, and there are inevitably payoffs working both ways. Otherwise, either the relationship isn't friendship (rather, compulsion and/or manipulation) or it isn't destined to last very long. Perhaps the oldest text of the Western written tradition is the enduring Babylonian tale of friendship and mutual assistance exchanged between Gilgamesh and

Enkidu. Also Homer's recounting of Achilles and Patrocles, the stirring medieval romances featuring Roland and Oliver, the Knights of the Round Table, Don Quixote and Sancho Panza, and more recent if lighter fare, such as the Lone Ranger and Tonto or Butch Cassidy and the Sundance Kid. In all these cases, favors are *exchanged*; never is one friend only a giver and the other only a receiver.

As to those fabled Musketeers, even they weren't all that self-abnegating. Throughout Dumas's swashbuckling novel, the implication was clear: buckles aren't swashed simply for the fun of it, nor just to do good. Either they are payback for assistance rendered in the past or they are done in the hope of generating a comparable behavior to be directed toward the current do-gooder sometime in the future. When our four heroes (Athos, Aramis, and Porthos—the original Three Musketeers—plus D'Artagnan, the fourth) are needy and poor, "the hungry friends, followed by their lackeys, are seen haunting the quays and guard-rooms, picking up among their friends abroad all the dinners they could meet with." This generosity on the part of the Musketeers' friends and acquaintances is encouraged by Aramis, who points out that "it was prudent to sow repasts left and right in prosperity in order to reap a few in times of need." Biologists call it "reciprocal altruism." Regular people call it friendship.

Here is Aramis, once again (who seemed to have an especially acute sense of the role of reciprocity in mediating relationships among nonrelatives). Aramis has just received some money from his girlfriend, whereas D'Artagnan has been poor and hungry for some time. "My dear D'Artagnan," says he, "if you please, we will join our friends; as I am rich, we will to-day begin to dine together again, expecting that you will be rich in return." The rules are clear, even among these established buddies. They all share money and food; in fact whenever they pawn a ring—which they do regularly, seeming to have an infinite supply of precious jewelry—they share the money evenly between them, no matter who originally owned it, and even if it was a family heirloom or lover's keepsake. The Musketeers constitute a kind of inchoate Marxist co-op, everyone making sure that the others can eat, drink, and be merry in safety and comfort.

This friendship among the Musketeers is especially intense because of the situations of great risk in which they find themselves. It's a familiar story, reflected, for example, in Shakespeare's famous wartime rallying speech, entrusted to Henry V: "We few, we happy few; we band of brothers; for he today that sheds his blood with me shall be my brother." Unsaid but clearly implied: he who chickens out isn't.

Camaraderie among the Musketeers is thus based as well on a kind of "I've got your back" theory. Dumas's heroes live in a very violent, dangerous time in which people kill each other merely for being disrespectful and in which traitors and double-crossers abound. They are the "inseparables" in part because there is safety in numbers, and they have made a commitment to help each other as much as possible. Thus, when D'Artagnan goes on a dangerous mission to England, they all go with him even though there is nothing in it for them (at least, not on the surface). They all risk their lives, with only D'Artagnan getting to his destination; the rest are left on the road in various fights and other encounters.

Because *The Three Musketeers* is really about D'Artagnan, it might seem that they assist him without any expectation of positive payback, but after D'Artagnan returns from England he undertakes the highly risky course of going out by himself, leading a bunch of fancy, valuable horses given to him by Lord Buckingham and which he means to give, most generously, to his buddies. In the course of events, D'Artagnan attempts to find and rescue the other Musketeers; after all, they went with him and sacrificed for him, so he will sacrifice for them by looking out for their safety. (Isn't that what friends are for?)

While it warms our hearts, friendship based on reciprocal benevolence is strangely delicate, always teetering on the uncertainty that whoever gives might not get back. Kin-based altruism, by contrast, is more secure: after one individual does something to benefit a relative, it doesn't matter whether the recipient is especially grateful, whether he or she reciprocates sometime down the road, or if the good deed is even identified as such. Part of the charm of selfish genetics is that the altruist's payoff inheres directly in his action, regardless of what the recipient does or doesn't do. Any benefit to the recipient automatically bounces back to the donor as a result of their shared genes.

This is a lesson that Blanche DuBois could have learned. "I have always relied," she famously acknowledges in Tennessee Williams's *A Streetcar Named Desire*, "on the kindness of strangers." Not necessarily a bad policy, but only if those others are likely to play ball, and that, in turn, depends in large part on whether you are in a position, and of an inclination, to reciprocate when called to do so. Otherwise, there is little reason for those strangers to continue to help you, and much reason for them to act less benevolently. In Williams's play, Blanche also relied on the kindness of her kin—notably her sister Stella, with whom she moved in when she needed a place to live. But Stella turned out to be sexually in thrall to the earthy Stanley Kowalski (played in the movie version, torn T-shirt, rippling muscles, and all, by a young and sexy, "Stella!"-screaming Marlon Brando). And Blanche turns out to be helpless and hapless, sexually violated by Stanley and left to the not-so-tender mercies of a notably unkind, late-arriving crew of operatives from the Louisiana state mental hospital.

Altruism based on reciprocity involves a short-term asymmetry: the altruist gives while the beneficiary gets. What's to keep the beneficiary from gathering in his benefits but refusing to reciprocate when and if the opportunity arises? This is why relying on the kindness of strangers is so risky. What if, once D'Artagnan becomes wealthy, he snubs Aramis and doesn't pay him back after all? We can assume that if this were to happen, their friendship would end pretty quickly, just as it does in our own twenty-first-century world when a couple repeatedly has dinner at another's house but doesn't invite them over "in turn." What, for instance, is likely to happen to those who keep receiving Christmas cards from others while not sending out any of their own?

At the same time, reputation counts, and people often restrain themselves or sacrifice on behalf of a friendship, so long as it is one that has endured, which is to say, so long as the friends have already shown themselves to be reliable reciprocators. At one point in *The Three Musketeers*, the evil Cardinal Richelieu has just offered D'Artagnan a high office in his own guards—a real honor, and very tempting—but he refuses, at which point the cardinal warns that given D'Artagnan's penchant for getting in trouble, and considering the enemies he has made and the schemes he has been involved in, our fourth Musketeer is in serious danger. To be safe, the cardinal insinuates, he really should take up the cardinal's offer. D'Artagnan again refuses. After this,

> D'Artagnan went out, but at the door his heart almost failed him, and he felt inclined to return. But the noble and severe countenance of Athos crossed his mind: if he made the compact with the Cardinal which he required, Athos would no more give him his hand, Athos would renounce him. It was this fear that restrained him, so powerful is the influence of a truly great character on all that surrounds it.

It isn't always easy, but, as Paul McCartney once sang—and Athos, Aramis, Porthos, and D'Artagnan would doubtless agree—it is often at least possible to "get by with a little help from my friends."

In a sense, reciprocal altruism is plain common sense: one good turn deserves another. Its echo resounds whenever we assess someone as "reliable," "trustworthy," or "somebody you can (or can't) count on," as well as in such laments as "What did I do to deserve that?" or the satisfying "She had it coming." But sometimes it takes a while for common sense to become scientifically legitimate. In this case, the problem is as follows: when genes aren't shared and thus nepotism (aka kin selection) isn't at issue, is there some way that natural selection can still promote altruism?

The answer is, it can.

Here is the idea. Imagine you have some food and are about to eat it. Along comes someone else who begs for a portion. If you give in and share, there is less for yourself. Of course, if your hungry importuner is a genetic relative, you should be generous—that is, altruistic—and all the more so if you are closely related. You can also be expected to be more generous if he or she needs the food more than you do, less so if you can really use the extra bite yourself. But there is an additional set of circumstances in which it would pay your genes to donate food to the beggar, *even if the two of you are not related at all.*

The key provision is that in the long run, the ultimate benefit of being altruistic has to overcome the cost. In other words, there must be a good chance that sometime in the future the tables will be turned—in our example, literally. If the recipient of your generosity, for example, will someday have food when you don't, and if your good deed will be remembered and repaid in kind, then reciprocity may be a tasty feast for everyone involved. (And in this case, once again, the act isn't really altruistic at all! Thus are the Musketeers—for all their friendly collegiality—revealed as, at heart, the three must-get-theirs.)

It sounds simple enough, but actually these are demanding, rigorous conditions, which probably don't occur very often. The problem is that as soon as you have given some food to a beggar, unrelated to you, your evolutionary bank account has gone down by one notch, while the beggar's has gone up. This wouldn't be a problem in the long run *if* you will eventually gain more than you lost by donating the food in the first place. Not impossible, for example, if you have just killed a large animal, since you probably wouldn't require every bit of the meat. For a hungry beggar, by contrast, just one slice might mean the difference between survival and starvation. So you lose a little; he gains a lot. If sometime later *you* are starving and your beggar buddy has hit the jackpot, it could be a good trade all around: give a little when you are fat and happy in return for a likely assist when you're really in need. In some ways, the transaction is equivalent to a healthy person banking some of her bone marrow to be used later, if necessary, when the situation is dire. But when it comes to bone marrow, there is no question that the donor will be able to retrieve the investment. In the case of reciprocity, on the other hand, there is a huge and lingering doubt: the beggar/beneficiary might *not* pay you back, or might not be around even if he is inclined to do so. It's a risk, sometimes a big one. Perhaps this is what Polonius, in Shakespeare's *Hamlet*, was driving at when he advised his son, "Neither a borrower nor a lender be."[1]

Remember, after the first act of altruism, you (the altruist) have lost something—in our example, some food, which translates into some fitness, the basic biological currency—while the recipient has benefited. What is to stop him or her from profiting from your generosity, then snubbing you when payback time rolls around? It is more blessed, we are told, to give than to receive. But it is awfully tempting to take and not to repay. (Maybe that's why giving is so universally blessed!)

In any event, this is the major difficulty that any system of reciprocal altruism must confront. Economists refer to it as the "free rider problem," referring to the ever-present temptation of taking advantage of another's benevolence. "Good people," of course, don't do it. Take, for example, one of those high-minded souls encountered by Jack Kerouac in *On the Road*:

---

[1] If Polonius were only worried that his son might not be paid back, he presumably would have left it "Don't be a lender." The problem with being a borrower is that then *you* are expected to pay back or lose your friend.

I was just about giving up and planning to sit over coffee when a
fairly new car stopped, driven by a young guy. I ran like mad.

"Where you going?"

"Denver."

"Well, I can take you a hundred miles up the line."

"Grand, grand, you saved my life."

"I used to hitchhike myself, that's why I always pick up a
fellow."

Besides what economists call the free rider problem, there are
other difficulties as well, all of which must be resolved for reciprocity to work. For example, altruist and beneficiary must have a good
chance of meeting again later. Otherwise, a debt incurred cannot
be paid back. Hence, reciprocity isn't anticipated among total
strangers, who are likely to melt away into an anonymous crowd.
Part of the early hippie ethos—celebrated and to some extent created by Kerouac in his book—is that crowds need not be anonymous and that treating people as reliable reciprocators might
become a self-fulfilling prophecy. There must also be enough likelihood that at some time the tables really will be turned, that the
beneficiary will be in a position to reciprocate and repay the debt,
and that he will in fact do so when the opportunity arises. This
notoriously didn't happen among most of Kerouac's generation, so
the benevolent, prosocial, indiscriminately altruistic hippie ideal
has largely fallen by the wayside, victimized in part by the fact that
crowds are too large and too anonymous to promote reciprocity.
(To be sure, there are still bumper stickers that urge us all to "per-
form random acts of kindness," but relatively few actually do so.)

If a youthful hippie never grows up to own a car or if
D'Artagnan were just an average schlemiel, then picking up a
hitchhiker or buying D'Artagnan a meal wouldn't be terribly wise.
Given D'Artagnan's demonstrated competence with a sword, however, Aramis's "altruism" shows not just generosity but some cagey
evolutionary wisdom. (We're not so sure about the hitchhiker.)
The beneficiary must also be able to recognize the altruist and not

dispense repayment to others who don't deserve it. But above all looms the temptation to cheat.

Most people assume that cheating is nasty, unfair, maybe even despicable. And there is probably a good reason why this is so, why cheaters generally evoke such intolerance. In fact, it may be precisely *because* reciprocity is so important to people and at the same time so vulnerable to cheaters that the nonreciprocator is singled out for such criticism. "There is no duty more indispensable," wrote Cicero, "than that of returning a kindness. All men distrust one forgetful of a benefit."

Pity the poor cheater, however, for she is doubly tempted. First she gains by receiving something for nothing; then she gains yet again by ducking out when it is her turn to reciprocate (if she *does* reciprocate, then she would instantaneously be losing something, however small, just as the initial altruist did). Of course, the cheater may really be forgetful, as Cicero suggests, but it seems more likely that just as there can be Freudian slips, there are "Freudian forgets," or rather, biologically mediated inclinations to deny one's obligation. Maybe beggars can't be choosers; they can, however, be cheaters.

Emile Zola's huge multivolume panorama of human foible and folly, *The Human Comedy*, includes many examples of such moral defection, notably including *Nana*, the tale of a beautiful and heartless woman who takes love and money from many, promising (and sometimes giving) sex in return, but no love. Nana is vain, shallow, stupid, voluptuous, and a genuine, 100 percent cheater, not only in the customary sense of contemporary country ballads ("Oh, your cheatin' heart") but also in the deeper, biological sense of someone who fails the basic criterion of reciprocity, leaving havoc in her wake.

The situation, however, is not hopeless. Just as there are costs to reciprocating (hence temptations to cheat), there are also some good reasons to do one's part and play by the rules. Most important, if cheaters can be identified and then punished, this in itself would make cheating costly. Such punishment could be administered directly, as by physical punishment or some form of reprimand, or indirectly, by excluding the cheater from subsequent exchanges of favors. Biologist Robert Trivers first opened the topic of reciprocal altruism to scientific scrutiny in a landmark paper published in 1971, when he was a graduate student at Harvard, just as he was to open biologists' eyes to parent-offspring conflict three years later. Although Trivers pointed to a few possible animal examples, he also suggested that the requirements for reciprocal altruism are so stringent, and by the same token the temptations to cheat are so great, that full-blown reciprocity might well be a human specialty. Trivers even coined the phrase "moralistic aggression" for the peculiarly intense pressure that people exert upon suspected cheaters in an effort to bring them into line and keep them there. Hell hath no fury like an altruist whose generosity is not reciprocated.

That, at least, is the theory. The practice—at least among animals—is best demonstrated by that favorite of horror stories, the vampire. Not Bram Stoker's novelistic version, nor the much mythologized Romanian nobleman, Vlad the Impaler, but *Desmodus rotundus*, a species of bat that exists only in Central and South America, not Transylvania. These creatures don't actually suck blood; rather, they lick it after making a tiny incision with their needle-like incisors. And their preferred prey is livestock—cattle and especially horses—not people. (There are two other species of vampire bat, white-winged and hairy-legged, which feed mostly on bird blood and about which very little is known.) In Central America, where they have been most carefully studied, vampire bats are reported to land on the mane or tail of their victims, although one of the authors has seen them in the cattle country of Colombia, landing on the ground nearby, and then tiptoeing incongruously, shoulders hunched high, apparently trying not to awaken their prey.

Belying their nasty reputations, vampires use a buddy system. They are, if you please, reciprocating altruists.

Vampire bats roost in caves or hollow trees, in groups of eight to twelve adult females, including their female offspring (young males leave home early). Gerald Wilkinson of the University of Maryland, who has studied these creatures for many years, finds that vampire bats' daytime roosts are not made up of close relatives, however. Instead, female vampire bats within these roosts establish long-term associations, often lasting several years, and sometimes more than ten. These creatures are female musketeers. (It may also be noteworthy that despite their small size, most bats have a long life span, which in itself seems to be favorable for reciprocity, since it would increase the chances of eventual payback.)

What do vampires share? Food. To put it frankly, they regurgitate blood to each other. A well-fed bat has a distended belly, easily visible to the human observer and presumably even more obvious—and attractive—to a hungry bat. The solicitor licks under the potential donor's wing, then her lips; if successful, she gets a vomited meal of blood in return. This may sound less than delightful, but for a vampire bat, it is the very stuff of life. Such sharing is important, since one-third of all vampire bats under two years of age come back from their nocturnal flights empty-stomached, generally because the cows or horses on which they attempted to feed woke up and brushed them away. This wariness by their victims poses a serious problem for the bats, since they need to consume 50 to 100 percent of their weight in blood every twenty-four hours, and if they fail to obtain a meal just two nights running, they can starve to death. All vampire bats come back hungry on occasion, and it appears that individuals who are successful one night are liable to fail, unpredictably, on another. So, the life of a vampire bat is one of constant alternation between success and failure, which satisfies that key requirement for reciprocal altruism: recipients and donors often trade places.

This helps them avoid what has been called the banker's paradox: when we most need help, we are typically least able to reciprocate. Thus a bank is most eager to lend money to those who need it *least*, that is, those who are the best credit risk. As it happens, a starving vampire bat is about as good a credit risk as one who is fat and happy.

Wilkinson found that bats establish relationships of reciprocating regurgitation, and furthermore, that such pairs are composed only of those that have been together at the roost at least 60 percent of the time. In addition—and as expected by reciprocity theory—the cost of donating blood is less than the benefit of receiving it: a recently fed bat can save the life of its roostmate at relatively little cost to itself. Wilkinson also found that well-fed vampires direct their bounty toward others who are especially needy and close to starvation. And finally, bats that have been starving and received mouth-to-mouth transfusions are likely to reciprocate the next time around, when their hunting has been good and the previous donors are in need. It is not clear whether there are any cheaters among vampire bats, but these animals evidently can recognize each other as individuals, so it seems likely that any cheaters could readily be made to suffer a dire penalty for nonreciprocation: denial of food when they need it.

Whether human beings are natural-born killers is still up for debate, but we are definitely natural-born reciprocators, despite the glum warning of Welsh writer Alice Thomas Ellis: "There is no reciprocity. Men love women. Women love children. Children love hamsters." It is probably significant as well that whenever it comes to such exchanges, our emotions and sense of fairness are immediately engaged. One good turn deserves another—we all give at least lip service to this bromide, partly because it is hammered into us by our teachers, our families, our codes of morality and ethics, the constant prodding and insistent concern of society at large. Might there not also be a deeper, biologically based inclination as well, one that probably involves a complicated mix of tendencies, including—but not limited to—"reciprocate when necessary" and "cheat when possible"? Maybe social rules wouldn't push so hard for reciprocity if people were naturally inclined to play fair most of the time, to return good for good without the urging of ethical principles and moral teachings.

Or perhaps this is a false dichotomy if ethical principles are in fact externalized instinct, reflecting our intuitive sense that moral behavior is in our long-term self-interest. But it's not likely: even though natural selection does not operate importantly at higher levels such as groups or species, social groups nonetheless exist, and not surprisingly, they seek to indoctrinate their members to behave in ways that contribute to their own success.

Nonreciprocators, those who take and do not give, are quickly singled out as selfish undesirables, people one had better not associate with. It probably takes a fair amount of intellect to achieve this: you have to remember who got what in the past, and whether he or she gave back. It is even possible that our braininess is due in part to precisely these demands. And it may not be coincidental that vampires, notable reciprocators that they are, also have the distinction of being the brainiest of all bats.

Essentially, reciprocity is a social contract, of the sort that operates in our most intimate, day-to-day lives. It is so powerful, in fact, that most people are discomfited to receive a handout without some prospect of repayment. Charity is devoid of reciprocity, to be sure, and thus it is notably hard to take. Consider this account in *The Grapes of Wrath*, by John Steinbeck (of which more later). Here, a woman is remembering how she once took charity:

> "We was hungry—they made us crawl for our dinner. They took our dignity. They—I hate 'em! . . . Mis' Joad, we don't allow nobody in this camp to build theirself up that-a-way. We don't allow nobody to give nothing to another person. They can give it to the camp, and the camp can pass it out. We won't have no charity!" Her voice was fierce and hoarse. "I hate 'em," she said. "I ain't never seen my man beat before, but them—them Salvation Army done it to 'im."

Even so, most people are uncomfortable when expectations of reciprocity are made explicit, just as friendship itself is somehow supposed to transcend "mere" considerations of payback and the troubling question "What have you done for me lately?"

As with so many aspects of human behavior, it seems that the dignity of an act varies inversely with the extent to which it can be explained; for many, to understand the underpinnings of our behavior is to deprive it of legitimacy. To these readers, we apologize, but we do not retract! Like language, reciprocal altruism is clearly learned, and it follows rules that are handed down by local tradition. Just as all human beings use language, and all languages have certain deep structures in common, all people engage in some form of reciprocity, patterns that are shared worldwide and that everyone can understand at some level. Although generosity is praised, reciprocity is expected.

"There is some benevolence, however small," wrote David Hume in 1750, ". . . some particle of the dove kneaded into our frame, along with the elements of the wolf and serpent."[2] That "particle of the dove," responsible for our most benevolent, altruistic inclinations, is the same part of human beings—as well as wolves and serpents—that responds to the adaptive call of either kin selection or reciprocity or both. And that writes about it.

In theory, reciprocal altruism is quite different from kin selection. It could even operate between individuals who are members of different species, since at the genetic level, reciprocity is promoted by paybacks that benefit genes within the body of the individual doing the behaving rather than through relatives. For this reason, "reciprocity" is a better term than "reciprocal altruism," since it refers to a process that is actually selfish, working at the level of the individual as well as his or her genes.

A large proportion of human behavior—both real and depicted in literature—might well be encompassed and in a sense explained

---

[2] David Hume, *An Enquiry Concerning the Principles of Morals* (Oxford: Clarendon Press, 1975).

by adding together the combined effects of kin selection and reciprocity. With whom, for example, do people interact? Offspring, mates, friends, and those with whom we do business or exchange information. Of these, the first relates to nepotism and thus kin selection, whereas marriage represents a mixed case by which people typically marry nonrelatives and create genetic relatives. The last two—friends and business associates—are ripe for reciprocity. (And cheating.)

Pure kin-selected altruism is probably rare: most people generally expect some kind of reciprocity even from their relatives. And although pure kin selection without reciprocity may be infrequent, pure reciprocity without kin selection is comparatively common. It is, we suggest, what friendship is all about. "The only reward of virtue is virtue," wrote Ralph Waldo Emerson. "The only way to have a friend is to be one." We count on our friends. And they count on us. Put more strongly, we identify someone as a friend if, and often only if, we *can* count on him or her. What do we count on friends *for*? For reciprocity: for the reliable, useful, and pleasurable exchange of favors, assistance, valued company, sympathy, shared interests, and so forth. And, if you are a musketeer, for saving one's life when needed.

But that's not all.

"A friend," we learn in Shakespeare's *Julius Caesar*, "should bear his friend's infirmities." Think of how often the phrase "That's what friends are for" pops up when someone does a good turn for another. At the same time, doesn't "One good turn deserves another" also imply that if you fail to do someone a good turn, you might well be ignored in the future? Or that if you have received a good turn, failing to pay it back would be a wrong turn indeed?

It may be cynical to point out that friendship ultimately rests on the expectation of reciprocity. But cynicism and validity are not mutually exclusive. When it comes to business associates and others with whom we interact but do not strictly consider friends, relationships are governed even more objectively and impersonally by the expectation of getting fair value in return for our offerings. We exchange goods or favors, for example, with the shared expectation that each side is being fairly recompensed. Even a simple request for information—such as the time of day—is repaid with a "thank you," which acknowledges the small debt and also, in a sense, confers a degree of status upon the donor.

Among chimpanzees, interestingly, being nice is often a matter of selfish tactics in disguise. There is a method to the beneficent madness of chimps who give food away. As primatologist Frans de Waal puts it, "sharing is no free-for-all." Or, as Marcus Aurelius noted in the second century, "The art of living is more like wrestling than dancing."

Examining more than five thousand food transfers among chimpanzees housed at the Yerkes Regional Primate Research Center, in Georgia, de Waal and his associates found that "the number of transfers in each direction was related to the number in the opposite direction; that is, if A shared a lot with B, B generally shared a lot with A, and if A shared little with C, C also shared little with A." De Waal also reports, interestingly, that chimpanzees don't insist that reciprocation always take place in the same currency. For example, "A's chances for getting food from B improved if A had groomed B earlier that day."[3]

Robert Trivers, the guru of reciprocal altruism, has pointed out that systems of reciprocity are likely to be inherently unstable, relying on a variety of psychological and social mechanisms in order to keep them going. Diverse psychological traits and social teachings may in fact owe their existence to the pressures of reciprocal altruism. To take one example, the Golden Rule is a statement of idealized reciprocity: Do unto others as you would have others do unto you. And while it's true that there exist such injunctions as

---

[3] Frans de Waal, *Good Natured* (Cambridge, Mass.: Harvard University Press, 1996), 153.

"Whomsoever shall smite thee on thy right cheek, turn to him the other also," lessons similar to the Golden Rule have been identified for most of the world's religions and ethical systems. They are especially important since, as we've seen, when those others are truly "other"—that is, unrelated—there is a powerful yet subtle pressure to behave more selfishly.

When cheating is obvious, retaliation can be an equally obvious response, at least among creatures intelligent enough to recognize the transgression. Human beings are experts at blaming one another for what they have or have not done, whether their behavior was warranted given previous events, and so forth. "Friendship is friendship," goes an old Chinese proverb, "but accounts must be kept." Punishment for nonreciprocation—although implied among vampire bats—has thus far been reported for only one nonhuman animal species, and it should surprise no one that this animal is the highly intelligent chimpanzee. Here is an account by de Waal, describing a complex encounter among captive chimps at the Arnhem Zoo in Holland:

> A high-ranking female, Puist, took the trouble and risk to help her male friend, Luit, chase off a rival, Nikkie. Nikkie, however, had a habit after major confrontations of singling out and cornering allies of his rivals, to punish them. This time Nikkie displayed at Puist shortly after he had been attacked. Puist turned to Luit, stretching out her hand in search of support. But Luit did not lift a finger to protect her. Immediately after Nikkie had left the scene, Puist turned on Luit, barking furiously. She chased him across the enclosure and even pummeled him.

It is easy to imagine Puist saying to Luit: "I helped you. Why didn't you help me?" It seems that the wisdom of reciprocity is no more lost on chimpanzees than it is on humans. And much of this wisdom seems to come from the penalty of being caught refusing to pay back the good turn that one has received.

For another example, de Waal compares the behavior of two adult female chimpanzees, Gwinnie and Mai:

> If Gwinnie obtained [food] . . . she would take it to the top of a climbing frame, where it could easily be monopolized. Except for her offspring, few others managed to get anything. Mai, in contrast, shared readily and was typically surrounded by a cluster of beggars.

Later, Gwinnie, with her stingy personality, encountered more resistance and threats when she begged food from the others. De Waal concludes, "It is as if the other apes are telling Gwinnie, 'You never share with us, why should we share with you!' "

In short, reputation matters. As a result, people scramble to associate themselves with the ideals of kindness, goodness, and benevolent altruism, although actually practicing them is often a different matter. In Shakespeare's *Richard III*, there is a hilarious scene in which Richard—one of the most despicable, altogether unredeemable villains in literature—is trying to convince the citizens of London that he is ethical, altruistic, and trustworthy. So he arranges to be seen reading the Bible, something he assuredly does not do when left to his own devices.

Friendship is not just a guy thing, nor is reciprocity. In fact, given that males are biologically primed to be if anything more competitive than females, we might expect female friendships to be more pronounced than their male counterparts.

Indeed, "sisterhood" is reputed to be powerful, and never more so than when it is backed by reciprocity. In Rebecca Wells's *Divine Secrets of the Ya-Ya Sisterhood*, the mother-daughter team of Vivi (mother) and Siddalee (daughter) are going through a rough patch when the Ya-Yas—Vivi's band of stubborn and endearing girlfriends, who go back more than sixty years together and are now "bucking seventy"—sashay in and conspire to bring everyone back together. They get Vivi to send Sidda "The Divine Secrets of the Ya-Ya Sisterhood," a scrapbook of their early years together.

As Sidda enters into the early lives of this tribe of Louisiana wild women, she comes to appreciate the power of relationships in their lives, and her own. We meet Vivi, Necie, Teensy, and Caro, growing up in central Louisiana during the 1930s and 1940s, and through Sidda's eyes we learn how her mother suffered and survived, leaning all the while on her Ya-Ya friends and being leaned on in turn.

The Ya-Yas' most divine secret is their reciprocity. When Necie is unable to accompany the others to see the premiere of *Gone With the Wind*, Vivi writes her daily letters:

> You asked me to write you about every little thing, and that is just what I'm going to do. I'll save everything and we can paste it into my Divine Secrets album when we get home! . . . So that is our day, Countess Singing Cloud. And every single word is true. And when we get home, we will act things out for you. . . . Well, we all slept real late, especially me who was a real lazyhead after staying up all night writing to you. . . . You are our blood sister, remember, and blood sisters can never really go away from each other, no matter how lonesome train whistles sound in the night air.

Vivi's letters are detailed enough to tell an entire story that goes on for about thirty pages. Writing so much is itself a sacrifice on her part, one of many that each of the Ya-Yas makes for each other. Then when Vivi has a breakdown and runs away, the Ya-Yas look after Vivi's kids. Here are excerpts from Vivi's letters to each of her friends talking about her children and her gratitude:

> Teensy Baby . . . That beautiful white gown you gave her [Sidda]. How did you find something so perfect? . . .
>
>   Caro Dahlin . . . My dearest friend—I am . . . at a loss for

words to thank you for all you have done for me and my gang. Taking care of my boys for almost three solid months. . . .

Dear dear Necie . . . You were the one who kept my world running while I was gone. . . . The ten thousand basketball games and altar-boy practices and Girl Scout and Brownie meetings and dentist appointments and God knows what else. Baby doll, you must have *lived* in your station wagon between taxiing your kids *and* mine.

Rebecca Wells's gem of a novel is filled with poignant little reciprocation moments, and also telling cases of nonreciprocation, as when Lyle Johnson refuses to do Vivi a favor, but she eventually gets around him and then adds, " 'Lyle, I'm looking forward to the day when you have to ask *me* for a favor.' Mama winked at me, and I winked back." There is a lot of winking in *The Divine Secrets of the Ya-Ya Sisterhood*, a paean to the widely acknowledged power of female friendship, as well as to the typically unacknowledged impact of reciprocity.

Nor are the Ya-Yas alone. The world abounds in beautifully realized accounts of women's reciprocity: old, young, and in-between. Terry McMillan's *Waiting to Exhale* gives us the earthy, hilarious tribulations of Bernadine, Gloria, Robin, and Savannah, four thirtyish African American women who struggle with men in modern Phoenix, supporting each other all the while, sometimes literally holding one another up (depending on the vagaries of alcohol and other events). And Amy Tan's phenomenally successful *The Joy Luck Club* owes much of that success to its meticulous description of how four aged Chinese women, seated around a mah-jongg table in San Francisco over a span of forty years, offer friendly sustenance to each other's past as well as to their present and future via one another's daughters.

Interestingly, even though the biological theory of mutual exchange is not sex-specific, there seem to be relatively few accounts of male-female friendships based on pure reciprocity; perhaps this is because such relationships, uncontaminated by sexual overtones, are themselves rare.

When it comes to depicting bonding and friendship among men, John Steinbeck is our top candidate. If not the most profound, his portraits are at least the most generous, warmhearted, and sympathetic of any in literature. Steinbeck country is the realm of reciprocity.

Probably the finest buddy novel in modern times is Steinbeck's *Of Mice and Men*, the tragic, beautiful, bittersweet tale of Lennie Small, a dim-witted but well-meaning giant, and George Milton, "small and quick, with restless eyes and sharp features." The two travel the dusty roads of rural California, dreaming of someday owning their own land. As George explains to Lennie,

> "Guys like us, that work on ranches, are the loneliest guys in the world. They got no family. They don't belong no place . . . [but] with us it ain't like that. We got a future. We got somebody to talk to that gives a damn about us. . . ." Lennie broke in, "But not us! An' why? Because . . . because I got you to look after me, and you got me to look after you, and that's why." He laughed delightedly.

George is smart, a bit of a schemer, and—when necessary—a liar, but with a good heart. Lennie could never survive without him, and indeed, his uncontrolled strength constantly gets the two of them into trouble. On the other hand, George is able to benefit from Lennie's physical capacity as a worker. Theirs is a reciprocating system: "We kinda look after each other," acknowledges George. "He ain't bright. Hell of a good worker, though. Hell of a nice fella, but he ain't bright. I've knew him for a long time."

At one point, when Crooks, one of the ranch hands, teases Lennie that maybe George had gotten hurt and won't be coming back from a night on the town, we get a hint of Lennie's protectiveness:

Suddenly Lennie's eyes centered and grew quiet, and mad. He stood up and walked dangerously toward Crooks. "Who hurt George?" he demanded. Crooks saw the danger as it approached him. . . . "I was just supposin'," he said. . . . Lennie stood over him. "What you supposin' for? Ain't nobody goin' to suppose no hurt to George."

Later, when Lennie has accidentally killed a young woman and is about to be hunted by an angry posse, we hear George announcing reciprocally, "I ain't gonna let 'em hurt Lennie." At the novel's end, it is ironically George who kills Lennie, but he does it humanely, with immense sadness, in a final, desperate act of friendship and kindness, the best that down-and-out people—committed to helping each other—can come up with in a cruel and brutal world.

In another of his great stories of reciprocity, *Tortilla Flat,* Steinbeck chronicles the denizens of a particular stretch of Monterey, California, populated by the "paisanos." This varied band of merry men share Mexican, Indian, Spanish, and Caucasian backgrounds as well as a cheerful fondness for booze, women, each other's company, and the avoidance of hard work. Danny, Pilon, Jesus Maria, Big Joe Portagee, and the Pirate consume wine by the gallon and whores by the brothelful. There is, however, a moral code—in a word: reciprocity.

Big Joe Portagee was happy to be with Pilon. "Here is one who takes care of his friends," he thought. "Even when they sleep he is alert to see that no harm comes to them." He resolved to do something nice for Pilon sometime.

Everyone in *Tortilla Flat,* it appears, resolves to do something nice for someone else sometime. And often they do. Mostly they exchange favors, and although they do not explicitly keep track, implicitly everyone maintains careful accounts:

It is impossible to say whether Danny expected any rent, or whether Pilon expected to pay any. If they did, both were disappointed. Danny never asked for it, and Pilon never offered it. The two friends were often together. Let Pilon come by a jug of wine or a piece of meat and Danny was sure to drop in and visit. And, if Danny were lucky or astute in the same way, Pilon spent a riotous night with him. Poor Pilon would have paid the money if he ever had any, but he never did have.

The dust jacket of our copy of *Tortilla Flat* describes the book as follows: "A story of love, laughter, and larceny in an uninhibited private world." Uninhibited by many standards, but rigid when it comes to the unwritten demands of friendship. In fact, the expectations of reciprocity are so ingrained that our bighearted band of rascals even convince themselves that they had behaved according to "code" when they hadn't, as in this exchange, in which Pablo and Pilon complain that one of them—Danny—has had the bad grace to hint at money that he is due:

> "We have been his friends for years. When he was in need, we fed him. When he was cold, we clothed him."
> "When was that?" Pablo asked.
> "Well, we would have, if he needed anything and we had it. That is the kind of friends we were to him."

One of the vagabonds—the Pirate—used to live in a chicken coop with his five dogs, earning twenty-five cents a day for hauling kindling into town. The others contrive to get hold of his money, which they estimate at about a hundred dollars, but are stymied when he relies on *their* friendship, asking them to help him keep it safe. It seems that the Pirate owes a gold candlestick to St. Francis, in thanks for having cured one of his dogs. When they learn that the Pirate is planning to use the money to repay this debt, they—who had been planning to steal it—now guard it diligently. The responsibilities of reciprocity are instantly appreciated and respected, even if the debt holder is a plaster saint.

Danny is the central character in *Tortilla Flat* and the social glue that holds everything together. He also owns the house where everyone lives but for which no one, it seems, pays rent. This introduces a constant, mild undercurrent of good-natured guilt, since, as we have seen, favors are supposed to be repaid. And so there recurs throughout the book a heartwarming, almost childlike eagerness on the part of Danny's friends to "do the right thing" and "make it up" to him. Thus, when the house they had previously been occupying burns down and all are invited to come and live in Danny's place, the paisanos celebrate Danny's generosity, also immediately offering to repay him:

> Although no one had mentioned it, each of the four knew they were all going to live in Danny's house. Pilon sighed with pleasure. Gone was the worry of rent; gone the responsibility of owing money. No longer was he a tenant, but a guest. In his mind he gave thanks for the burning of the other house.
>
> "We will all be happy here, Danny," he said. "In the evenings we will sit by the fire and our friends will come in to visit. And sometimes maybe we will have a glass of wine to drink for friendship's sake."
>
> Then Jesus Maria, in a frenzy of gratefulness, made a rash promise. It was the grappa that did it, and the night of the fire, and all the deviled eggs. He felt that he had received great gifts, and he wanted to distribute a gift in return. "It shall be our burden and our duty to see that there is always food in the house of Danny," he declaimed. "Never shall our friend go hungry."

Part of the humor of *Tortilla Flat* derives from the fact that these high-minded hopes are never quite realized, but at the same time, the friends keep trying to meet their responsibilities. Toward the novel's end, they attempt to find a treasure, committing themselves to using it to repay Danny:

All the idealism in Pilon came out then. He told Big Joe how good Danny was to his friends. "And we do nothing for him," he said. "We pay no rent. Sometimes we get drunk and break the furniture. We fight with Danny when we are angry with him, and we call him names. Oh, we are very bad, Big Joe. And so all of us, Pablo and Jesus Maria and the Pirate and I, talked and planned. We are all in the woods, tonight, looking for treasure. And this treasure is to be for Danny. He is so good, Big Joe. He is so kind; and we are so bad. But if we take a great sack of treasure to him, then he will be glad. It is because my heart is clean of selfishness that I can find this treasure."

Of course he doesn't. The important thing, however, is that he tries.

People also try to behave decently, and even altruistically, throughout Steinbeck's acknowledged masterpiece, *The Grapes of Wrath*. Their accomplishment is to do so reciprocally. As the novel opens, Tom Joad agrees to disclose his past to a truck driver who gave him a ride to his family farm. Even though he would rather not divulge this information, Tom recognizes it as a kind of exchange: "You been a good guy. You give me a lift. Well, hell! I done time."

Reciprocity means more than sharing information, though. At one point, Tom Joad and his friend Jim Casy have come across Muley Graves, who has killed a rabbit. Tom and Casy are hungry, and ask to share:

> Muley fidgeted in embarrassment. "I ain't got no choice in the matter." He stopped on the ungracious sound of his words. "That ain't like I mean it. That ain't. I mean"—he stumbled—"what I mean, if a fella's got somepin to eat, and another fella's hungry—why, the first fella ain't got no choice. I mean, s'pose I pick up my rabbits an' go off somewhere an' eat 'em. See?"

Later, when the Joad family is debating whether they can afford to take Casy with them on their trip, Ma says they must:

"It's a long time our folks been here and east before, an' I never heerd tell of no Joads or no Hazletts, neither, ever refusin' food an' shelter or a lift on the road to anybody that asked. They's been mean Joads, but never that mean. . . . One more ain't gonna hurt; an' a man, strong an' healthy, ain't never no burden."

The last part is redolent with reciprocity. The Joads will do Casy a favor by taking him along, but he will be expected to pull his weight and contribute what he can. A man, strong and healthy, ain't never no burden because he'll help out, as friends are expected to do.

Such exchanges permeate *The Grapes of Wrath*, a novel that could have served as a sourcebook for Trivers's now-classic article that opened the eyes of biologists to the world of reciprocity. For example, when Grampa dies in the Wilsons' tent,

"Fine friendly folks," Pa said softly. . . . "We're thankful to you folks."

"We're proud to help," said Wilson.

"We're beholden to you," said Pa.

"There's no beholden in a time of dying," said Wilson, and Sairy echoed him, "Never no beholden."

Al said, "I'll fix your car—me an' Tom will." And Al looked proud that he could return the family's obligation.

A bit later, Ma Joad is once again thanking Sairy Wilson for being so kind, whereupon Sairy's response hinges on reciprocity. She feels safe because she knows that others will help her, in large part because she has helped them: "Sairy said, 'You shouldn' talk like that. We're proud to help. I ain't felt so—safe in a long time. People needs—to help.'"

Sure enough, the Joads end up helping the Wilsons, combining forces in order to keep their two trucks running. The families cooperate by lightening the load on the Joads' truck, while Al and Tom constantly monitor the Wilsons':

Ma said, "You won't be no burden. Each'll help each, an' we'll all git to California. Sairy Wilson he'ped lay Grampa out," and she stopped. The relationship was plain.

Steinbeck's people are notable for recognizing and acting upon the bond of friendship and solidarity, which, although heartwarming, also possesses a consistent logic, born of necessity: "A man with food fed a hungry man, and thus ensured himself against hunger." Toward the book's end, Ma Joad is thanking the neighbors for helping when Rose of Sharon's baby was stillborn:

> "You been frien'ly," she said. "We thank you."
>   The stout woman smiled. "No need to thank. Ever'body's in the same wagon. S'pose we was down. You'd a give us a han'."
>   "Yes," Ma said, "we would."
>   "Or anybody."
>   "Or anybody. Use' ta be the fambly was fust. It ain't so now. It's anybody. Worse off we get, the more we got to do."

Maybe John Steinbeck went too far in idealizing the poor and the downtrodden. But he also captured some deep truths, paralleling this observation by Albert Camus in the closing lines of his great novel *The Plague*: "What we learn in a time of pestilence: that there are more things to admire in men than to despise." Steinbeck also recognized—without need of evolutionary theory—the important principle that kin-based altruism is (in a manner of speaking) closely related to reciprocity-based altruism. Consider, for example, this account of the camps of the Dust Bowl migrants:

> And because they were lonely and perplexed, because they had all come from a place of sadness and worry and defeat, and because they were all going to a new mysterious place, they huddled together; they talked together; they shared their lives, their food, and the things they hoped for in the new country. . . . In the evening a strange thing happened: the twenty families became one family, the children were the children of all.

The Grapes of Wrath goes on to make a momentous claim, one that is widely acknowledged today but was new in the 1930s, a time that hadn't yet absorbed either an ecological conscience or an evolutionary sensibility. That claim—although not stated in so many words—is that reciprocity extends beyond interpersonal friendship to encompass the connection of people to the land. For that relationship to be healthy, it, too, must be reciprocal. If treated well, the land will reciprocate; if not, it won't. In Steinbeck's world, "the bank"—representative of uncaring industrial capitalism—supplants the genuine, interdependent, interpersonal relationships that make for a caring, just, and healthy society. The relationships among Steinbeck's poor folks are all rich and warm by contrast with the "inhuman" sterility of the bank. Here, in an intercalary chapter, the bank's representatives are trying to explain why the "real owners" must leave, even though they have worked the same land for years:

> Sure, cried the tenant men, but it's our land. We measured it and broke it up. We were born on it, and we got killed on it, died on it. Even if it's no good, it's still ours. That's what makes it ours— being born on it, working it, dying on it. That makes ownership, not a paper with numbers on it.
>
> We're sorry. It's not us. It's the monster. The bank isn't like a man.
>
> Yes, but the bank is only made of men.
>
> No, you're wrong there—quite wrong there. The bank is something else than men. It happens that every man in a bank hates what the bank does, and yet the bank does it. The bank is something more than men, I tell you. It's the monster. Men made it, but they can't control it.

Sure enough, a few pages later, we are given this description of a bulldozer and its driver, once the bank got its way and took control of the land: "The man sitting in the iron seat did not look like a man: gloved, goggled, rubber dust mask over the nose and mouth, he was part of the monster, a robot in the seat."

A healthy man-land relationship is reciprocal and productive. By contrast, that between machine and land is likely to be neither:

> The man who is more than his chemistry, walking on the earth, turning his plow point for a stone, dropping his handles to slide over an outcropping, kneeling in the earth to eat his lunch; that man who is more than his elements knows the land that is more than its analysis. But the machine man, driving a dead tractor on land that he does not know and love, understands only chemistry; and he is contemptuous of the land and of himself. When the corrugated iron doors are shut, he goes home, and his home is not the land.

Finally, any consideration of friendship and reciprocity among Steinbeck's souls must revisit the famous final scene of *The Grapes of Wrath*, in which Rose of Sharon grows from being a whiny girl into a real, caring woman, wise in the ways of the world and the need to give if you are to get. Her baby having died, she gives her milk to a starving man.

> For a minute Rose of Sharon sat still in the whispering barn. Then she hoisted her tired body up and drew the comforter about her. She moved slowly to the corner and stood looking down at the wasted face, into the wide, frightened eyes. Then slowly she lay down beside him. He shook his head slowly from side to side. Rose of Sharon loosened one side of the blanket and bared her breast. "You got to," she said. She squirmed closer and pulled his head close. "There!" she said. "There." Her hand moved behind his head and supported it. Her fingers moved gently in his hair. She looked up and across the barn, and her lips came together and smiled mysteriously.

10

EPILOGUE

Foxes, Hedgehogs, Science, and Literature

In one of his most influential essays, "The Hedgehog and the Fox," Isaiah Berlin expanded on a well-known observation by the ancient Greek poet Archilochus: "The fox knows many things, but the hedgehog knows one big thing." Archilochus had been contrasting Athens, a multifaceted, foxy city-state if ever there was one, with Sparta, which, like a hedgehog, was single-minded. But Berlin, a philosopher, saw in these zoological contrasts a metaphor for comparing intellectual styles (Shakespeare was a fox, Dante a hedgehog, Tolstoy a fox who desperately wanted to be a hedgehog). In *Madame Bovary's Ovaries*, we have looked a fox squarely in the eyes and called it a hedgehog.

Human beings, while basically animals, are also something more—animals *plus*. Many believe this plus to be a soul; most biologists maintain that specialness resides in humanity's plus-sized brain and that language, imagination, culture, symbolism, and self-consciousness all result from big-braininess. But however you slice it, no objective observer worth his salt, upon studying the life-forms of planet Earth, would conclude that human beings are in any sense nonbiological.

"What a strange scene you describe and what strange prisoners. They are just like us." This comes from Plato's *Republic* (and is also used as an epigraph in José Saramago's *The Cave*). One consequence of being the same species is that everyone is astoundingly like everyone else. What a strange scene indeed! And yet how much stranger, how much more astounding, if literature were to represent people who in any deep sense were *not* "just like us."

According to Joseph Conrad in *'Twixt Land and Sea*, the creative artist speaks to

> the subtle but invincible conviction of solidarity that knits together the loneliness of innumerable hearts; to the solidarity in dreams, in joy, in sorrow, in aspirations, in illusions, in hope, in fear, which binds men to each other, which binds together all humanity—the dead to the living and the living to the unborn.

Throughout this book, we have sought to point out that the solidarity of which Conrad speaks so movingly is born of a shared biology, and that we are bound together in dreams, joy, sorrow, and so forth precisely because we are bound together by an evolutionary past formed of a continuous thread: the double helix of DNA.

"But, but, but," some might protest, "there is so much more to literature than *that*." Of course there is. Biology isn't *the* key to understanding and appreciating literature. It is a key. A skeleton key of sorts, which opens more doors, permits more access, and sheds more light than any of its more narrowly designed alternatives.

At the same time, even the most devoted biology buffs should beware hardening of the categories. One characteristic of human nature, it seems, is a yearning for simplicity, often achieved by setting up fundamental dichotomies: yes/no, black/white, either/or, humanities/science, culture/biology. The world, however, is rarely composed of such straightforward alternatives: shades of gray abound, and culture *and* biology, the humanities *and* the sciences interpenetrate and illuminate rather than oppose each other.

"I am large," bragged Walt Whitman. "I contain multitudes." All of literature—and not just Whitman's contribution—is large.

It, too, contains multitudes, and among these, biology has its rightful and hitherto neglected place.

Within biology, evolution, too, is "large." Indeed, according to philosopher Daniel Dennett, "evolution is the greatest idea, ever." Certainly it isn't the only idea, or even the only idea worth entertaining . . . but equally certainly, it deserves attention not only from biologists but from serious readers as well. And evolution, the fundamental driving force of the living world, also contains multitudes. If, as Henry James wrote, "it takes a great deal of history to produce a little literature," it also takes a great deal of biology to make up something as large as the human literary imagination.

Regrettably, however, there is a long-standing dispute between science and the humanities when it comes to tapping the wellsprings of human nature. More than seventy years ago, Max Eastman, in a book whose title does a fine job of summarizing his quest (*The Literary Mind: Its Place in an Age of Science*), concluded that science was on the verge of answering "every problem that arises" and that literature, therefore, "has no place in such a world." He was wrong on both counts. First, science seems unlikely to have all the answers (ever), and second, literature has its place and always will—all the more when thoughtfully combined with science. This has been our lofty goal in *Madame Bovary's Ovaries*, although we have admittedly sought to bring it down to earth by leavening both literature and science, here and there, with a bit of levity.

Eastman's perspective has nonetheless been repeatedly rediscovered and rebroadcast (more often, interestingly, by humanists than by scientists). Consider this, from playwright Eugène Ionesco, in 1970:

> I wonder if art hasn't reached a dead-end, if indeed in its present form, it hasn't already reached its end. Once, writers and poets were venerated as seers and prophets. They had a certain intuition, a sharper sensitivity than their contemporaries, better still, they discovered things and their imaginations went beyond the discoveries even of science itself, to things science would only

establish twenty-five or fifty years later. . . . But for some time now, science has been making enormous progress, whereas the empirical revelations of writers have been making very little . . . can literature still be considered a means to knowledge?

As though to balance Ionesco—the humanist distrustful of the humanities—Noam Chomsky is a scientist who is radically distrustful of science: "It is quite possible—overwhelmingly probable, one might guess—that we will always learn more about human life and human personality from novels than from scientific psychology."

The truth, almost certainly, is in between. Literature is unquestionably a means to knowledge, and so, without doubt, is science (for our purposes, biological science). The good news is that we needn't discard either. In fact, it would be foolish to do so, just as it would be foolish to define oneself as exclusively a fox or a hedgehog.

It is now more than half a century since C. P. Snow warned about the existence of "two cultures"—the humanities and the sciences—which rarely meet. Snow's observation was valid then and, by and large, has remained true ever since. But these days, as John Brockman has pointed out, a kind of "third culture" has been emerging, generating a new natural philosophy that examines our place in the universe by combining insights largely from the natural sciences. Shouldn't our perceptions be as wide as the subject we seek to perceive?

"Every man, wherever he goes," according to philosopher Bertrand Russell, "is encompassed by a cloud of comforting convictions which move with him like flies on a summer day." This is true even of the most open-minded people; indeed, maybe one of the most comforting convictions is of being open-minded! It is also true of serious practitioners of literary criticism, too many of whom are comfortably convinced that theirs is the only way to read. At the same time, Russell's warning doubtless applies to the notions set forth in this book as well: literature is more than just a manifestation of human DNA, and yet how could biology *not* be relevant to literature?

In his magisterial *History of English Literature*, written in the late nineteenth century between the appearance of Darwin's two masterpieces, *On the Origin of Species by Means of Natural Selection* and *The Descent of Man and Selection in Relation to Sex*, the French scholar Hippolyte Taine struggled to glimpse an evolutionary conception of literature, reveling in the fact that modern science finally "approaches man." More than a century ago, Taine suggested that science "has gone beyond the visible and palpable world of stars, stones, plants, amongst which man disdainfully confined her. It reaches the heart, provided with exact and penetrating implements." How much more penetrating are the analytic implements of today's biology! Taine's approach was relatively primitive, emphasizing the importance of a writer's inherited tendencies as well as his or her cultural and historical circumstances. Modern biological science has come a long way since then, although by and large, literary theorists have not noticed.

Maybe they still won't. That's okay with us, since our concern is not with the official, scholarly establishment of theorists and critics but with readers, those people who—almost literally—consume novels and plays, seeking sustenance along with pleasure.

We have based our approach on the conviction that literature, after all, is by human beings, about human beings, and for human beings. And whatever else they are, human beings are *beings*, biological creatures through and through, from beginning to end, ashes to ashes and dust to dust, hydrogen and oxygen and carbon and a sprinkling of sulfur, potassium, calcium, sodium, iron, and phosphrous, shaken and stirred and winnowed and selected by millions of years of evolutionary history.

If there is a single take-home lesson to be derived from the progress of biological science, from Darwin through the outset of the twenty-first century, it is continuity. People are natural, organic, biological, evolved critters, just like every other natural, organic, biological, evolved critter on this planet. When the great biologist Julian Huxley warned against what we called "nothing butism," the tempting oversimplification that because we are animals we are nothing but animals, his point was well taken, but it can also be usefully turned around: just because human beings are capable of great leaps of imagination and intellect and are also possessors of complex culture, this doesn't mean that we are nothing but creatures of imagination, intellect, and culture. We are also animals.

Evolutionary psychologists John Tooby and Leda Cosmides have argued that people "should be interested in evolutionary biology for the same reason that hikers should be interested in an aerial map of an unfamiliar territory that they plan to explore on foot. If they look at the map, they are much less likely to lose their way." Or as William Faulkner put it, "The past isn't dead. It isn't even past." It still persists, in our hands, our hearts, our heads, and in the most revered and beloved creations of our intellect and imagination. Human beings can no more walk away from their biology—or from their creative, artistic imaginations—than we can outrun our shadows or stand apart from our own thoughts. And when we read, seeking perhaps to gain deeper insight into ourselves, or maybe just to enjoy a good story, we can be all the more dazzled by human creativity and all the more grateful for our shared humanity in direct proportion as that reading is enriched by the insights that modern biology has to offer.

Thus, in calling attention to Madame Bovary's ovaries, we have no wish to ignore the rest of her anatomy, nor to diminish her as a person, as a creation, or even as a metaphor. Rather, throughout this book we have suggested that reading makes more sense and is also more fun when informed by modern science's current knowledge of biology and of human nature. We come to expand the appreciation of literature, not to limit it. Human nature pulses inside every writer and, when artfully communicated, is understood by every reader, because it is so deeply shared. It is the breath and beat of living organisms embodied in an organic world of sex, blood, food, fear, anger, love, hopes, trees, animals, air, water, sky, rocks, and dirt. Now that biologists have begun clarifying their perspective on what it means to be human, it is time to look for it—for ourselves, in the deepest sense—where it has always been: in our greatest, most resonant stories.

Moreover, the path is open to all. You needn't be a trained biologist to proceed. In fact, as a Darwinian reader you have an advantage over traditional scientists, who, after all, don't typically learn about discoveries firsthand but rather by reading other people's accounts. By contrast, literature—the original data for anyone wanting to practice Darwinian lit-crit—is there for anyone to encounter directly. So try spicing up your reading with a bit of biology. Go ahead, dive in, swim about, look around, and see what you can see. Most likely, it will be yourself.

Acknowledgments

We thank Malcolm Scully for warmly embracing the first incarnation of this project as an article in *The Chronicle of Higher Education*. Also our agent, John Michel, for telling us there was a book "here," for finding it a happy home, and then, going beyond the call of agently duty and improving it. Editor Bill Massey at Bantam Dell was doubly astute: pointing out just where our arguments needed sharpening, and also encouraging and supporting us when they stood on their own. Micahlyn Whitt was wonderfully effective at shepherding this project through production, making it easy, at least for us! Also helpful: the students of Honors Seminar 397 at the University of Washington, and particularly Kevin Comartin and Rachel Liebman, who came up with more than their share of good suggestions.

We also want to thank and congratulate . . . each other, for being such compatible coauthors and showing that—theory notwithstanding (see Chapter 8)—parent-offspring conflict needn't be inevitable. We are delighted, in addition, to thank those writers, from Homer to Rebecca Wells, who provded us with the tasty material upon which we have feasted, and to Charles Darwin and his intellectual descendants, for giving us the utensils. Most of all, we express our deepest gratitude to the many millions of creatures, going back in an unbroken line to the primordial Precambrian slime, who gave rise to evolutionary biologists as well as writers of fiction, including us, you, dear reader, and everyone else.

—David P. & Nanelle R. Barash

About the Authors

DAVID BARASH is currently Professor of Psychology at the University of Washington and the author of two dozen books, including *The Myth of Monogamy*, written with his wife, psychiatrist Judith Lipton.

NANELLE BARASH is currently studying biology and literature at Swarthmore College. This is her first book . . . although probably not her last.

INDEX